·SOIT·AMIABLE·

COAT OF ARMS

Soit Amiable

The description of a Coat of Arms always uses the technical language of the Heralds and is difficult for us to understand. The meaning, however, is more simple and describes the family for whom it has been granted.

In this case, the armour and helm represent my military background, the plumes and the feathers our loyalty to the Crown, the Five Rosary beads my five children. The two shield patterns in blue are the bell shape for leather and textiles which represents one side of my family trade since the 1500s and the transverse dovetail joints their occupation in carpentry since the 1600s.

Perhaps the most important item is the family motto – Soit Amiable – (a pun on Bellamy) which urges us as a family to be loveable and friendly to all peoples.

"Vair per pale counterchanged on a Bend Argent a Bendlet dovetailed Azure and for the Crest upon a Helm with a Wreath Argent and Azure Rising from a decade of the Rosary in a circle the Beads Gules (five manifest) a cubit Arm in Armour gauntleted proper grasping two Ostrich Plumes proper their spines Azure and between them a Rose erect Argent barbed seeded and slipped proper Mantled Azure doubled Argent as are in the margin hereof more plainly depicted to be borne and used for ever hereafter by the said Lionel Gale Bellamy and his descendants" – *(Extract from Grant of Arms dated 2 March 1984)*

SQUARING
THE CIRCLE

A FAMILY STORY

BILL BELLAMY

First published in 2009

ISBN 978-0-9550911-3-1

James Bellamy
10 Wellingborough Road
Mears Ashby
Northampton
NN6 0DZ

james.bellamy@jtbellamy.com

Printed in Great Britain by Stanley L Hunt (Printers) Limited, Rushden, Northamptonshire

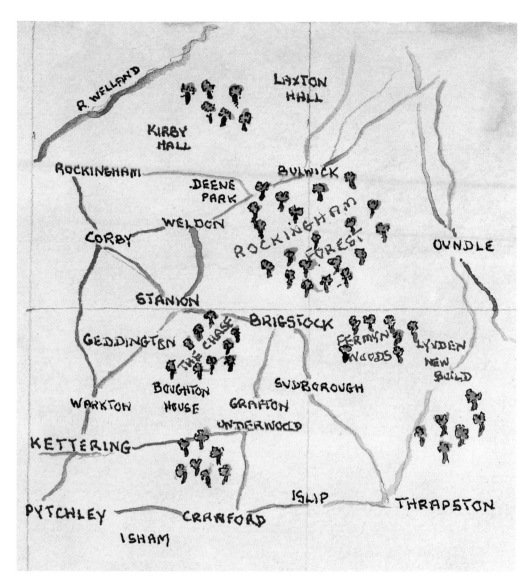

Map of Brigstock and surrounding area

THIS Indenture made the ___ Day of ___ in the ___ Year of the Reign of our Sovereign Lord ___ by the Grace of God of the United Kingdom of *Great Britain* and *Ireland* King, Defender of the Faith, and so forth, and in the Year of our Lord 18__ ___ Church Wardens of the ___ *Winsfield*, That ___ And ___

___ by and with the Consent of his Majesty's Justices of the Peace for the said ___ whose Names are hereunto subscribed, have put and placed, and by these Presents do put and place ___

Overseers of the Poor of the said ___ or thereabouts, a poor Child of the said ___ Apprentice to ___ aged ___

dwell and serve from the Day of the Date of these Presents, until the said Apprentice shall accomplish his full Age of ___ to according to the Statute in that Case made and provided: During all which Term, the said Apprentice his said Master faithfully shall serve in all lawful Businesses, according to his Power, Wit, and Ability; and honestly, orderly, and obediently in all Things demean and behave himself towards his said Master, and all his during the said Term. And the said ___ for himself, his Executors and Administrators, doth covenant and grant to and with the said Church Wardens and Overseers, and every of them, their, and every of their Executors and Administrators, and their and every of their Successors for the Time being, by these Presents, That he the said ___ the said Apprentice in ___ shall and will teach, and instruct, or cause to be taught and instructed in the best way and manner that he can ___

And shall and will during all the Term aforesaid, find, provide, and allow unto the said Apprentice meet, competent, and sufficient Meat, Drink, Apparel Lodging, Washing, and other Things necessary and fit for an Apprentice: (*provided always*, That the last mentioned Covenant on the said his Executors and Administrators, to be done and performed, shall continue and be in force for no longer Time than Three Calendar Months next after the Death of the said ___ in case the said ___ shall happen to die during the Continuance of such Apprenticeship, according to the Provision of an Act passed in the Thirty-second Year of the Reign of King George the Third, intituled, " An Act for the further Regulation of Parish Apprentices") And also shall and will so provide for the said Apprentice, that he be not any way a Charge to the said ___ Parishioners of the same; but of and from all Charge shall and will save the said ___ harmless and indemnified during the said Term:

In Witness whereof the Parties aforesaid to these present Indentures interchangeably have set their Hands and Seals the Day and Year first above written.

Sealed and delivered in the Presence of

Charles Margere J *John Bellamy*
William Margere

WE whose Names are here under-written, Justices of the Peace for the ___ aforesaid (whereof one is of the Quorum) Do consent to the putting forth ___ an Apprentice according to the Intent and Meaning of this Indenture.

Banns of Marriage between Thomas Bellamy & Martha Bullevant both of this Parish
were published in the Church Jan. 28 & Febnuary the 4 th & 11 th by me Wm Davies

No. 97

Thomas Bellamy ——— of this Parish Widower ——————
and Martha Bullevant ——— of this ——————— were

Parish Minister
Married in this Church by Banns
this nineteenth Day of February in the Year One Thousand Seven
Hundred and twenty six by me Wm Davies

This Marriage was solemnized between Us { The Mark + Thomas Bellamy
                                          Bellamy + Martha Bullevant

In the Presence of Tho B Wilmore
                   John Barrett

Banns of Marriage Between James Bellamy of this Parish and Lucy Ward
of this Parish & were published July 5 th 12 th and 19 th 1812

No 155   James Bellamy ——— of this Parish
         and Lucy Ward ——— of this ——————— were

Parish
Married in this Church by Banns
this thirtieth Day of July in the Year One Thousand Eight
Hundred and twelve by me Phil Greenwood Vicar
                                      James Bellamy

This Marriage was solemnized between Us { The Mark + of Lucy Ward

In the Presence of Thos Morris
The Mark + of Elizabeth Day   The Mark + of John Ward

Banns

This is to Sertifie hom it may consarn that Thos Bellamy Bares hear of lived three years and A half during the hot time A Very faithful honest Servant

With me Edwd Bramptoon, Warkton

April ye 8 1793

Apriel 3d 1793

He is Very Honeste man and a good Caracter for what i no from me

Wm Downing
Grafton

Thos Eyet
Grafton

April 1= 1793

He is Very Honast man for what i no from me

John Jones
Grafton

Joseph Beeby
Ringstead

A Fidoury
Ringstead

Henry Hudsen
Ringstead

I do think with the above writen Gentlemen that Thos Bellamy of Grafton is an honest Man & of fair Character Witness my hand Wm Bidwell

Reference

viii

CONTENTS

ILLUSTRATIONS

The sketches on the front cover were drawn by Bill

INTRODUCTION

"If you are a good boy then you can sit by the fire with me and listen to Jack Payne". It was my mother speaking and this offer was the final pleasure for me to enjoy before I was bathed in days which, at this distance anyway, seem to have been filled with happiness. It would have been about 5.15pm on any winter's evening in 1926. A fire would have been burning brightly in the sitting room grate at number 3, Silver Street, Kettering whilst my mother, whom I remember then as warm, gentle and cuddly, sat, holding me on the sofa, as we waited with blissful anticipation for the return of my father from his office in Northampton.

I thought that my mother was the epitome of beauty and I still recall with the utmost clarity her brown eyes, her long auburn hair, which at night time hung down to her waist, during the daytime was coiled around her ears in the then fashionable telephone coils and her slightly aquiline nose set in her smooth soft-skinned features. She was a dress designer before her marriage to my father and her dress sense was the envy of her friends. Even Auntie Peggy, my dress making Aunt, followed "Olive's marvellous taste". She not only bought cleverly but her accessories ensured that things always looked a little different and she stood out in the crowd. It was this, plus her vivacity which bowled my father over when he met her in London during the winter of 1921. He had been sent up to London from Kettering, sponsored and chaperoned by his elder brother, Leslie, Auntie Peggy's husband, to train as a leather salesman like his father before him.

My father was a good looking man, and was 'promised' to a most suitable young girl, Ivy Loake, who was waiting for him in Kettering. She, having been vetted by his mother, was thoroughly approved and thus accepted by his whole family. He had known her for a long time, but after he had abandoned his original career as a school teacher to train as a leather salesman, and gone up to London, freed from the disciplines of the maternal house, he was perhaps more amenable to change!

The Bellamy Family were one of the leading Congregationalist families in Kettering and District. Discipline was strict and after the death of her husband, Joseph, in 1918, the mantle of authority had fallen squarely on my grandmother, who accepted it with apparent relish. Her decisions were absolute, one did not argue, her word was not to be disobeyed. Even at the tender age of three, I was aware of Granny Bellamy's commanding presence, the quiet power which she exercised over her two surviving sons and her daughter, and the awe in which she was held by the world at large. She was after all, as my father explained so often to my slightly mutinous mother, the eldest daughter of the so-called "Rich" Bellamys of Brigstock, whilst her husband came from the "Poor" branch in Kettering. My father had been brought up to believe that his father had been very privileged to be allowed to marry her. My mother had never met her father-in-law, as he had died in 1918, but clearly, she held the view that he must have been a saint, and that her mother-in-law, having been left on the shelf until she was an old woman of 27, was very lucky to catch him! This did not make for easy relationships and certainly coloured my views, as although I admired her and was greatly influenced by her, I found Granny Bellamy very cold, and in later life I was the grandchild who subsequently carried the war into the enemy's camp!

The Bellamys of Brigstock and of Kettering shared the same roots but some centuries separated them in terms of direct relationship. Both family's antecedents are firmly based in eastern Northamptonshire and the village of Brigstock itself was the focal area, certainly from the late 17th Century onwards. The term "Rich" when used in the family context refers to the fact that one branch consisted of millers, master shoemakers, butchers, master carpenters etc whilst the other was directly involved in manual labour on farms, or as carpenters, or footwear operatives. Of course there were many 'cross-overs' especially in the late 19th century, but at the time of which I am talking, the story still stood. Most families of that time must have comprised a similar mixture. However the unbreakable bond which united them, and smoothed out the social difficulties, was that of Congregationalism. They were staunch believers in Almighty God and upholders of the Reformed Church. This epitomised their faith and they clung to it steadfastly.

They were an articulate group, and, being totally certain in their faith, were undaunted, in so far as any public expression of their religious views was concerned. Despite this they did suffer some sense of isolation within the mainly Anglican communities in which they lived. I have the impression that criticism, having to obtain licences for weddings in their own church and so forth, in no way deterred them from their single-minded Low Church convictions; in fact, if anything it strengthened the bonds of family. I find that I can readily relate to this obstinacy over matters of faith and morals or indeed of social principles. My own re-actions and indeed actions are so often a carbon copy of theirs. For instance, in 1794, James Bellamy became the focus of village opposition to the Duke of Buccleuch when he was seeking to enclose Geddington Chase. This, in 1977, was mirrored by my opposition to Lord Althorp over the destruction of 27 miles of mature hedgerows in the parish of Brington. Life is repetitive, only the players change!

A person who was to have a great influence on my life was my father's young sister, Edna. He was the apple of her eye and in all the years that I knew them, I never heard either of them find serious fault with the other. She was a large handsome woman, like her mother and was married to a good looking, charming extrovert, 'Bunny' (Bernard) Shrive. He was very popular and gregarious whilst she was straitlaced, family orientated and very proud of her Bellamy lineage. I both respected her and loved her, and in return, at every stage of my life, she was very kind to me, and later, to my own family. Granny Bellamy was as critical and intolerant of Uncle Bernard as she was of my own mother and in later life they both blamed her for many of their marriage problems.

One's life is not influenced by only one half of one's parent's families. My mother's family came from London and her mother, Helen Isabella Gale, was the absolute antithesis of Granny Bellamy. She was warmly affectionate and caring in everything that she undertook and, although I am sure that their moral outlook was the same, both being staunchly Low Church, Granny Gale was as demonstrative and warm as Granny Bellamy, although undoubtedly a good person, was cold and aloof. It was very much the parable of the tax collector and the Pharisee and Granny Bellamy appeared to me as the latter, a stickler for the rules, and for good manners, but unforgiving. She was clearly very aware of her position in Kettering society, and, personally, I felt that she behaved accordingly. In all fairness, this was not borne out by the obituaries or by the sense of loss expressed by so many people on her death.

Granny Gale loved all those in need with an open heart regardless of their faults, appearance or social position. She too was brought up in a strict Low Church atmosphere. Her mother, Olivia Gigg, an orphan, was educated in the Quaker tradition and, later, was a founder member of the City Temple in London. After the death of her husband in 1926, Granny Gale continued to work as a Foremistress in a leading curtain and upholstery company, Shingletons. At the same time she devoted herself to caring for her widowed mother and, later, for my mother and myself, when we came up to live with them in London. In 1954, aged 75 and living alone in London, she gave up work and came to live with us in Great Brington, Northamptonshire. Despite increasing frailty, she remained as patient, understanding and as loveable as ever. She died in her 97th year in 1976 and is buried in Brington churchyard. She, of all my relations, had the most profound influence on my life. I took copious notes of her recollections and they form the basis of much that I shall write about concerning the distaff side.

It is curious how traits run in families, not only physically and genetically, but also spiritually and emotionally. Sometimes they jump generations and re-emerge when those who would have recognised them as attributable to their own kith and kin, are already long since dead. In the case of prominent families where records exist either as portraits, marble busts, written accounts or even legends, we all nod wisely and say amongst ourselves "what do you expect when his grandfather did this or that!" or "she looks exactly like her great grandmother (poor thing!)" or something of that order. Where records are not available it becomes more a question of family traditions handed down from one generation to the other. For many reasons, I have found researching our family history to be intensely interesting. Of course it has added to my sense of belonging and of having a firm place in the world. It has provided me with an intriguing and often very frustrating detective problem, but most of all it has created in me a feeling both of a strong rapport and of continuity with my ancestors. Time and time again I have found that a comment, a newspaper cutting, a trade, or even the choice of a christian name have evoked in me a response which is clearly one of instinctive understanding. Given the same set of circumstances I would have done that, or said that, just as they did. I hope especially that this will become self evident to those who read this, and that this sense of belonging and of understanding will be shared by my children's children and all the generations to come. I believe most strongly that families offering stability, which then flows out in the form of love for those around them, make the greatest possible contribution to humanity. They can do this much more easily if their sense of personal security is based on a firm faith which they practise as a witness to their belief in Almighty God.

Nothing is new,"Patient endurance attaineth to all things" said the great Saint Teresa of Avila in the 16th century whilst Saint Therese of Lisieux in the late 19th Century, showed us that it was by following the "Little Way" and doing the so-called simple things of life well, that we would come to God. No mountain is too high to climb if we have the necessary determination and will. We are never presented with a problem which cannot be resolved but we always need the help of God and we nearly always need some help from other human beings. I have found that this latter aspect is helped immeasureably by the sense of belonging. In the same way that we never know where the 'ripple' effect of an evil act will finish, so it is with a good action. Whatever good action you offer freely and with love, will be returned a thousand fold and often in the most unexpected way. It will not only enrich your life but also the lives of those around you. This is what the word 'family ' means to me. This book is about such a family.

Bill Bellamy

CHAPTER 1
The Bellamy Family 1523 - 1918

Early in my childhood I remember hearing my grandmother Bellamy say that she was descended from the "rich Bellamys" and her husband, Joseph, from the "poor" side of the family. It was not said as a derogatory remark, but a statement of fact. It was something that puzzled me. To me, a Bellamy was a Bellamy, like a dog was a dog, so what was different?

In 1997 the Northamptonshire Record Office asked me to write about my life as a child in the 1920s and 1930s and it presented me with an opportunity to look back into the history of the Bellamy family. Granny Bellamy had indicated that both families came from the Brigstock area of Northamptonshire and I often wondered if, by chance, the rich and the poor lines could have sprung from the same root.

Assisted by Andy North of the Northamptonshire Record Office, I tracked the family back as far as the early 1500s. At that time they were based in Stanion and a Thomas and a William Bellamy appear on the Stanion Lay Subsidy, which is a Henry Vlll tax list. During the ensuing years William and John Bellamy appeared frequently in the Court Rolls of Presentments in Stanion, a village adjacent to Brigstock, as they surrender or transfer properties to a variety of people. The following three examples are indicative of the activity:-

1581 William Bellamy was admitted as youngest son of his father to a mesuage.
Also mentioned in 1596 and 1598 William Bellamy surrenders all his houses in Stanyon in fee remainder to his own right heirs.
In 1596 William senior and William junior mentioned.

They were members of the grand jury and clearly a family of some standing.

By the end of the sixteenth century the name appears all around that area, spreading into Weldon, Deene and very strongly into Brigstock. Much of the personal detailed evidence at that time is circumstantial. Births and deaths were not recorded in Brigstock until the end of the sixteenth century and, unfortunately, the earlier baptismal register for Brigstock has been lost and, although the recording began under Henry VIII in 1538, the existing one for Brigstock does not start until 1640. However, there is a very strong line of William Bellamys starting in Stanion early in the sixteenth century and running through into Brigstock. William must have been well known to the Montagues of Boughton House and the Brudenells of Deene Hall as a number of manorial records during this period show. When Lord Montague died in 1619 in his Will (see following extract) he left a cloak to William Bellamy and a sum of £10 to his wife Elizabeth, a sign of favour. This William Bellamy was described as a shoemaker in 1638 - he was resident in Brigstock, but still a property holder in Stanion. His elder son William was born in 1638, Samuel in 1642(RIP 1644) and his daughter Elizabeth in 1645.

Extract from Will – William Montague of Little Okely 1619 – 100
William Montague of Little Okely, to be buried in the Northside in the chancel of the parish church of Little Okely.
To my servant John Moore and the rest of my servants to have a mourning cloak and every maid servant a mourning gown
To Elizabeth Bellamy ten pounds
To William Bellamy a cloak

William, then aged 20, married Mary Francis on 24 September 1658. There is no trace of the Francis name in Brigstock but a Mary Francis, daughter of John Francis, was christened in Kingscliffe in 1635 or 1637, both of which fit the time frame. The family were active in the Brigstock area manorial records throughout this time.

William had four children by his first wife Mary. The eldest son William was born in 1664 being the heir to his fortunes, which were substantial. Mary died in 1667, and William married again. His second wife, Ann, bore him four male children and possibly a daughter, Sarah, and others. He was a very successful man, trading as a cordwainer and a baker. In the Manorial Court Fines for 1675 he was fined 3 shillings and four pence for "breaking the assize of bread", so Trading Standards were active even in the seventeenth century! He played an active part in village affairs, for instance as a certifying signatory. The 1674 Hearth Tax records show that he owned four hearths, which establishes him as a man of property. He was an assessor for the Poll Tax in 1697. This was a tax raised by King William and the assessors drew up the list. One of these shows him as employing a maid servant.

His will was drawn up on 19 February 1696, and appears to have been written in a state of great urgency, caused by a severe illness. The introduction reads as follows:- *"In the name of God Amen, I William Belamy now being taken very ill but very sensabull and of perfect memory, blessed by God for it. I doe hear comit my soul into the hands of god through the Lord Jesus Christ and my Body after death to be bureyed acording to the Chreshon Buriall with my lands and my goods to be disposed of as followeth. I do appoint*

Ann Belamy my wife and William Belamy my son my soul Ectecters of this my last will. I give unto my son Samuel the sum of six pounds within twelmonth. I give to my son John a hundred pounds: to be paid in two years time. I give unto my son James A hundred pounds: to be paid in two years time. I give unto my son Thomas the sum of six pounds: I give to my son Samuel the sorold horse: I give unto William King my grandchild five pounds to put him to Apprentice. I give unto Ann Chandler and Eliszbeth her daughter and Will Chandler her son three ginness. I give unto Elisabeth Stanion my daughter and Elisabeth her daughter and Joseph her son three ginness. I give unto Margrey Palmer my daughter and John King her son two ginness. I give unto Sarah Bellamy my daughter one ginne and this my Last Will to be proformed by them hom I have above monshoned my Ectecters the day and year Above Ritten in witnes hear unto I have set my hand and seal. Sealed and delivered in the presance of Mo Chandler, William Leigh, Jane Cunnington, William Bellamy. (Will proved 14 March 1704/5)". For full details see Appendix A.

However he subsequently recovered, although perhaps health impaired, as there is no reference of his taking any further part in official matters. It was a generous will under which all his children benefited. He acknowledges Sarah as his daughter although we have found no record of her baptism. He died in 1704 and the major part of his property - his businesses, his bakers shop etc - went to his eldest son, William. Substantial sums, £100 or more, were left to his sons Samuel, John and James, but to his eldest son from his second marriage, Thomas, he left £6 only. It is difficult to know what to read into this, although as the eldest son of a second marriage it is possible that he may have inherited elsewhere. The daughters and their children were left smaller amounts.

As it was the custom for the eldest son to take on the business of the father and as such William may already have had the bakery under his control, so when William senior died the will only dealt with those items which were still owned by the parent.

The Will was not proved until 14 March 1704 when the inventory of his goods and chattels was listed and totalled £10-11-6d. Clearly one can only hazard reasons for the will being written as it was, with Thomas only receiving £6, whilst Samuel received £120 and the *sorold* horse, and John and James, the latter of whom we have no christening record, £100 each, all being substantial sums. I would like to think that Thomas had taken over that part of William's affairs which did not relate to baking and as such had benefited from his father's generosity already. We shall never know!

However, the records of the Montague Estate show:-

18th February 1701 Thos Bellamy for work done at Weekly Hall (Montague Estate) £1.14s.4d.

This could well be a payment for contract work.

His grandson Thomas continued the same tradition. Wood expenses -

1801 31st December- paid Thomas Bellamy & Co a bill for cutting hedges and diking in Grafton Park Wood £14-7-8

1804 Paid Thomas Bellamy for felling underwood, cutting out stakes and faggotting long wood and making fences £19-3-4

Next year, again Montague Estate records:-

9 July 1702 Paid Will Bellamy ye first payment of ye land tax of 4s per pound for part of ye Chase etc belonging to Brigstock - £10-0-0.

Grazing rights, on which tax was payable, was the custom for the landlord to settle and recover from the tenant.

It would appear that William is already a tenant, cordwainer and baker, whilst Thomas appears as the independent provider of services. Genealogy and family history show that this was the point at which two of his children parted in terms of wealth. Whilst son William's heirs and successor became known later in the family as the "rich Bellamys", son Thomas' financial situation seems to have lagged behind at some point and his heirs became known as the "poor Bellamys". Both lines were united when, on 3 April 1893, two hundred years later, Joseph from the "poor" married Lily from the "rich". The Family Tree (The Circle) shows the seven generations from William to Lily Bellamy and the six generations from Thomas to Joseph Bellamy.

It would appear that William died unexpectedly, as his inventory is supported by an administration bond empowering his wife Elizabeth to be his heir and successor. Appendix B shows this and underlines the wealth which followed this line of 'Rich' Bellamys.

The family of this eldest son William found their success as butchers, graziers, millers and cordwainers (shoemakers). Throughout their genealogical tree there was a high measure of financial success. However, not all their enterprises succeeded and the Northampton Mercury for 21 September 1805 advertises John and Edward Bellamy, both late of Brigstock, butchers, graziers and chapmen as declared bankrupt. They were required to surrender themselves to the commissioners. His eldest son William set the standard as a Master Shoemaker and was the only Bellamy who I have found to be referred to as Mr, which signifies his high place in that society. Tombstones at that time, added the word "Gent", for men of importance in the community.

Both sides of the family were deeply committed to the Reformed Church, mainly Congregationalists. It is interesting to note that under the Commonwealth, 1653-1660, marriages did not have to be celebrated in church and only marriages before a Justice of the Peace were legally valid. These were recorded by an official actually called "the parish register", which is rather confusing and he was appointed by the parish into what was a purely civil appointment. Provided that weddings took place in the presence of a magistrate, they could be announced in the market place or take place in the church porch. It would appear that the vicar in the 1660s, Master Whiston, was a member of the Reformed church and as such not acknowledged as the Church of England incumbent. In the Northamptonshire and Rutland clergy list he is described as "clerk" and "intruder". In 1659 he signed the church register as "Vicar" but after the restoration, when Charles II came to the throne, the word "pretender" was writtten under his signature! The Bellamy family in Brigstock appear to have been members of the Reformed Church from a very early date and as such were "dissenters". The religious roots ran very deep and, as a child in the 1920s, the rectitude of the Low Church attitude to Christianity was dinned into me by the elders of my father's family.

William married Elizabeth Stanyon in 1728. The marriage was by licence in Benefield. This was possibly because the vicar there was more relaxed about marriage by licence. He then carried on his father's business as a cordwainer in Brigstock. The same trade was followed by his eldest son, William, who married Judith Bell in 1760. This family tradition was continued by their eldest son, John, who married Rebecca Barns in 1793 and whose second son, Thomas, cordwainer and grazier, married Mary Brett in 1830. Unfortunately, she died in the following year and in 1832 he married Sarah Preston by whom he had eight children.

The eldest son of this marriage was William John who was born in 1836. He was then a journeyman shoemaker and, as the 1851-1861 census shows, he lived with his parents at home. His father and mother owned a large house in High Street, Brigstock. He was, however, constantly on the move and when working in the Gloucester/Worcester area he lodged with a widow in Cheltenham Spa, called Mrs Ding. He was appointed as a Master Shoemaker and in 1863 he married her daughter, Rebecca. They lived in Brigstock, moving into his father's house at Hall Hill, then Sudborough Road, where they brought up their eleven children. Their daughter Lily, born in 1866, was my maternal grandmother and thus was descended from the rich Bellamys, completing one side of the family circle.

Turning now to the "poor" Bellamys, in 1692, Thomas married Mary Stanion, the daughter of Thurlbie Stanion, scion of a well known local family. There is a wedding recorded in 1607 between Eyzabethe Belamye and Thomas Thurlbye junior, so, historically, there were connections between the two families explaining the provenance of the name.

I have found no record of the trade that Thurlby followed, but he does not appear as a wealthy member of the family. In 1734, when he was twenty years old, he married a widow from Stanion, Mary Watts. They had no children and when she died in 1748, he married Elizabeth Starsmore by whom he had two sons, Thomas in 1750 and John in 1752. Thomas found work as an agricultural labourer, did not settle in Stanion, but by 1770 had moved to Grafton Underwood.

On 18 March 1770, he married Sarah Plowright in the church of St James there. His brother John and John Corley, probably the Parish Clerk, were witnesses. Sarah was a Brigstock girl, her father, William, having married Sarah Hall there in 1732. Sarah had four brothers and sisters, all of whom appear in the Brigstock or Stanion registers.

Thomas was listed in the 1771 and 1774 ballot lists for the Militia, which made him liable for service should his name be drawn. Each term was for three years and if one wished to appeal it had to be made promptly and direct to the Constable who at this time was Mr Eyott. This list shows five Bellamy names in Brigstock with their trades - one was a butcher, one a cordwainer and three were carpenters.

Their first child, Mary, was born in 1771, a second Elizabeth in 1773 and finally, John on 20 July 1775. He died on 14 August followed by his mother on 27 October. As if this wasn't enough, their daughter Elizabeth succumbed in January 1776. It must have been hard to be a widower, working the land and trying to care for a four year old child. Thomas married again on 19 February 1776. Re-marriage was a speedy essential as the men had to earn wages and had little time to care for their children. Most remarried after about three months. His second wife, a local girl, was Martha Bullevant. The wedding was by banns, again at St James, and the two witnesses were Thomas Bradshaw and John Barrett, the latter probably the Parish Clerk. The union produced seven children, the youngest James being born in 1792.

Having eight children must have placed a great strain on a labourer's wage. We have little data from the late 18th century but in the Grafton Underwood church safe we found the record book of John Bland, overseer of the highways, which contains the following entries:-

1818   1 July to Thomas Bellamy 7 days 15d per day - 8/9d
        5 Sept to Thomas Bellamy 8 acres stone breaking – 2 shillings per day 16 shillings
        5 Sept to Thomas Bellamy 7 days at 15d per day - 8/9d
        Oct to Thomas Bellamy   18 acres as above 2/6d a day - £2-5-0
1819   18 November - 9 days work 9/-

The work on the highways was a local responsibility paid for out of local taxes and may well have been used here both to help a poor man out of difficulty and, at the same time, save potential costs to the parish.

Work such as this did not appear to be his mainstay income, as there is evidence of his being well thought of by the local farming community to whom he must have hired his services. In the Buccleugh papers for April 1793 there are the following "Certificates of Inform" all apparently written on one sheet of paper:-

"This is to Sertifie hom it may consarn that Thos Bellamy Barer hear of lived three years and a half during the hot time – A very faithful honest servant – with me Edw Brampton, Warkton April 3 1793"
"April 3 1793
He is Very Honest man and a good Carrector for wot is no from me
M Downing   Thos Eyet
Grafton   Grafton
"April 4 1793
He is a very Honest man for wot is no from me.
John Jones   Joseph Beaby   F Sidbury   Henry Hudson
Grafton   Ringstead   Ringstead   Ringstead"
"I do think with the above written Gentlemen that Thomas Bellamy of Grafton Underwood is an honest man of fair Character Witness my hand Wm Bodwell"

These references were requested so as to show that Thomas was fit to be a tenant of the Buccleugh Estate and were provided by some of the farmers who employed him. It also illustrates that he covered a number of farms in other villages, which were some distance from Grafton Underwood. As the crow flies, Warkton is two miles whilst Ringstead is six.

The wage figures for 1818, which is somewhat later, give some indication of the likely daily rate, ie usually about one shilling per day. In the same Buccleugh papers there was reference to the fact that after the Enclosures Act in 1777 Thomas was registered as one of the cottagers "who have no commons", ie no common land. He rented twelve perches from the estate, ie approx 360 square yards for ten shillings per annum.

Where possible the wives or young daughters would take on work which could be performed in the house, thus raising extra income. Reeling or winding thread was one of these tasks and his second wife Martha did this work. The report of the Northamptonshire Quarter sessions of February 1794 refers to this:-

"Be it remembered that on the 21st day of February in the year of Our Lord one thousand seven hundreds and ninety four, Martha Bellamy of Grafton Underwood in said County is duly convicted before me, Cecil Maunsell Esq, one of His Majesties Justices of the Peace in and for the said County on the Oath of John Eddings, Inspector of Worsted yarn, of reeling false and short yard in and for which offence I do adjudge her to have forfeited the sum of five shillings, exclusive of the charges attending the said Conviction this being the first Offence against the said Statute given under my hand and seal the day and year above written some wool of jersey which she took to spin, contrary to the Statute in that case made and provided".

One senses his sympathy and thus the light sentence. Five shillings was still five days work for her husband!

Earlier in this Chapter reference was made to the staunch adherence of the Bellamys to the Reformed Church. Thomas may well have been an adherent, but it was a local requirement between 1754 and 1837 for all marriages to be called by banns in the local parish church. His marriages conformed to this and he was married in the church at Grafton Underwood and not by licence. It was costly to obtain a special licence which came from the Diocese of Peterborough and equally it was wise to remain in the vicar's good books in case of need. Study has shown that many Bellamys, of strong congregationalist outlook, were married at great expense, by licence.

The following entry appeared in the register of Births and Deaths in Brigstock:-

"In the year 1777 some of the Dissenters refus'd paying the Clerk his wages alleging they had no right as being Dissenters but the clerk put them in the Spiritual Court, and they were lost and pay'd fifty pounds charges. T Keene vicar". Brigstock dissenters were still alive and active!

Martha, Thomas' second wife, died in November 1805 and in February 1806 he married a widow, Sarah Tebbutt, some ten years older than himself. Her husband who died in May 1803 was the son of Richard and Sarah Tebbutt of Brigstock, who were married in 1731, he being born in September 1735. This marriage lasted until her death in 1826 when she was stated as being 85 years old.

It is relevant to an age, where travel was not easy, to see how the family remained in the general area of Grafton Underwood and Geddington. James the youngest son moved away and found work in the general area of Kettering. Mary, the surviving child of Thomas' first marriage, was married to John Wright in 1763 and, although his son Thomas seems to have remained in the village and followed in his father's footsteps, it seems likely that the others, as they became able to leave the family house, sought employment elsewhere.

The records show that Thomas junior remained in the village. He appears in the 1841 census and died in July 1846. Thomas senior died in Grafton Underwood and was buried in May 1828 aged 79 years. His son, John, was a householder in Church Hill, Geddington at the time of the 1841 census and had a housekeeper, Jane Daunt, also 60 years old. John appears as a witness at a wedding in St James, Grafton Underwood between John Bird and Susannah Thompson in December 1822. Another son, William, is recorded as working on the roads in Grafton Underwood in 1824. There appears to be no reference to Elizabeth, Samuel or Ann.

Thomas' youngest son, James, trained as a joiner. Clearly from the reference to these carpenters in the Militia List many took up this job. His wedding to Lucy Ward took place in Pytchley on 30 July 1812, a day after his twentieth birthday. Lucy was the daughter of John and Olive Ward, farmers of Great Addington near Woodford. They were married in All Saints church at Pytchley by banns and the marriage certificate shows Mr Greenwood as the vicar, both being described as "of this parish". The witnesses were Lucy's sister Amy and a friend Elizabeth Day. All signed the register with a mark. The Ward family were still farming in Great Addington in 1874, viz Whellans Directory and it seems strange that the young couple were not married in the local church, which incidentally is also All Saints. It was to be a long and happy marriage lasting until their deaths within two months of each other fifty four years later.

It has not been possible to trace their whereabouts for the first nine or ten years during which time four of their children were born, but it seems probable that the advent of their fifth child, John, in 1821 triggered their move to Kettering, probably to Wadcroft where they were living at the time of the 1841 and 1851 census. Wadcroft contained a lot of the working class people in Kettering, outworkers for the shoe trade and the like and was situated on the east of the Rothwell Road but close to the town centre. James and Lucy had ten children, nine boys and one girl. Joseph (1) was born on 27 January 1835 but was a sickly child and died in March; his brother, Joseph (2) being born on 27 November 1835, the youngest son and their tenth child.

Samuel, their eldest child, himself a carpenter married Mary Parish in 1837. The 1851 census shows them as living in Nags Head Lane, Kettering and he, by then aged 38, was already a Head Carpenter. They had five children, four boys and a girl. The eldest Joseph was described as a carpenter, aged thirteen, whilst his brother George, aged nine, as an agricultural labourer. Work experience began early in the 1800s! When their son George married he moved to Silver Street, Kettering where, by coincidence, my parents and I lived from 1923 to 1927, but in 1865 he moved back to Wadcroft, which seems to have remained the family base.

The second son Thomas became a head sawyer, marrying a local girl Elizabeth and they lived in Newland, moving to Gas Street by the time of the 1851 census. Gas Street is very close to Wadcroft. The fourth, Frederick, also followed his father becoming a sawyer, settling with his wife, Mary Ann, at the Rose and Crown yard, as did the sixth, James, who married another Elizabeth and had eight children, four boys and four girls. Emma, the only daughter, married William Reesby, a butcher, in 1856. They had two children, Elizabeth and William. By 1874 William had his own shop in Montague Street. During the early 1860s Emma's brother, James, and her husband William became very active in their faith and on 21 August 1864 all nine children were baptised in the Gold Street Independent Chapel.

William, the third son, took a different line, becoming a cordwainer and, with his wife Mary, lived in Northall Street. This seems to have influenced Septimus who also became a shoemaker, probably an outworker stitching and making welts etc for shoes. With his wife Mary he moved next door to his parents in Wadcroft. The youngest brother Joseph, lodging with them, becoming a shoe maker as well.

Only one son, their fifth, John, broke away from the family work pattern, qualifying as a bricklayer and by the time of the 1851 census was described as a head bricklayer. He married a girl from Rhyall in Rutland, the third daughter-in-law with the name Elizabeth, and moved into 57 Mount Pleasant. By 1874 he had his own builder's yard in Victoria Street and then moved to a house in Alexandra Street. They had five children, three boys and two girls.

Lucy and James' youngest son Joseph, seven years younger than their eighth child, married Catherine Watson on 3 March 1855. He was twenty years old and she eighteen. The wedding took place in the Parish church of St Peter & St Paul in Kettering, in accordance with the ceremonies of the established church and was by banns. The witnesses were Elizabeth Bellamy and James Wrigley. Catherine's parents worked in the silk weaving trade which was very much in decline at that time. Her father Jacob was a silk weaver whilst her mother was a bobbin winder. One can well imagine them pointing their children towards the expanding shoe trade, Catherine becoming a shoe binder, whilst her brother Henry, aged eleven, was an assistant shoe maker. After their wedding, Catherine moved to Wadcroft from 40 Uppingham Road where she had lived with her parents. Joseph made good progress in his trade and in the 1866 census he is described as a journeyman shoemaker. They had ten children.

At some point after the 1851 census, delighted, I feel sure, with the way that their family had found good employment, Lucy and James moved in with their son James at 6 Swan Street, Kettering where they both died in 1866, he on 5 April and she on 20 June. This couple are truly inspirational in all their attributes and I believe that they left a long and valuable example which the whole family should try to emulate.

Catherine's first child Alfred was born in 1855 followed by nine others, the youngest, Joseph, being born on 28 March 1866. All were raised in Wadcroft, the crowded housing area of Kettering, in which the Bellamy family had settled earlier in such numbers. Unfortunately, my grandfather, Joseph died before I had the privilege of meeting him and I have no clear recollection of contact with any of his surviving brothers or sisters. His father, after whom he was named, was a shoe-maker, an outworker, and thus he was brought up as a member of a large family group, poor and hardworking, most in one way or another being dependent on woodworking or the footwear industry for their prosperity, so from his earliest days, he was brought up surrounded by the mysteries of wood and leather. His parents, Joseph and Catherine, were active members of the Independent Chapel in Gold Street, as were his aunts and uncles, so he lived in a strong Christian environment.

It is clear that Joseph possessed a very enquiring mind and that his schooling at the 'British School' in Kettering not only served to whet his appetite for education in the broadest sense of the word, but awoke in him an almost missionary desire to see the benefits of education spread throughout the county. Apart from the 'Dame's School', this was a period in history when schooling and certainly secondary schooling as we know it today, was very much the exception. Boys and girls were expected to be contributing to the family income from a very early age. His own parents were married at 19 years of age and when his mother registered his birth, she signed the register with a cross.

He was modest but ambitious and appears to have decided very early on in his life, that he did not wish to spend his life in a factory producing footwear or be an outworker like other members of his family. His success at school helped him and when he was twenty-two he became a commercial traveller using his technical knowledge to sell shoes rather than make them. He spent the first twenty two years with F G Abbot, and then joined Messrs Sargeant and Co, of Rothwell. He covered a very large area for both firms, although much of his travelling was in the south-west of England. It was there that his deep love of painting found so much satisfaction through his contacts with the Newlyn School. He did not possess a motor car. Cars in those days were only owned by the wealthy. Long distance travel was by train and then one continued by horse and trap or on foot, to call on the customers.

In later life, having achieved a far greater social standing than his parents enjoyed, he served on many Education Committees, and spoke at Adult School meetings throughout the County. He was active in many societies and was one of the prominent founders of the Workers Educational Association in the County of Northamptonshire. This Association had been started by Albert Mansbridge in 1903. A self educated man himself, he inspired Grandfather with his methods and determination to permit working men to obtain higher education. Grandfather played a major role in developing the Adult schools in Gold Street and in London Road, Kettering. This educational work, running alongside his membership of the Toller chapel, was a part of his Christian mission. He served as the Treasurer to a small local mission 'Children's Free Breakfasts' (see Appendix C) based on Tanner's Lane, Kettering during the winter of 1887/8 when he was twenty-two. This mission served no less than 5761 breakfasts during that year to impoverished children; no mean achievement, as poverty was rife. It seems logical that politically, he would have leant towards Liberalism. This was before Socialism existed as a political party and, as a Liberal, he was able to act independently of the 'Establishment'. He was a strong character and a person who perhaps today, would be considered as rather 'Left wing'. In his day, Chapel, Boot & Shoe Trade and Liberalism ran together in Northamptonshire and Joseph was a long serving and very active member of the Kettering Liberal Club.

Whilst working hard to educate others, he didn't cease to broaden his own interests and was for instance, one of the first people to acknowledge the genius of Northamptonshire's own poet, John Clare, who had died in the asylum in Northampton in 1864. Clare, the son of a poor labourer, loved the countryside and wrote copiously about it in terms readily understood by his contemporaries. He had been largely forgotten, but his poetry appealed to Grandfather, both for his knowledge of nature, and his very clear, fresh and uncomplicated verse. I believe that he wrote a number of articles about Clare but so far have been unable to obtain copies. He certainly gave lectures on the subject. A verse from Clare's "Universal Goodness" illustrates the natural empathy between them:

I look on nature less with critics eyes
Than with that feeling every sense supplies
Feelings of reverence that warms and clings
Around the heart whilst viewing pleasant things

Wherever he went he visited the antique and curio shops. My Father, Ronald, often remarked that his father couldn't pass a shop without looking into the window and added, that his return from a week's working away was always a source of great excitement, as, nearly always, he had found some item to add to their collection. These purchases were not always a cause for harmony between the parents and *"Father often returned to a somewhat cool reception!"* He stood in some awe of his wife and, apparently, very often, he contacted one of his children at the house on his arrival at Kettering station to announce that he had purchased yet another item and needed help! My father, or one of the other children, then sped down to the station both to see what it was and then help him to smuggle the item into the house! It was said that nothing cost over five pounds, still a handsome sum in those days.

This love of antiquity, of art, of porcelain, medals and books, was shared by his wife, Lily, although she often disagreed with her husbands open-handedness. Their house although cluttered with objects, was a treasure trove of lovely things. As a child, I remember most especially, what seemed to me to be hundreds of tiny china and porcelain mementoes of visits to various towns. Plates, saucers, little jugs, weird ornaments, miniature shoes and so-on, all inscribed with the name of a town, with perhaps some message, 'Welcome to Dartmouth' or similar. They were displayed on shelves running at picture rail level around the rooms. In later life, I thought that they were rather vulgar, but I wish I had them now!

His wife to be, Lily Bellamy was the second child in a family consisting of seven girls and four boys. From the earliest days, she was reputed to be the strongest character amongst all the children and very domineering. I do not remember much about my great-aunts or uncles, as our ways did not cross very often. However, Adelaide (Auntie Addie), who was four years younger than Granny, became my favourite aunt. I loved my visits to see her and to stay in her lovely house and park in Sutton Coldfield.

To say that Granny was proud would be to denigrate the enormous quality which emanated from her. She was a good wife, a devoted mother, she shared her husband's ambitions, was tolerant of his weaknesses and proved to be of remarkable support in all his interests. In her own right she achieved as great a prominence in the field of Sunday School education as her husband did in Adult education. She was not only an indefatigable temperance worker but also President of the Kettering Branch of the British Women's Total Abstinence Union. She was an incisive speaker and her "fine presence, and winning manner" (Kettering Evening Telegraph 1934) ensured that her presence on the platform was in great demand.

She was admired, respected, feared and loved in one way or another by those who knew her both in the Chapel and at home. She was placed high upon a pedestal by her admiring husband and her children and she revelled in the authority that this gave her. However, her decisiveness, her straight talking, without thought of the hurt that it may cause or the offence that it may give, and her very poise and graciousness, were inhibiting, certainly to me, smarting under some, probably highly deserved ticking off. I cried once on Auntie Addie's shoulder, and she remarked that she had always found that *"Lil had a very powerful personality"* whatever that may have meant. To me, there was no warmth in her and she engendered respect but little love. Equally, I never heard my father talk of her with the warmth of love but only with respectful obedience to her wishes. I feel that my grandfather had a difficult life and his warm nature, idiosyncratic life style, and bohemian outlook was more at ease in Newlyn than in Kettering. A cartoon of him, which I remember seeing but cannot trace, depicted him as others saw him, both loveable and eccentric. However despite these differences, they both made the marriage work.

Right and wrong for Granny Bellamy were etched in black and white and forgivenesss was not readily given. I learned from her a lesson that I have never forgotten. We are all full of faults, but pride and the harsh judgement of other people, are amongst the most insufferable. It is neither necessary nor desirable to expose others faults in too blunt a way. A blemish ignored often goes away

William John and Rebecca Bellamy and family 1892

Joseph Bellamy and his wife Lily Bellamy 1920

18a

The Bellamys Boxing Day Warkton 1910

The Bellamys Christmas 1914

quicker than one which is drawn to the attention of the world. I don't think that we would have agreed on this latter point!

Joseph and Lily were married in Brigstock, in the Parish Church of St Andrew on 3 April 1893; they were both 27 years of age. The witnesses were her father, William John and her sister, Adelaide. There is no guest list and thus no evidence that any member of Joseph's side of the family was present, only the other half, the Brigstock Bellamys. Grandfather was worldly wise by this time and had doubtless exercised all his charm and experience to win over this proud, rather haughty eldest daughter of a master shoe maker. Social distinction was all important in Victorian times, she was middle class whilst he was working class, but, despite the difficulties, her father must have been impressed by him, as he gave his consent.

This marriage between Joseph Bellamy of Kettering and Lily Bellamy of Brigstock in 1893 closed the circle between the two sides of the family which had started with William Bellamy in the late 1600s.

Great-grandfather, William-John, was a tough father and such permissions were not always given easily. I always loved to hear Aunt Addie recount the story of her engagement to Uncle Bob. Bob Streather was a Brigstock building labourer of little account when he fell in love with her and she with him. Her father told him that he could not marry his daughter and that he should go away and look for one of his own kind, adding that he could return and ask once more if and when he had his own pony and trap and some prospects. Off went Uncle Bob to Birmingham, worked like a Trojan and twelve months later returned not only in his own pony and trap but also with money in his bank account, and a building firm of his own! Permission was granted! Later he made a mint of money, built half the new houses in Sutton Coldfield and in Market Harborough and purchased the estate of Moor Hall, Sutton Coldfield for his beloved Addie. They always made my father and me very welcome there.

Mature, ambitious and well suited in interests and temperament, Joseph and Lily settled down quickly to raising their family. They set up home in 38 Mill Road, not far from where Grandpa's family lived and pursued their various trades. Their first child, Raymond, was born on 20 February 1894, Lionel, in June 1895, Leslie, in September 1896, my father, Ronald, in January 1898 and finally their daughter, Edna, in October 1899. Sometime early in 1900 they moved to their final home at "Kenilworth", Tennyson Road, Kettering.

From the very first, the children were subject to absolute obedience. It was unthinkable to question any instruction given by Mother. This seems to have been the normal practice in Victorian times. Discipline was strict and this was reflected in church attendance. Chapel every Sunday morning and evening, whilst, in the afternoon, Sunday School ensured that they were well versed in the Bible. Granny herself was a Sunday School teacher and, when they moved from 38 Mill Road to 'Kenilworth' in Tennyson Road, they left the Toller Congregational Chapel in Gold Street and joined the architecturally more modern Chapel in the London Road. There, she took, if possible, an even more active role in teaching and in other good works. My father always said that Chapel on Sunday although deadly serious and boring, could be hilarious too. Apparently the male members of the Bellamy family had excellent loud voices but were tone deaf, sang at the tops of their voices and created musical mayhem.

Despite the demands of their family, their church and their educational work, they managed to continue to expand their interests in many directions, their house becoming a centre for art and literary activities. Grandfather continued with his study of Northamptonshire poets, of which there are many, became an acknowledged expert and this was one of the subjects on which he lectured. As we said earlier, he was one of the first people to study the works of Northamptonshire poet, John Clare, and did much to bring his poems to the attention of the public. Clare spent much of the last years of his life in St Andrew's, but despite this, Grandpa considered his poetry to have great quality. Grandpa's library, which I can remember clearly, was located in the back parlour of their house. It comprised over a thousand well chosen books, or so my Father told me. *"You will be able to read them all when you are old enough"* he said, but they all looked terribly stuffy and as far as I could see, contained no pictures, so I took this more as a threat than an honour! Clearly, the books were not there for show, but were used diligently by my grandfather and I was told that the eldest son, Raymond, who was schooled at Laxton Hall, Oundle and London University, was the most intellectual of the children, shared this love of reading.

Their marriage seems to have been very well regulated prior to the start of The Great War in 1914 which altered life patterns for ever. All the children were at school, working hard and doing well in their classes. I have two attendance medals for their second son, Lionel, after whom I was to be named. He won a bronze medal from the Kettering Education Authority *"for punctual attendance every time the school was opened during the school years ended 1906"*. He received the silver medal in 1908, when he was thirteen years old. My father always said that you had to be very ill indeed to miss school and there was no chance of *"Fooling, Mother!"* Whilst mother looked after them at home, father broadened their interests at the weekend. The house was always full of interesting people, artists such as Walter Gash, John Parks and Frank Salisbury were close personal friends and the subject of Liberalism drew local politicians to the house. Grandpa travelled for both his firms and clearly was away many days of the week. By chance we found an entry for a Temperance Hotel in Penzance for 1 January 1901. He didn't take New Year holidays!

During this period William John died. He and his wife Rebecca, were living in Regent Street, Kettering at the time and the newspaper reports for both of them are highly complimentary. William John was ill for two years and died in 1907, whilst Rebecca lived on until January 1915.

Many stories of life at 'Kenilworth' were told to me by my father. Apparently, when they were very young, there was a period when Leslie was jealous of my father and some rivalry existed between them. One fateful day Ronald was peering down the well which was situated at the rear of the house, Leslie was standing next to him, when suddenly and (inexplicably!) he found himself tumbling down into the water, some ten feet below. His loving brother put the wooden lid back on the well head and danced around it singing *"Ronnie's down the well-ell , Ronnie's down the well-ell!"*. Luckily the maid heard him, rushed out, lifted the lid and with great presence of mind, using the clothes prop, hooked my father rather ignominiously by the braces. She then screamed for assistance and Granny came out and together they heaved the soaked, belligerent and unbowed figure of my father from the well-shaft. History does not relate what happened to Leslie.

My father was the smallest of the five children and at the age of twelve or thirteen, his younger sister, Edna, towered above him. However, he made up for his lack of size by having all his father's charm and tact. Auntie Edna, who loved him dearly throughout his life always said that *"even with Mother, he could charm the bird's off the trees and he got away with murder"*. Praise indeed! In fact my father was 5 foot 8 inches high, 1.5 inches shorter than I was, but he never struck me as a small man. He was certainly very persuasive, very courteous, perhaps rather old-world in a way. I never remember seeing him lose his temper, angry yes if one had done wrong, but always well in control of himself. Temperate in his behaviour and in his language, loved by women, but very popular with men as well. Auntie Edna used to say that he reminded her of her father and I think that this was probably very true. He too, was certainly a character!

On Sunday mornings after church, it was the habit of the head of the family to take the offspring off on some monumental hike which kept them out of the way until that almost religious and prodigious meal, 'Sunday Lunch', was ready. They walked, talked, looked, listened and learned. Grandpa was a born teacher, lessons were fun and the subjects varied. One day they might be on the great fossil hunt, another day art, the difficulties of the footwear trade, politics, poetry, paintings, copper and brass artifacts, porcelain, in fact, a seeming infinity of subjects. My father found that these times with his father were wonderful and although he always maintained that he knew nothing about anything, I believe that he knew a little about everything and that this sprang from the development of an enquiring mind from these early days. I have deliberately tried to model my outlook to people and subjects in the same way. The other attractive facet of grandfather was that he combined all this with a fine sense of humour. Life was never dull and the most boring subjects sprang to life. An article in the local newspaper after his death in 1918 says:- *"Kettering is distinctly the poorer by the death of Mr Joseph Bellamy, who was at one and the same time an antiquarian of note, geologist, art critic, an omniverous reader, well versed in natural history - and withal one of the best of good fellows, with a keen eye for anything beautiful, and he has greatly aided the Kettering Museum by his contributions of fossils and "finds" of the neolithic age and the Roman settlement. His favourite subjects at the local adult schools comprised antiquities, natural history and the lives of Northamptonshire poets."*

Fossils were a constant source of interest both to him and to the children. During the early part of this century the iron ore workings which fed the smelting furnaces all around Kettering, depended on the open quarry system. There was a complex of these quarries in the Cransley area, but new excavations were taking place all the time, especially about three to four miles out of the town on the road towards Rockingham. This side of the town was a favourite direction for grandfather's Sunday strolls and he homed in on the new quarries like a genuine addict. Auntie Edna always maintained that she was allowed less physical involvement than her brothers, but admitted that she watched avidly, as the boys ranged up and down the almost vertical quarry sides bringing their discoveries to their father. Iron stone is found in the Jurassic systems formed some thirty million years ago, and to excavate it, they have to disturb the accompanying limestone rock formations which hold wonderful treasures for those whose eyes have been opened. The discoveries brought back to their father by his devoted 'hounds' formed the large 'Joseph Bellamy Fossil Collection' which is still housed in the Kettering Museum. It must have devastated their Sunday clothes and certainly their highly polished Sunday boots but I can't remember any adverse comments on this from my father! Strangely enough this interest was shared by Giles, our son, and, in the 1980's, he and I enjoyed expeditions to the Weldon and to the Cransley sites to collect geological specimens.

Grandfather was deeply interested in the countryside in all its aspects. One of his favourite walks took them out towards Rushton Hall, the home of the Treshams in the 16th century. The road, which wound it's way towards Pipewell and Oakley was a very narrow one, and was bordered by an avenue of magnificent oak trees. Grandfather was incensed to see that these were being choked by ivy which encircled their trunks and gradually strangled their growth. Accordingly, on one of the Sunday walks, he took a small axe and aided by his children, cut the main trunks of the ivy and left it to wither. The deed was not noticed immediately, but some time later the land owner discovered what had happened, was furious, found out who had perpetrated this outrage and issued a summons against grandfather for trespass. Tradition, as recounted to me by Leslie, Edna and my father, stated that he was sentenced to pay a twenty shilling fine or serve a week in prison. Grandfather was so incensed by the injustice of the Court's decision that he decided to serve his sentence and achieve local fame as a man who was prepared to suffer for his principles! It does seem in character. I believe that his friends decided it would be stupid to do this and paid the fine!

His interest in art led him to purchase many paintings, including some by Frank Salisbury, who had recently painted large canvases for the newly furbished Houses of Parliament, some of the cartoons or drafts for these were also in the collection. I was always fascinated by one of these, which was in Uncle Leslie's house and which depicted helmeted soldiers, with spears, swords and ancient muzzle loading guns.

His closest friend of many years was Mr Walter Bonnar Gash, art master at the Kettering Grammar School and himself an accomplished artist. He painted Lily and Joseph's portraits in 1906. At some point, these were sent to an exhibition in the Derby Art Gallery and after many years, found their way back into the family. Of course never having met my paternal grandfather I cannot make a personal judgement as to the accuracy or not of the man depicted in that painting. I certainly knew my grandmother however, and I find it a strikingly accurate and perceptive portrait of her. Her poise, her distinguished features, her unchanging stateliness of dress and demeanour and her strength of character, come through most forcibly. I feel therefore that the man in the picture is grandfather as he truly was, painted by a man who knew him well. A strong face, ruddy complexion, freckled, as one would expect, with his auburn hair swept back from his forehead, a full moustache and a strong chin line, but all this dominated by his eyes which were deep brown with more than a glint of humour in them. Eyes incidentally which follow you round as you walk past the oil painting! I can see my Uncle Leslie and my father as carbon copies of the upper half of his face, both with the same wide foreheads and both with their hair swept straight back. *"There were no mirrors in the trenches during the war so you just combed it back"* my father told me! My aunt bore a striking physical resemblance to her mother.

In addition to his local contacts, grandfather developed a strong affinity with the members of the Newlyn School of painting in Cornwall. He acquired a quantity of paintings of that school, mostly by John Anthony Park, who clearly had become a very close personal friend. I have a letter from him, in which he says *"It is interesting to know that the Kettering Art Gallery possesses my pictures. Mr Bellamy was a great friend of mine. I have always enjoyed his friendship and interesting personality. I expect the Bellamy family have several pictures of mine etc"*. Many others owned by cousins, showed that he did buy from other artists there, such as A Beaumont. His interest in art took him into the circle dominated by the well known Victorian artist Sir Alfred East, brother of a wealthy shoe manufacturer, and himself a philanthropist. Mr East, who was a leading light in Kettering society, became a close friend of my grandfather and they met frequently in the local 'Art-set'. In 1904 Mr Alfred East decided to endow a museum and gallery as a gift to his home town, Kettering. Grandfather was one of the people who helped him with the layout and with the choice of the exhibits. Some of the showcases contained his fossils, which still form the nucleus of the Kettering collection.

Art exhibitions were held there, as indeed they are to this day, showing the work of a variety of artists local and otherwise. Together with Walter Gash, he helped to organise these, often submitting pictures from his own collection. His wife shared his love of painting and 'Kenilworth' walls were covered with pictures to the extent that no wallpaper surface was visible. It was surprising that neither of them showed any inclination to paint pictures themselves and none of their children were artistic.

During this immediate pre-1914 period, life must have been very full and rewarding to them. I have only one photograph taken around this time and that I believe dates from 1910, as Grandfather is wearing a mourning band, probably for King Edward the V11th. He looks the epitome of vigour, humour and health, walking stick in hand, moustache well pointed and a deerstalker firmly in place. Next to him is Lionel, aged about 16, then my father, Ronald, aged 13, also with walking stick in hand. In later years he never seemed to be without one! His sister, Edna, long haired, elegant in her Sunday hat and fur collar, aged 12, was already taller than him by several inches. Standing to her right is Leslie, aged 15, a very good looking young man and, according to my father, very conscious of it. Finally the linch pin member of the family and the "*apple of his mother's eye*" (Uncle Leslie's comment!), the eldest son, Raymond, aged 17. Already he was showing that scientific bent which was to take him into higher education and, ultimately, to work as a scientist with British Celluloid in Sponden near Derby. The only child to achieve academic prowess, he was educated at Laxton Hall, Stamford followed by a B.Sc from London University.

On 4 August 1914, war was declared and all this happiness was to be disrupted or destroyed by the ghastly war which ensued. The first to volunteer was Lionel followed in 1915 by Raymond, then Leslie and finally the youngest, Ronald, in 1916. In August 1916 Raymond was commissioned into the 4th Battalion of the Northamptonshire Regiment, posted to the South Wales Borderers, gassed at Cambrai and was seconded to the Royal Flying Corps, becoming an Observer. The airforces were under command of the army and the navy at this time, the R.A.F. being formed in April 1918. He ended up, home service only, as an instructor in the R.F.C. at Reading College. He was eventually discharged in February 1919 and then resumed his scientific work at Derby. My father told me that, strangely enough, he worked on the further development of poison gas.

Lionel volunteered in 1914, probably in May or June. He joined the 4th Hussars and went with them to France, fighting with the Regiment at Ypres, where during the first four months of 1915 they were very heavily engaged. In the photograph taken at that time, he is wearing 4th Hussar uniform and looks very young and vulnerable. The photograph that I have, bears the date "*Christmas 1915*", but I believe that this was added later and is an error, as in 1915, bored with the new role of the cavalry, and wanting to see more action, he transferred to the Royal Irish Regiment. He returned on leave in 1915 and the Gash portrait of him dated 1915, shows him as a full Corporal, looking a very seasoned soldier, rather older than his twenty years and wearing the uniform and hat badge of the Royal Irish Regiment. A local newspaper article in 1915 reported:-
"*Lieutenant Raymond Bellamy and Corporal Lionel Bellamy, both serving in France, were fortunate enough to be out of the trenches and knowing that they were not far away from each other endeavoured to meet, with the result that they met on Tuesday last in a French village behind the firing line*". It went to add that Uncle Leslie was under orders for France whilst, Ronald, too young for overseas service was with the Motor Transport in London.

Uncle Lionel was involved almost continuously in the battles of the Western Front and finally, wounded for the second time, was hospitalised in Cork. His Record of Service, dated 2 May 1918, states "*No longer fit for war service*" and he was discharged through wounds on 10 May 1918. In fact, his actual return home was delayed until the following November, presumably due to enforced "Hospital Blue" convalescence in Ireland. At the beginning of November 1918 he sent a telegram to "Kenilworth" which reads *"Discharged through wounds letter follows love to all Lionel"*. I have attached the original telegram to the back of the Gash portrait. He was also given a certificate, No 405594, issued by the Officer i/c Records No 12 District, which awards him a War Badge for services rendered to H.M.'s Military Forces since 4 August 1914. His army number was 8294-The Royal Irish Regiment. He was a courageous man, unflinching in seeking to serve in an active capacity.

Leslie joined as a Trooper in the Household Cavalry, number 119. He was a cavalryman from his immaculate tunic to his shining boots, and this pride of appearance he maintained all his life. He was transferred to the Grenadier Guards, Number 30780, finally training as an Observer, like Raymond, but serving in Observation Balloons rather than the R.F.C. On many occasions I tried to draw Uncle Leslie on the subject of the war but he wanted to forget all about it and told me very little. I understood from my father that his work as an observer was mainly carried out from a balloon although he did actually fly as well. His record of service gives no clue as to his activities whilst his war medals were awarded through the Grenadier Guards H.Q in 1921! - all very confusing. The photograph taken of him during the Army of Occupation in 1919, shows him well mounted and in full uniform. He was gazetted as a Lieutenant, wears an R.A.F. cap badge and on his chest is the badge of an Observer. My father said that he had served with great distinction. He was discharged in November 1919, and in 1920, to his mother's undisguised pleasure, married his long time sweetheart, Peggy Tovey, who came from Suffolk and spent much of the war with Granny Bellamy in Kettering. He then commenced his career as a Commercial Traveller in the Footwear Industry, following in his father's footsteps but selling components for shoe making.

The youngest son, Ronald, my father, was posted to the Royal Corps of Transport in 1916. Before serving in France he was trained as a motorcycle rider and served as a Don-R. He appeared to have enjoyed his war *"a few hairy moments"* he said to me once, but again, like most first world war veterans he was keen to forget about it and talked but little. Again Walter Gash drew a fine portait of him. He too looks very young and vulnerable. I think that this silence is normal in those who have been engaged in fighting a war. It took about 20-30 years for we 1939-45 War veterans to start talking freely about our experiences and of course for those who fought in the First War, there was only 21 years between one conflict and another. He served on in the Army of

Occupation, but the two photographs which date from this period, make it difficult to determine where he was stationed. He does however appear to be enjoying life thoroughly and I am sure that he revelled in the freedom which service life allowed.

Although all four of them survived the conflict, the effect on my grandfather was devastating. My father told me that to him, every day was a torment, every post or telegram a nightmare and that his health suffered accordingly. In 1914 he was a young and healthy man, 48 years old and in his prime. The war and the worry that a member or members of his family would perish proved too much for him to bear. All around him, his close friends mourned their sons, killed or wounded in action and the odds seemed to be stacked against his own sons surviving. He continued all his educational work, worked in the Chapel and the Liberal Club for servicemen's welfare, continued to sell for Sarjeants, travelling with difficulty in trains filled by service personnel, and did all that he could at home. His wife, apparently physically much stronger, did the same and was in the forefront of a number of local charities involved in war work. She, outwardly anyway, remained poised and calm, accepting all the anxieties and supporting her husband.

When, all his sons safe, peace was declared, grandfather was in a low state of health and succumbed almost overnight, to the flu epidemic which ravaged England. The second wave of this flu in 1918 took the lives of 2.3 million Europeans and it is said that more people died worldwide from Spanish flu in a few months than were killed during the whole of the 1914-1918 war. Grandpa died on 30 November 1918, three weeks after the Armistice had been declared. Even at this time when sudden death had been so common, he was deeply mourned by a large and varied section of the local community. The Liberal Club flew their flag at half mast, glowing obituaries were published in the local press and the Chapel was filled to overflowing at his funeral. He was buried in the Kettering Churchyard. Shortly before his death, he visited Newlyn for the last time and his friend, John Park, painted his portrait. In seven years he had changed from being a zestful, auburn haired, vigorous young man to becoming a white haired, drawn and careworn old man with sunken eyes. He was 52 years old.

After her husbands death, Granny continued to live at "Kenilworth" in Tennyson Road, accompanied by Auntie Edna and, after his discharge from the Army, my father joined them. Uncle Lionel became a commercial traveller, but the war had both debilitated him and turned him into a heavy drinker. Granny, as President of the Temperance Society would not allow him to live in the house. In any event he wished to live his own life, built a wooden hut in the back garden of Kenilworth and lived there. It must have been a heavy burden for Granny to bear with her strong views on alcohol. Uncle Raymond had married Kathleen Durant during the war, and with their sons, Raymond and Ivan, moved to Sponden, near Derby. Uncle Leslie married Peggy shortly after his discharge from the R.A.F. in 1919 and gave her no concern, so by 1920 they had all settled back into civilian life with the Great War put firmly behind them.

The Bellamy Circle

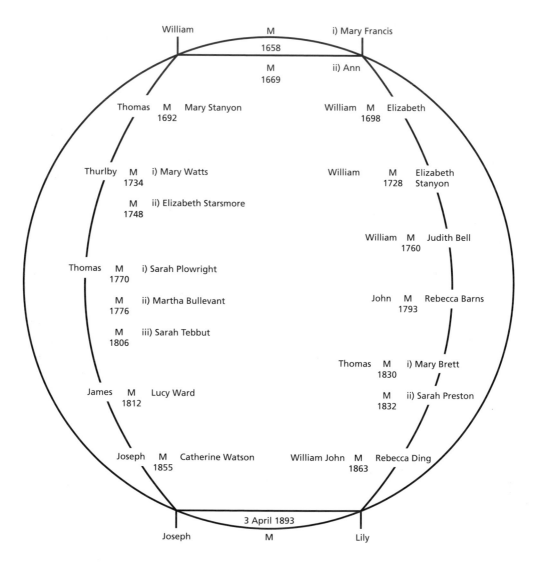

William   M   i) Mary Francis
1658

M   ii) Ann
1669

Thomas   M   Mary Stanyon
1692

William   M   Elizabeth
1698

Thurlby   M   i) Mary Watts
1734

M   ii) Elizabeth Starsmore
1748

William   M   Elizabeth
1728   Stanyon

William   M   Judith Bell
1760

Thomas   M   i) Sarah Plowright
1770

M   ii) Martha Bullevant
1776

M   iii) Sarah Tebbut
1806

John   M   Rebecca Barns
1793

Thomas   M   i) Mary Brett
1830

M   ii) Sarah Preston
1832

James   M   Lucy Ward
1812

Joseph   M   Catherine Watson
1855

William John   M   Rebecca Ding
1863

3 April 1893

Joseph   M   Lily

CHAPTER 2
Maternal parents - Gale/Gigg

I have not researched the Gale and Gigg families as a genealogical study. However, I took copious notes of what Granny Gale said whilst she was still alive and those form the substance of this section of the book. Grandpa came from a well-to-do background, his father George Gale being a solicitor and then Agent to a Mrs Bird, a substantial property owner of Phoenix Lodge, Brook Green. He married Louisa, nee Hammond, and they then had eight children. Louisa died shortly after the birth of her daughter, Edith, and her husband took to drink, living, it is understood, on the interest from £2000 investments. His wife had been a great friend of his patron, Mrs Bird, who then very generously paid for his children's education, clothed them and generally looked after their welfare. She seems to have been a very generous lady.

Grandpa, Frederick, was the sixth of their children and was born in 1873, baptised at St Paul's, Hammersmith on 22 May and made his first Holy Communion at St Marks, Hammersmith on 29 May 1887, when he was fourteen years of age. Despite this early religious upbringing, he did not remain a regular church goer. He had four brothers and three sisters. Two of his brothers, Ralph and George, qualified as solicitors and another, Tom, became solicitor's clerk. After the War, Tom got into severe financial difficulties over client's funds and was hustled off to the U.S.A. to get the scandal out of the way! He went to Detroit and I have a letter to my mother from his daughter Irene Gale dated 8 November 1921 on which she says that at last she had found a job. She was *"the last girl the man had employed"* so life was not easy for them.

However my Grandfather was not legally minded, he should have been born with great wealth, as he was by nature a dilettante, loving music, fishing and working with his hands. Initially, he lived on his inheritance but eventually set up as a cabinet maker with a small shop. He met my grandmother in 1898 and, according to her, swept her off her feet. He was a very personable young man, apparently comfortably off, but with little prospect of a financially secure future. There was little contact with his brothers and sisters and I have never to my knowledge met any of them. I formed the impression that Grandpa, an individualist, was the "black sheep"!

This did not deter Granny, who was considered by her father, who she adored, to be "headstrong" and for better or for worse, she married him in the Autumn of 1899 at Hammersmith Parish church. She wore a mauve velvet blouse, trimmed with guipure lace, a mauve suit and a velvet hat. The wedding was early, at 9.30 am, and after it they went back to a reception at the family house, 7, Wells Road., where they spent their wedding night. She was 20 years old on 14 April 1899. Then they went to live over the shop which Grandpa had rented at 78, Askew Road, Shepherds Bush.

My grandmother's family, Gigg, on her father's side were descended from a George Gigg, the stud farm manager to the Marquess of Ailesbury and he lived at Luton Lye in the Savernake Forest, Wiltshire. George had six daughters including a set of twins and three sons. The eldest son, George, died young; the second, Richard, emigrated to Canada where he became a rancher, returning to England to become Land Agent to a Mr de Sallis, who lived near Virginia Water and the third was her father, John. He was a first class amateur horseman and from a very early age, helped both his father and the Race Horse stud manager by breaking in young horses and subsequently training them. This promising career was brought to a sudden dramatic halt by a terrible fall which left him partially crippled for life.

Despite his injuries, he was determined to make his own way and he managed to get an engineering apprenticeship to the G.W.R. at Hungerford. He worked hard and showed great inventive skills which singled him out to the extent that the London manager of G.W.R. Engineering made a special visit to Hungerford to interview him, saw his work on developments and posted him to London. He had been married prior to going up to London, but his wife, aged 24, died in childbirth, his little daughter being still-born. Once there, he immersed himself in development and investigation work. Whilst studying some "new working" on the line between Aldgate and Aldgate East, his party was struck by a train and one was killed, one lost a leg and his close friend, Stephen Hobbs, lost a foot. Stephen had introduced him to his second wife, Olivia Carter Gigg, who he married in 1875 in the Quex Road Chapel of which she was a founder member.

My great-grandmother, Olivia Gigg (née Carter Gigg) who I got to know very well, as she lived at Wells Road until her death in 1934, was always a source of some mystery to her family. She was born in 1847 and christened at Christchurch, Spitalfields. When she was three years old, her father, a manager in the London Docks, was said to have died of the plague, but there is some doubt about this. Her mother, Marion, was a Quaker but later became a free-lance missioner working for the City Temple. Marion had three sisters - Alice married a jeweller called Seymour, Olivia married a fruiterer called Pritchard, a very kind man and one of great-granny's Trustees. Her mother died when Granny Gigg was 17 and thereafter she was brought up by her third aunt,

Helen, who had married a rich Greek merchant, named Mr Gegrocki. They had lived in Greece but returned to London and set up house in Stamford Hill. Mrs Gegrocki was a very wealthy woman. Granny Gigg had a private income until she was 21. She collected this from a solicitor called Powell at Old Sargeants Inn every month.

She took after her mother, who was a devout Christian, remaining as such all her life, and worked in the City Temple Parish. Strangely enough the vicar at that time was called Bellamy! She lived at Stamford Hill until her marriage, when she was 28 years old. She always concealed her age from Granny and from her husband, as she was older than him. As a result she did not draw her Lloyd George pension of 10 shillings per week until five years after it was due! My Grandmother was furious when she found out, although this was not until after her mother's death. *"Vanity, vanity"* she exclaimed!

The Great-Grandparents were married in 1875 and subsequently had six children; Richard in 1876, Nellie (my Grandmother) in 1879, William in 1881 and Alice in 1883. They then moved out of their house in Albert Road, Kilburn and went to Vespan Road in Shepherds Bush, where Arthur was born in 1886. Meanwhile, Great Grandpa had been engaged by Sir William Crooks and Mr Spanaletti, great financiers and the founders, I understand, of G.E.C. He was employed as a specialist development engineer and worked on a variety of projects including aircraft. Sir William bought for them the house in Adelaide Grove where they lived until 1896. In 1888, May was born but she died after six months. Some of the children were born at Queen Charlottes Hospital where Dr Platt was her gynaecologist.

Great Grandpa's work went well and, with the new company, he patented his new switchgear in the late 1880's. This was named the B.K.O. Switch because, as described by Mr Spanaletti, it was *"A bloody knockout!"* He then developed the principal of the automatic doors which are used on Tube trains etc, also patented, and the company went from strength to strength. Sir William's two sons left University in the early 1890's and Great-Grandpa became their friend and mentor until his death in 1906.

Granny Gale enjoyed a very happy childhood, she worshipped her father and was devoted to her mother. She was full of anecdotes concerning him. As the eldest girl she did a lot of the chores and helped in the dressing and entertainment of the younger ones. In the evenings when they were not playing musical instruments or singing, her father often talked about his childhood in Wiltshire. The family home there was very substantial and his father took his

31

responsibilities to his employees on the Estate very seriously. There was great poverty but no actual starvation. Meat was a rare dish for the poor, who lived mainly on bread and vegetables, and his wife used to provide soup or stew every weekend for those in need. At Christmas they would hand out joints of beef or chickens. The farm hands had their breakfast with the family in the kitchen at a long oak table and those without wives ate their supper there as well. After this, his mother would sit in the beechwood chair which now stands in our hall, and read the bible to the assembled company.

In the great winter famine of 1889, my Great-Grandmother ran a soup kitchen from her house. She tried to make all feel at ease by giving them some work to do so that they felt that they had earned it rather than receiving cold charity. Apparently, one day, a poor man with wife and five children came to the door, he was an upholsterer. She looked around and found the old chair from her mother-in-law's house which needed re-seating and asked him to do it. He stripped it, repadded it and covered it in black oil cloth as was the custom of the day. When Granny Gale came to live with us in 1954, amongst other furniture was this very drab old chair. We wanted to dispose of it but she told us this story, which incidentally I very much doubted, and so we put it in the garage for "re-doing some day perhaps". When we moved to Great Brington we needed another hall chair, so we sent it to the Blind Shop in Northampton. They telephoned in great excitement to say that the seat was stuffed with newspapers from December 1889, was originally rush seated and should they re-rush seat it! I never doubted Granny's memory again!

Great-Grandpa was a devoted husband and, each day, his wife had breakfast in bed, with tea and a boiled egg. The children ate with him and always had Allinsons brown bread, and a quart of milk. They were not allowed sweets except on Sundays when each of them had four, placed on the mantelpiece. At Christmas each had three presents and for Granny this was a doll, a book and a stocking filled with fruit and nuts. She often told the story of them crossing the Goldhawk Road one day when she was a teenager. *"Nellie"* he said *"Promise me that you will take special care now that these bicycles are on the roads. You can't trust them to avoid running you over like you can a horse!"* She recalled that the Goldhawk Road was sand and gravel at the time. The family were active in chapel matters and Granny used to go on the annual Sunday School Tea. She remembered clearly going on one outing to Ealing and picnicking under the trees in Sandy Lane, now part of the North Circular Road.

Granny had always possessed a lovely voice, and even shortly before her death, was able to sing beautifully and easily. Her father insisted that she should develop a trade and learn to earn money, so at 15, she trained as a seamstress, qualifying very quickly as an expert in curtains and covers. She trained at Whiteleys, where there were some 200 girls in the workroom. Apparently at the age of 19, she was appointed as the sewing room foremistress at Whiteley's on a wage of 22 shillings a week. She talked of the huge stockroom and the rats which used to slither over the bolts of cloth. Apparently she said that she had an affair with the manager and that they were planning to run a way to the U.S.A. together. Luckily this all fizzled out when she met Grandpa! After her marriage, she moved from Whiteleys to Shingletons in Hammersmith. My Mother, Olive Helen Louise, was born on 25 May 1900 so this prevented her from working for a while.

On 1 February 1901, the funeral of Queen Victoria took place in London. It was a day of mourning but a great spectacle. Granny, Grandpa and another man friend of theirs, went up to Hyde Park, walking there from Shepherds Bush and -her words- *"Closing the shop for 6 hours!"*. When they got to the funeral route and the entourage appeared, *"They lifted me up and I saw Prince Edward and the Kaiser whilst they only saw the top of their hats! The massive crowds were full of respect for them but we all loved Queen Alexandra most as she moved amongst the people more. The old Queen was virtually retired although we used to see her a great deal in an open landau at Virginia Water and Egham. She loved that part of England."* They often went down to Virginia Water to see her favourite uncle, Richard, who was a Land Agent there.

As a young girl she had trained at the Royal Opera House under Mr Bloor and sang professionally at concerts and as an after dinner entertainer. She had had many admirers, numbering my grandfather amongst them. She continued to do this and became very well known. In 1905 she joined the chorus at Daly's Theatre in the Strand. She loved it, stayed with it for five months and made friends with most of the stars of her day including Elaine Terry. This led to her being picked by Seymour Hicks, who had seen her at Dalys. He offered her a singing and chorus role in "The Cherry Girl" at the Vaudeville Theatre in the Strand. She was now on the road to stardom and Grandpa, who attended most of her performances, was delighted. However when the demand for her to be "kind-hearted" to some of the more important theatre goers was mooted, she refused and was sidelined. She left the theatre life very disillusioned but continued to sing professionally at dinners etc. I have her concert programmes from 1907-1926. She sang at a wide range of hotels and restaurants. Her agreement with an agent, Tom Alfred Brooks, bound her to four concerts in the summer/autumn of 1908 at five shillings per concert.

Grandpa was not making a living as a cabinet maker, although the quality of his work was excellent as can be seen by the examples of his mahogany table, corner cupboard and small chest-of-drawers, which we have at home still. Being a very popular man and gregarious, it was suggested that he should open a tobacconist shop, where his friends could meet! They remained in Askew Road. His visiting card reads:-

'Fred Gale. Wholesale and Retail Tobacconist. Pipes cleaned, mounted and repaired for the trade.' I have his silver cigarette case and the initials on it are "F.A.G."!

I have the impression that although they made a little money, it was insufficient to maintain them and Granny did a great deal of singing. The Programmes which have survived relate to the period 1907-1926. They show her singing at places like the Café Monaco, Piccadilly, Molinari's, Old Compton Street, Boileau Arms Hotel, Barnes, River trips, Open air concert in Hampshire, Chelsea Town Hall and so-on. The Agents letters speak well of her and she was in demand. The business, however continued to go down-hill until eventually they were declared bankrupt and the bailiffs were called in. Granny recalled this as one of the worst moments of her life. However she was lucky in one respect, as one of the Bailiffs advised her to declare certain items as her personal possessions, such as the piano and the musical instruments so vital to their life, these were then excluded from the appropriation and sale. They then moved to 5, Wells Road to live with her mother, widowed in 1906.

This must have been a very difficult moment in their marriage but they bounced back. Grandpa took a job as salesman to Cherry Blossom Boot Polish and Granny became the foremistress at Shingletons, by now a major curtain and covers maker in Hammersmith. She remained with them for 55 years. Her wages at this time were 21 shillings per week! Lower than Whiteleys.

One day Granny told me a little about the tobacco shop and I wrote it down - verbatim - *"When we ran the tobacco shop the tobacco was sold by the ounce of course, but then most people smoked pipes. It cost 6d to 9d per ounce and they put it directly into their pouches. The favourite was Glasgow Mixture. We sold cigarettes at 6d to 9d per ounce as well including lady's thin ones and scented ones. Snuff was the thing that I disliked selling most, especially when the poor old washerwomen used to come in at lunchtime and ask for a pinch to keep them going until night. Great red raw hands and they used to press a button into the ball of their thumb before coming into the shop so that the pinch would take nearly a quarter of an ounce! I was wise to them but felt so sorry for them that I couldn't stop it. They worked all day, 12 hours at the tub, for 1/6d. First class ironers got 2/6d and ordinary ironers 2/-. The shirts were delivered clean and ironed for 4d each. I remember that your grandfather had three white ones each week for 1/- or there was trouble! There was a man who worked the clothes boilers at the laundry, poor man, he always looked parboiled but I don't know what he earned."*

During all this time my mother was being educated at St Stephens School in the Shepherds Bush Road. She was a popular girl, but a moderate student who excelled both at music and sewing. Her upbringing was fairly liberal for those days, although she attended church and chapel depending on whether she accompanied her mother or her grandmother. Grandpa loved to go out, not only for walks, or for his beloved roach fishing, but to the theatre or any other any social event which was on offer. As a family, and individually, they were always in demand. Entertainment was very much self-made and Grandpa was an accomplished cellist, violinist, oboist and pianist. Granny sang, whilst my mother played the piano, and the ukulele. She too, possessed a pleasant tuneful voice but more suited to popular songs. Grandfather had the facility of hearing a song once at a show and coming home and playing it on their piano, whilst Granny retained the words of the songs. Together, they were always up to date with the latest hits.

The Great War was in full swing and a young man called Harold Turnage had been billeted on the family. He was an orphan whose parents had lived in India. I believe that he came early in 1915, and soon became one of the family. He had volunteered whilst living in India and so had no immediate family here in England. He then went off to France and was badly gassed. I found an envelope from him to my mother, marked "On active service" containing a card with a dried flower arrangement and "A Souvenir from France" printed on it. After his convalescence, he returned to the house as a war invalid, with severe breathing problems, an object of hero-worship by many young girls including my mother. He was fast accepted as a son of the house and called Granny "Mum".

In 1916, when she was sixteen, my mother left St Stephens School and was apprenticed to a dressmaker. She was very adept and showing promise especially on the design side, was trained with a view to going up to the East End into the "Rag-trade" proper. She was very proud of her first week's earnings and spent them all on buying a black and white fairy print which was framed and given to her mother. It is now in the possession of my daughter, Sarah Sacarello. Later she bought a very nice small brass figure of a nude girl carrying a parrot on her fore-arm. We still have this and were amused by Connie Manning when she was our "Daily", as she was too embarrassed to clean it! She thought it was naughty!

During his convalescence in the next two years, Uncle Harold and my mother spent most of their time in each others company. Inevitably the relationship developed until, my mother said, they had almost drifted into their engagement in 1919. This was accepted by the family and fairly widely known by their friends but whether or not they announced it and exchanged rings etc I never knew. They both loved the Theatre and the Music Hall which they attended frequently, either alone or with my grandparents. They got to know many of the Artists, were invited to many parties and often went back stage.

As peace came and life started to return to normal, my grandfather returned to work for Cherry Blossom. Meanwhile my mother became very friendly with the Wales family - five brothers, the sons of a big wholesale butcher from Smithfield Market. They were great sportsman, all educated at Christ's Hospital and prominent "Old Blues". The five of them played in the Old Blues Rugger Team at one time. 'Syd', the fourth brother, also played left wing for Middlesex. He was especially devoted to my mother, wanted to marry her and stayed as her faithful devotee until after her death, when, at the age of forty-seven, he finally married. In addition to these very close friends, both my mother and Harold were active members of the Tennis Clubs and his other passion in which he excelled, swimming. He became one of the champion swimmers of the Penguin Club, one of the leading swimming clubs in the country. Life was good to them and they responded enthusiastically - a very popular couple, they were nearly always asked out together. This happy gang of young people became known as "Ollies Troop"! She was at the heart of them all.

The unknown nervous illness which was to dog my mother throughout her life had begun to evidence itself in a more positive way at this time. She had developed a serious nervo-muscular complaint, which we now know was Myasthenia Gravis, see Appendix D. In lay terms this is a disturbance of the nervous system leading to periods of paralysis in what appear to be perfectly normal muscles. This problem which often led to early death, was relatively unknown and untreatable and was to cause her great difficulties throughout her life. An extract from a medical report filed with letters from her Doctor, Dr Laurent, who was her specialist and became a world wide expert on the disease, states *"Patients with Myasthenia Gravis - a deficit of the chemical transmitter acetylcholine in their nerve endings - find the simplest of tasks, such as eating, speaking, turning over in bed, increasingly difficult."* Bearing in mind that medical science had not pinpointed the cause nor catologued the effect it is easy to understand that within this complaint lay one of the major reasons for my parent's subsequent marriage breakdown. Disabilities, mental or nervous, are treated with far more tolerance and understanding nowadays, than they were, even when I was a child. The Bellamys were not unusual but rather typified the attitude of their day, nerves are there to control.

Amongst my grandmother's possessions, I found a letter from a great family friend, Fred Corbet, addressed to "My dear Olive" and sent from S.S.Nankin, a P & O liner, en route for Calcutta, on 21 March 1919. In it, he urges her to see a Doctor regarding her nervous trouble *"Nervous complaints are not the kind of thing to be trifled with"*; this presumably was the onset of the Myasthenia Gravis, then refers to Harold's chest trouble and recommends a Doctor Levin who would be happy to treat them both free of charge. He concludes by saying *"I am glad that I met you for I feel sure that Harold's choice of a future partner could not possibly have been a better one"*.

In 1921 Uncle Harold decided that he should return to India, rejoin his firm, and make a better career for himself. Before the war he had just started to work as a clerical trainee for Davenport and Co, Engineers, in Calcutta. He returned to Calcutta but became increasingly unhappy. He had, so Granny told me, some native Indian blood somewhere in his ancestry. Somehow this became known and he was treated badly by his peers. He tried to see it through but this, coupled with continuing ill health made him decide to return to England. Unfortunately before this took place, my mother had met Ronald Bellamy in London and Harold had been appraised that his fiancée had become officially engaged to someone else. He was desperately unhappy and wrote a series of poems which he sent to my Grandmother. These are two of them:

Oh, since love is all so short, the sob so near the smile,
Blue eyes that always conquer us, is it worth your while?
and

When first I loved, I gave my very soul.   *There is no other joy I learned to know,*
Utterly unreserved to Love's control,   *And so returned to Love, as long ago,*
But Love deceived me, wrenched my love away,   *Yet I, this little while ere I go hence,*
And made the gold of life forever gray.   *Love very lightly now in self defence.*
Long I lived lonely, yet I tried in vain,
With any other joy to stifle pain.

On his return, my grandfather, Fred, obtained a position for him with Cherry Blossom Boot Polish at Chiswick. He married after my mother's death in 1945 and his wife had three children. He worked until he died in the 1960's.

Helen Isabella Gale (née Gigg)
"Granny Gale" early 1900s

Fred Gale, Great Musician
early 1900s

Olive Gale

CHAPTER 3
Ronald and Olive Bellamy 1922-27

When we look back on our own childhood, we realise how much we trusted the wisdom of our parents, and how uncritical and unquestioning we were of their actions. Now, as I try to review the rather eccentric life style which I was forced to adopt as a direct result of the somewhat mercurial relationship which was to develop between my own mother and father, I am astonished to realise how little I knew about it all. I saw events in isolation as they actually happened, accepted them, and carried on with life; it never entered my head to ask why or to try to change things. The ensuing history of my family is based largely on my recollections, supported, where possible, by contemporary comments or by extracts from letters. The interpretation of events is taken strictly from my own standpoint and as such some details may be flawed.

Although my father, Ronald, prior to his discharge from his military service in 1919, was described as serving in the Army of Occupation, the photographs I have of the period, show that he was still serving in France. One shows him as an exuberant youngster sitting with friends outside a large building labelled PSAP and the other sitting astride the statue of an immense stag with the caption "some animal – Don-R. He was, of course, a Don-R (motorcyclist messenger).

He told me that when he returned home, he decided to continue with his chosen career and train as a teacher. A photograph of him, taken in 1920 shows him immaculately dressed in a pinstripe suit and looking very young and debonair. He found both study and the restraints of life at "Kenilworth" tiresome, as during his service in the Army he had developed a taste for that freedom and activity which sedentary work did little to satisfy. Auntie Edna recounted that Uncle Lionel and he used to escape in the evenings, go out on the town and, returning in the early hours, come into the house via the neighbour's garden. My aunt, complaining to her mother that she was not allowed such freedom, was made well aware that her mother knew what was going on but that *"Their Mother was not going to help them on their way to Damnation!"* He had become more like his father, an entertaining extrovert. As his academic interest waned, but with strong opposition from his mother, he joined a leather company as a trainee leather salesman, planning to follow in his fathers footsteps. His great friend and mentor at this time was his brother Leslie, recently married to Peggy May Tovey, and now building a good reputation in Kettering and area as the salesman for a local shoe mercery business. In order to accelerate the learning process, Leslie arranged for him to go up to London to work in a tannery in the East End, hoping that this experience would make him a more marketable commodity in the Kettering area on his return. He went into "digs" in London, settled down for twelve months training and entered the social life as far as this was possible on the meagre salary which he received as a trainee. He was a keen sportsman, although not a distinguished one and he joined various groups to watch and play rugger, cricket and swimming. During his lunch break in the City one day, towards the end of 1921, he met Olive Helen Louise Gale and fell immediately and desperately in love!

My mother, Olive, also had started work as a trainee, but in one of the many couture houses which centred on the East End in those days. She had a flair for dress design and as such was beginning to climb the ladder in her firm. She was 21 years old on 25 May 1921 and celebrated it in some style. She was vivacious, attractive and very popular. She retained all of her 21st Birthday cards, which I have kept as well; there are some forty of them! Her friends were found in all levels of society but together with her fiancé, Harold Turnage, she enjoyed watching sport, especially tennis, rugger, and cricket. Harold loved my mother with a single minded devotion and accepted all the difficulties which were to ensue, whilst, in my lifetime anyway, she always treated him as a beloved brother. This was in 1919, so clearly by 1921 their engagement would have been well known and of long standing. Perhaps she felt a little trapped by it and it had become rather too comfortable a relationship for someone so young, who knows? My mother was always jealous if Uncle Harold had a girlfriend and I was present at a number of altercations. However, they never seemed to be very close relationships and he did not marry until three years after her death. Having broken off her engagement, her ex-fiancé rejoined his pre-war occupation with Davenports, Engineers in Calcutta. Before coming home, he wrote consistently to my grandmother including poetry, poignant and baring his grief.

Anyway, according to Uncle Leslie, my parents met, were immediately attracted to each other, forgot all their promises to others and ignoring all the difficulties decided to get married. To him fell the task of trying to explain all this to his outraged mother, after all it was due to him that Ron had gone up to London in the first place! His sister, Edna, was charged with breaking off the understanding which had been made, apparently, with the unfortunate Miss Loake in Kettering. I suspect that Granny Bellamy had a hand in this. Meanwhile the culprit kept a low profile in London! Olive faced the difficulty with her own parents and with her fiancé. All parties were upset and Ronald was no more wanted at the Gale household, than Olive was welcome at "Kenilworth". In the end the influence of my two uncles, Lionel and Leslie, prevailed, and an invitation was issued to "That Girl's" parents to visit the Bellamy stronghold. This after Lionel and Leslie had visited the Gales in London and been made most welcome. Granny Gale did not speak to me about the visit to Kettering except to say that it was rather an uncomfortable one, made bearable by the presence of Lionel, who she loved dearly!

Lionel's war experiences and wounds had made him a heavy drinker and he lived out in a wooden house in the garden of his mother's property, whilst she, eschewing all drink and still Chairwoman of the British Woman's Total Abstinence Union, simply ignored his problem, pretending that it did not exist. When the Gales arrived at the house and were escorted up to their room, Granny Gale told me that Lionel took my grandfather on one side and whispered, *"There's a bottle of Scotch in the wardrobe, Fred, and two glasses!"*. They blessed him for that! The result of the meeting was agreement that the wedding, although unwelcome, would go ahead although it did not have either parents willing blessing and both parties felt that it was being entered into with indecent haste and without proper forethought.

Whilst all this furore was going on, Edna, who had recently become engaged to be married to Bernard George Shrive, was trying to get on with the arrangements for her own wedding, planned for the following May. This was itself a major problem, as Granny Bellamy was not entirely enchanted with her choice of mate either! She expressed the view very forcibly, that she was marrying beneath her and the engagement had its problems because of this. Bernard was a handsome, well liked, hard working young man, popular in the town, an excellent cricketer and a general sportsman. He had been much encouraged and approved by Grandpa Bellamy, whilst he was alive, so Granny was bound to support his cause. In fact Auntie Edna always maintained to me that she was railroaded into her marriage by her mother. This runs counter to the views expressed to me by my own mother and father who said that she was very much in love with Bernard but, like her mother, had great difficulty in showing any affection.

They were planning to marry on 18 May, 1922 and I wonder whether there wasn't a bit of competition as to who would be married first! In the event her brother won the day and his marriage was solemnised at St Paul's Church in the Parish of Hammersmith on 12 April 1922. The bride was given away by her father, Frederick, and the best man was Leslie Bellamy. These two, plus her godmother, Aunt Alice, Granny Gale's sister, witnessed the wedding. My father was described as Leather Warehouse Manager, his father as a Gentleman (deceased) and her father as a Foreman Carpenter. Leslie's wife, Peggy, attended the ceremony as did Auntie Edna, but, apart from the Marriage certificate, I can find no photograph or written record of the event itself. The young couple then departed for a brief honeymoon in Cliftonville, before returning to work in London. There was at this time a very close affinity between Edna and my mother. The latter had a very smart three quarter length coat which she had made for her own trousseau and, incidentally, looks very good in it on one of the honeymoon photos. Auntie Edna wore it, after her wedding, as a "going away" coat and thus it was a part of her trousseau too. She too looked very smart and I have an excellent photograph of her too.

After Granny Gale died in 1976, I discovered that many of my mother's papers had been preserved. Amongst them was a bundle of love letters which my father had written to her. As far as I am aware, they were all dated prior to their marriage, but I felt that these were a strictly private matter and as such, I decided to burn them without reading any. I also found the enclosed note from my father to Granny, obviously written immediately after they were married. I feel that this is relevant, as it shows very clearly the feelings that my father had towards my mother and the relationship which already existed between him and Granny. This relationship remained one of love despite all the traumas which occurred. He helped Granny financially by giving her a small monthly allowance when his income permitted, not stopping it until the 1950's

"Mum. Goodbye 'only temporarily' soon we will return, never worry about Olive. She will always be safe and sound and happy. I think more of her than anything on earth and will protect and love her always. You have this small compensation. May God reward you for all you have done for our united good. We will always remember you. Always your loving children. Olive and Ron."

Family matters during this period were made even more difficult by the sudden death of Raymond, the oldest of the the four Bellamy brothers. He was by now the chief analytical chemist at the British Celluloid Works in Sponden, but still suffered from his war disabilities. His wife, Kathleen, had borne two children, Raymond in 1917 and Ivor in 1918, but now with their father dead they had to be re-housed and comforted. Ronald's course was coming to an end in London and plans had to be made to accommodate him and his wife, both impecunious. Granny Bellamy was always master of such situations but, in the event, Kathleen, who was a very independent woman, took her family down to her old hometown, Rochester, where she was still well-known, whilst Ronald and Olive were offered a room in "Kenilworth", joining sister Edna and her new husband, as well as brother Lionel. They accepted this gratefully, as a short term measure, and were fortunate in that Ronald secured a job as a salesman with a leather merchant in Northampton.

That summer they took a week's holiday in Margate. A postcard to Granny Gale written on 18 August 1922 says, *"We are splendid and look red. The sun glorious this morning. do you think this is like Ron's writing? Love Olive and Ron".* My father, who had a very distinctive type of print writing, had addressed the card and my mother's copy was almost undetectable!

It must have been a great trial for two sets of newly weds to live with a very capable and autocratic old mother-in-law in such a small house. The problem was exacerbated by the fact that neither my mother nor my Uncle Bernard was considered to be suitable partners for her children. Uncle Lionel was of great comfort to my parents, loved my mother dearly and when she became pregnant in the Spring of 1923, she promised him that if the child was a boy, then he would be called Lionel after her beloved brother-in law. I don't know how serious a promise this was intended to be, but my parents both told me later that they had decided to persuade him to accept the role of god-father and choose another name, when, suddenly and unexpectedly, in August 1923, staying at a hotel in Newton Abbot whilst travelling for his firm, he contracted blood poisoning and died. His general debility as a result of the war and of his drinking, preventing any chance of survival. The family were devastated, he was a most lovable, kind hearted man and left a great feeling of loss. The garden room was dismantled and carted away and, according to my father, so was a cartload of the empties, which Uncle Lionel had stacked under the floorboards. All trace of his presence in the garden was removed, and a new gravelled garden made in its place. One cannot fail to admire Granny Bellamy's behaviour during this incident, remaining totally calm, outwardly anyway, never referring to the incident and treated it as if it had never happened.

My mother had a very difficult pregnancy, complicated by her Myasthenia Gravis, although in many ways it was made more enjoyable because my Aunt Edna also became pregnant and the two of them shared the domestic difficulties. It had been their original intention that Olive's baby was to be born in London but owing to her general medical condition it was agreed that unnecessary travel would be unwise. The nine months dragged on until almost ten, before, on 1 December 1923 in the nursing home in Colwyn Road, Northampton, after a difficult drawn-out birth, using forceps (apparently typical of such cases, as later correspondence with her surgeon, Mr Laurent, indicates), she gave birth to a 9.5lb boy, Lionel Gale - Lionel, as promised, and Gale for her own family name. From the very earliest days I was called "Boy" by my parents, so as to avoid the name "Lionel". Actually, nobody called me Lionel except Granny Bellamy and Auntie Edna! My parents were then both warned very strongly, that to have a further child could prove fatal and should be avoided at all costs.

My advent meant that the housing problem at "Kenilworth" became very difficult. It was a substantial house but the main living room was narrow and contained the large dining table, whilst both of the reception rooms were very Victorian and full of valuable objects. Upstairs there was one bathroom which had to be shared by everyone. It was somewhat easier for Auntie Edna, in that as the daughter of the house, she knew the form, running the domestic side of things just as her mother had done always, but the birth of her baby was fast approaching too, so soon there would be two young babies in the house. My mother told me that Granny Bellamy put up with all this without voicing any complaint but her very demeanour underlined her disapproval of the way "modern couples" carried on.

My mother was, to use her words, *"trying hard to conform"* to her mother-in-law's life style but finding it very narrow and constraining. She had been entrusted with far greater freedom by her parents in London, and enjoyed the theatre, music hall and concert hall life in which they practised. She dressed very conservatively at this time and the first photograph of us taken together, when I was three months old, the famous Mr Speight being the photographer, shows her in very traditional clothes with a dark, possibly black dress and loose silk coat with a large collar, whilst I am in christening robes, my head on a silk cushion.

My father, as an ex-serviceman, always had a kind word and a shilling for the war wounded, and there were hundreds of them in Kettering at that time. Two especially became well known to me as I grew older. One, who had lost both legs on the Somme, wheeled himself around on a tiny padded platform with three armchair castors as wheels and sold newspapers and matches in Gold Street at the entrance to the Post Office Arcade. I was always allowed to buy a box. The other had lost one leg, and had a wooden stump and a crutch, which he handled incredibly well. He was an excellent carpenter and made many of my toys. One day my mother had taken me, as a very small baby, up to see some friends, who lived at the top of the steep hill on the Northampton Road out of Kettering. Apparently, as she turned the pram ready to go through their gateway, she lost her grip on the handle and off I sped down the hill with her screaming behind me. Luckily our friend, the one legged soldier was walking up the hill and managed to throw himself at the pram, was knocked over but held on and stopped what could have been a fatal accident. They never forgot his brave action and he was a frequent visitor to our kitchen when I was a child.

My cousin Edna Mary Rowena Shrive, was born on 20 March 1924 and, some time after that date, but I believe prior to Christmas, as my father once told me that 1924 was the first Christmas that they shared on their own, my parents moved out of "Kenilworth" and into 3 Silver Street, Kettering. It was a red brick terraced house situated in the centre of the town, and adjacent to the main cross roads of Gold Street and the Rockingham and Stamford roads. Directly opposite was the "Rising Sun" public house and behind our house next to the rear entrance, a small banana warehouse. I have a photograph of my mother pushing the pram wearing pure Edwardian dress with a large-brimmed sun hat and it is amazing to see how quickly fashions changed during the next two years. The house itself was surprisingly large, with two main and two small bedrooms plus a bathroom upstairs and a large living-cum-dining room downstairs. There was a very big kitchen at the rear and over that, a long, narrow, but well lit attic room which became my playroom. I was told once that it also housed, or previously had housed, the workshop in which Auntie Peggy (Uncle Leslie's wife) carried out her work as a dressmaker.

I certainly remember life there as fun. The house was always full of people, music and laughter. I went to bed early but if the noise woke me up then I was collected and brought down to be exhibited. Both my father and mother were keen partygoers and free of parental constraint, there was an active social life open to them in Kettering. She was very much the "Twenties" girl, moving readily into the fashionably shorter skirts, but at this time, retaining her long plaited earphone hair-style; a competent pianist, singer and ukulele player, she sang and danced whenever the opportunity arose. My father was a willing and uninhibited ally and together they made an attractive couple soon becoming leaders of the Kettering "Young Set". Auntie Edna always admired her brother and secretly, I think, envied the way that he had broken away from the sobriety of the Bellamy Congregationalist tradition but she couldn't bring herself to do that, and to her credit, she remained at home, her mother's loyal daughter, staunchly maintaining both traditional home-style and values. This precluded her from socialising, a fact which was to cause problems throughout her married life, as Uncle Bernard was as social and gregarious a man as his brother-in-law.

The friendship between my parents and the "Old Blues" in London flourished and there were frequent visits by members, especially the Wales family. At one time, when the five brothers played in the Old Blues First Fifteen, there was a newspaper article in the London Evening Standard asking if this is a record! Uncle Harold usually came with them and as a very small baby I can remember being tossed from one huge man to another, shrieking with pleasure, whilst ringing in my ears were the anguished screams of my mother! In 1925, to their great concern, my mother became pregnant again, this despite all the warnings given by the doctors. This time matters were considerably worse and her Doctor arranged for her to return to see the Specialist at the West London Hospital where she had been treated before her marriage. In view of the likelihood that she would lose the baby if nothing was done, he advocated an operation designed to help overcome some of the muscular difficulties that she was experiencing. She went into the hospital in May, leaving me with Auntie Edna and her daughter, Mary, so that my father could travel up to London as required. A letter to her parents, dated 19 May reads as follows:-

"Dearest Mummie and Daddie,

Just a little note to say that I am quite O.K. and not a wee bit downhearted,yet, mind you I can't vouch for tomorrow. There are two new patients in this afternoon. I like it quite well here now thanks and I feel sure that after this I shall really be better. I must be better it is not a bit of good. I shall look forward to seeing Jackie tomorrow he will make it much easier for me if I don't have chloroform. I am very 'happy' and not a scrap frightened or worried so don't you be please. All my love, Olive."

I am sure that my father did not really understand the seriousness of her general medical condition. "Nerves" was something which we didn't either have or talk about as Bellamy's, (my father speaking!). So, dominating this illness was the whispered idea that Olive suffered from nerves, a fact which "The Family" viewed as something which should be controlled, and if she didn't control them, then it was her fault and therefore reprehensible. Even in later life, when she had to inject herself every four hours so as to stay alive at all, with all the effort that this involved, he simply didn't seem to grasp that she really was a very sick woman. To her credit, she never blamed him for this and I think that quite genuinely he was incapable of believing that any illness with a nervous background couldn't be cured by a little self control. Perhaps this standpoint paralleled the stigma often endured by those who suffered "Shellshock" as a result of war, I don't know. Happily the operation was a success, as on 1 November 1925, Audrey Almond, was born and mother and child returned to Silver Street.

1926 began well for the young marrieds, my father, Ron as he was known, was promoted in his company and a brand new motor car, a Morris Cowley, became the joy of his life. It was almost polished out of existence and when not in use was garaged in the front of the banana warehouse adjacent to our backyard. By this time, the man who owned this warehouse had become a good friend to us all. He always seemed very old to me, but I don't suppose he was more than fifty years of age. He worshipped my mother, and spoiled us with a continual supply of bananas which he brought in great green bunches from London to hang and ripen slowly in the cold dark of his warehouse. He had a horse and cart and delivered his product to all the green grocers in the town. He was only a banana specialist and sold no other fruit.

During that summer, we went down to Devon and brought back with us a nanny called Dodie. She was a big comfortable Devonshire girl, had never left that county before, and was astonished at everything that she saw. She certainly found Kettering to be the very centre of social life. I think, looking back on things, that from the very start she was doomed to failure. She was a very cheerful person to have in the house but noisy and didn't know when to make herself scarce. Her great ambition always was to find a soldier and walk out with him. Our afternoon walks therefore, always took us in the direction of the new Drill Hall at the bottom of the Northampton Road, by the railway bridge. She had many admirers there, and I spent most of my afternoons racing around the Drill Hall instead of out in the fresh air. My parents got wind of this and she was forbidden to go in that direction so we started going "into the country" by walking demurely down Gold Street until we reached the "Electric Pavilion" cinema. There she quickly went in and sat in the back row with whoever was available whilst I sat in the row in front. For a time all went well, I didn't sneak, I enjoyed the sweets, the piano player and the ice-creams as well as the films, with artists such as Charlie Chaplin, Janet Gaynor and of course Al Jolson. Then, one afternoon, we saw "The San Francisco Earthquake". That night I suffered the most horrible nightmare and in my fear, I must have inadvertently given away our guilty secret. Whatever the cause, my parents found out the truth and Dodie was sent back to Devon.

At this time our greatest friends locally were the Mittens, who owned the "Rising Sun" opposite. They were a wonderful warm family, a large, bucolic, rumbling voiced father who could, and often did, pick me up in one hand and his wife, Minnie, ever smiling, cheerful, generous hearted and full of kindness to us all. Their eldest son, Jim, was a stoker in the Royal Navy. His leaves were memorable events, he too loved our family and appeared with exotic presents from places he visited. Their daughter, Gracie, was about twelve years old at this time and spent much of her free time playing with me. She became an ex-officio nanny and as Audrey was rather delicate and demanded more attention from my mother, so I spent more and more time over with them, being thoroughly spoiled. Their sitting room over the Public Bar looked out onto Silver Street and I could sit in the window and watch the passers by and at the same time keep an eye on our house which was almost directly opposite.

I was three years old at the end of 1926, and have very few memories of that period in my life. However, two events stand out with absolute clarity. In May there was the General Strike, and there was a great deal of to-ing and fro-ing in our house, and a general atmosphere of excitement. It didn't mean much to me, but one day after we had had tea at Barlow's Cafe, the social tea place of the town, I stood outside with my mother, accompanied by Auntie Peggy, and we looked over towards the Art Gallery and the bus stops. After a few minutes a single decker bus appeared with my father, dressed in his plus-fours, standing on the running board. I suppose he was riding shotgun to the volunteer driver. I can remember dancing up and down with excitement as I shared my mother's pride in his courage, and also that of my Godfather, Uncle Mattie Wilson, who played the same role on the bus which followed.

The second event took place in our house in November. My small bed room was at the top of the stairs and directly opposite, connected by the corridor but across the stairwell was that of my sister. Audrey was very sick, having caught the flu, an epidemic which had devastated the country after the war. On the night in question, I was put to bed as usual and woke up during the night. My bedroom door was always left ajar with a light burning at the top of the stairs. I looked through the bottom rails of my bed. I saw with great clarity, a beautiful lady in a blue and white gown standing with her hand on the half open door of my sister's room. I wasn't concerned or frightened, then the lady half turned and smiled at me and I snuggled down and went back to sleep. In the morning, I was woken up by the unusual movement in the house, and was then told that Audrey had gone to join the angels. Apparently, I responded by saying that I knew because I had seen the "Lady in Blue" coming to visit her. My mother often spoke of this to me later, but never offered any solution. There were no visitors to the house during that night, and only my parents were there.

We went up to London after Audrey's death, as my mother had to go into hospital for a few days. I stayed alone with my grandparents and have a very clear recollection of the happiness that I experienced with my grandfather, including the games that we played. It is the only memory that I have of him and it has made me realise how, in later life, one treasures such memories. Perhaps I am more especially aware of it now that I am a grandfather myself. He was a cabinet maker at this time and some of the lovely inlaid furniture that he made is still kept in our house. He had made a small wooden train for me, pulling three capacious open trucks. We played with this for hours on the floor of the front room. He was a very good humoured man, slight of build, but full of life and you were aware of his presence always. He was immensely popular, a good musician, pianist, violinist, cellist and oboist, always in demand and provided excellent backing for my grandmother. He loved the theatre and the music hall and, like Granny, he knew most of the performers. Among their special family friends were the Lloyds - Marie Lloyd, her husband and children. She often performed at the Shepherds Bush Empire which was just round the corner and then the whole family came back for a sing-song and a party. These parties went on into the small hours and a lot of alchohol was consumed! Years later, in Great Brington, where our parties usually ended by about two in the morning, Granny Gale stayed to the bitter end and scorned our lack of stamina! This at the age of ninety! Granny often spoke of Grandpa's astonishing musical ability and how they could go to a musical, hear a new score and he would then come home and play it from memory on the piano without any difficulty. He was not a particularly strong man, he smoked fairly heavily as most men did in those days but drank sparingly. He had suffered some stomach problems, but they had been considered as minor and he enjoyed reasonably good health.

Just before Christmas 1926, he was taken ill and rushed into hospital, seemed a little better although in acute discomfort and died on 27 December. My father registered his death on the 28th, so they must have stayed up in London. The death Certificate states that it was caused by a perforated gastric ulcer. 1926 had not ended happily and they must have prayed that the New Year would bring better news for the whole family.

The death of my sister meant that my mother and father had all the time in the world to concentrate on me and undoubtedly as a result I became very spoiled. I was showered with expensive toys at that time and I suppose that in many ways they were trying to compensate for the loss of Audrey. My mother had always been an avid reader and also loved drawing so, somewhat naturally, we spent hours drawing and reading together. Many of the drawings which I did were sent up to my grandmother in London and she kept all of them. I have a sheaf of them here now, and they are all of trains, horses and carts and of little match stick people. Some of them are signed and I found a note on the back of one, written by my mother, which reads - *"I think it funny that Boy signs B B and then BOY or else YOB"*.

Granny Gale came to stay quite often and she too was a great reader. I loved it when she read to me and it was during this period of my life that we laid the foundations of the love which was to remain between us for the whole of her long life. My great-grandmother living with her in London was known as "Little Granny" whilst she was known as "Big Granny". I delighted her at about this time apparently, by telling one of her friends in London *"I have a Grandmother*

Bellamy in Kettering, a Little Granny and a Big Granny in London but the best wun is the Big Wun!"

I have a photograph taken in 1927, of Granny Bellamy standing with my mother and I by some woodland. She is dressed in Black with a black straw toque hat, whilst my mother, with her now fashionably bobbed hair (shingled was the term), is in a knee length white dress with a scalloped hem line. I look very proper in grey shorts and a shirt and tie. Granny had her hand on my shoulder and we all look very happy together. My mother's hair, like that of my Auntie Edna, was originally of waist length and she was very proud of it. However, unlike my Aunt, she felt very strongly about staying in fashion. This affected her clothes and of course everything else, including her hair. So, off it came and she joined the "Shingled Set"! A cartoon in the newspaper of the time shows a girl, "Miss 1927" with the "new popular hairstyle" and goes on to report that *"the current rage for women to shingle their hair has led to an astonishing boom in the number of hairdressers"*.

By this time the Shrives had left "Kenilworth" and completed their move into 13, Bowling Green Road. Mary's brother, Stuart was born in September 1927 and thus this extra space was very necessary. Our respective mothers were still close friends and my cousin Mary and I were like brother and sister and, doubtless egged on by me, allies against authority. We spent a lot of time in each others company.

The first weekend of November in 1927 included the 5th, with Bonfire Night falling on the Saturday. This proved irresistible to the "Old Blues" crowd from London. A friendly rugger match was arranged and they all came down ready for some fun. The highlight of it all as far as I was concerned was the Firework display which was held in our yard. I imagine that it was highly dangerous for all concerned but then I was only allowed to watch from the kitchen window; that was until the final bang, for which my mother and I were invited outside. They had bought some large and very expensive rockets, which they lashed to our dustbin lid and then lit them, so that they exploded more-or-less simultaneously. Looking back on it I think that they were a little astonished, I certainly was, and everyone cheered wildly as the dustbin lid took off majestically into the night sky and, narrowly missing our roof, disappeared in the direction of Stamford. There was a moment of dramatic silence and then the most frightful clatter as the whole contrivance landed in the centre of the Gold Street crossroads. Everyone then dashed down the alleyway to the road, where my father was met by a rather cross policeman, who had been standing within a few yards of the lid as it arrived. One can imagine the notebook and pencil poised and an *"Ahem......is this your property, Sir"?* I don't think that charges were preferred!

My great friend and child companion for the last two years in Silver Street was Gerry Tate, whose family lived in a large apartment house a short way from us in the direction of the Toller Chapel. She was the greatest fun to be with and we developed a series of games which kept us occupied for hours with the simplest of stage props. We were inseparable and played endlessly, especially games of imagination, such as Dartmoor ponies caught in the snow and the like. She used to dare me to do things and I willingly accepted her challenges. One day we decided to follow my mother's example and do some sewing. I put my fingers and some cloth under the head of the sewing machine, whilst she put her foot on the treadle in order to find out what happened.. The predictable result was agonising; I fainted, fell and the needle pinned my hand to the sewing plate. My finger bled copiously and, as my mother tried to release me so the needle broke and remained in it. General panic set in whilst my distraught parent, who was only in the next room, had to send the maid for the doctor to extract the end of the needle. That taught me a good lesson and I have been somewhat wary of such machines ever since!

The winter of 1927 was very hard and Granny Gale came up by train to stay for Christmas. Very excited, we all went to the station to collect her. The car skidded as we turned into Station Road and nearly hit the railings round the gardens there. I thought it was wonderful. My mother screamed most satisfactorily and my father said we had *"Looped the Loop"*, an exercise which in the future I often begged him to carry out. He did this by wobbling the steering wheel, thus making the car do a series of "S" movements. I was an appreciative audience and always loved it. My main memory of that Christmas however,was that when we ran out of milk, my father decided to go to a farm on the Barton Seagrave road in order to get some more. I imagine that it was an excuse to have a drive on the snow. I believe that Christmas Eve had seen the worst blizzard in England for centuries. Anyway, we set off, and in places the snow was piled above the height of the car right back to the hedgerows. On the way back we stopped on the road above Wicksteed Park and had a snowball fight, Granny Gale joining in with great gusto. Of course, although to me she was very old, in fact she was only 48 and full of energy.

I have a strong impression during the first eighteen years of my life of winters which not only brought snow, sometimes very heavy, but also splendid frosts. Surrounding Kettering were a number of meadows which flooded very easily and, of coure, the wonderful Wicksteed Park. I learnt to skate at a fairly early age and I well remember my father buying a pair of skate boots for me in the late 1930s from a company manufacturing on the Rockingham Road. It would be wrong to say that I was a very good skater, but I was sure on my feet and the opportunities were amazing, for instance there was very thin water in the meadow prior to the Kettering Golf Course. This froze very readily and a large number of us younger ones from the town spent much of the Christmas holidays there. The fact that I could skate became a distinct advantage during the battles in Holland in 1944/45.

Christmas 1927 was also unforgettable for me as it was then that I received from my parents the present of the most wonderful pedal car. It was made by Lines Bros, and with it's dark blue bodywork and chromium plated radiator it looked like a bull-nosed Morris. It was every boy's dream car, equipped with running boards, spare petrol can, horn with rubber bulb and at the back a pannier that opened to take the shopping. The number was LB1 that made it very personalised! I was unable to be separated from it and drove out in it every day as we did the rounds, visiting the shops or calling on friends. My poor mother must have been driven demented, as doubtless half the time I needed a helping hand, not to mention a jolly good push! On one occasion that I still remember very clearly, we arrived at the main cross-roads in the centre of Kettering and my mother wished to cross over to visit Woodcocks store which was on the corner. The policeman, who was on duty controlling the traffic, spotted us, and majestically calling all the vehicles to a halt, waved us across. We both felt very proud.

One of the great events of the year for us was the Annual Hospital Fete. This was the major event during which we raised funds for the upkeep of our hospital. Everyone took some part but the crowning event was the Carnival Parade. This comprised dozens of floats manned, designed and decorated by all the organisations in Kettering. The whole town turned out to see the fun, at the end of which the Mayor chose the best float and presented them with the cup; a cup which was fiercely competed for. Usually my mother and father took part on one of the floats and I used to go over to the "Rising Sun", sitting in the window there to get the best view of the parade as it came along Silver Street and turned left down Gold Street. Minnie Mitten used to give me cash which we used to throw down to the collectors in fancy dress who accompanied the parade or, really thrilling, put it into the pouch presented to those in the upper windows by clowns walking on enormously tall stilts. It was always a wonderful day and we were all thrilled by it.

Mummy was always game for new excitements and when a new fire engine was delivered to a very proud Kettering Fire Brigade, as was their practice, they tested it on the hill at Rockingham, probably the steepest and longest in the county. We were due to have tea at the Castle that day so I was left in charge of the Saunders Watson's Nanny and taken with the other children to a view point on the S-bend whilst my mother and another lady joined the fire engine in the village. It was very impressive to see it grind up the hill, very smoky and extremely noisy, with my mother sitting between two firemen on the side. We also used to go to tea with the Wicksteeds in their lovely house overlooking the park which they gave so generously to the town. That was always fun because our mothers left us to our own devices and went off to play croquet. It had a marvellous garden for children with masses of bushes and places in which we could hide.

I was now four years old and the prospect of school began to loom ahead. My reading, writing and drawing, as my letters showed, was well above average, thanks both to my parents and to Granny Gale. I was really quite excited at the idea.

"Great Granny" Gigg holding her Great Grandson Bill 1924

Olive (née Gale) wife of
Ronald Bellamy 1925

Ronald Bellamy 1921

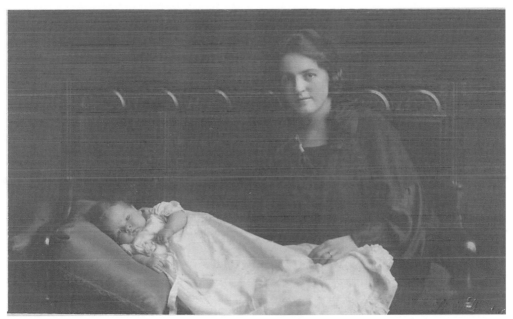

Olive Bellamy and Bill 1924

Olive Bellamy in Edwardian
clothing 1924

Bill 1925

Silver Street, Kettering

Hospital Fete

Bill 1927

CHAPTER 4
Ronald and Olive Bellamy 1928-31

The Spring of 1928 started badly. I contracted tonsilitis and was put into the Kettering Hospital for a tonsilectomy. The children's ward was straight ahead inside the front door of the old stone built building. I remember it as light and airy with a beautifully polished wooden floor. I was happy there and very well cared for. Apparently I was the first person in Kettering to have tonsils removed with a hot electric wire. I received a flood of visitors and, consequently, an almost unlimited supply of ice-creams! Shortly after I left hospital, I was playing with some other children at a friend's house and stumbled backwards as I went to retrieve a toy motorcar. I stood up suddenly close to the French windows, turned, lost my balance and tumbled straight through them, cutting my head deeply enough to warrant stitches. This provided another occasion for a spoiling. Funnily enough when in June 1944 I was wounded in the head by a German mortar fragment, it ran almost exactly along the faint line of the original scar.

Despite many friends, as an only child, I was often alone and although I was very occupied with reading and drawing, my comfort always was to be accompanied by my rather tatty Teddy-bear, Nina. I missed Nina later when I went away to school, but kept her by me on my bed throughout the holidays, only parting with her in 1941 when I joined the army! Sadly I then gave her away to our landlady's daughter, Muriel Sleath.

I found plenty of time for mischief. On one occasion, bored and ignored by my mother, who was desperately trying to cook the Sunday lunch, I turned on the gas in the oven whilst she was making the gravy on the top of the stove. A few minutes later she opened the oven door to put the plates in to warm. The resultant explosion was dramatic and I was astonished to see her blown out through the kitchen door and into the yard. Luckily the door was open at the time. My father came rushing in and picking her up took her into the sitting room and sent for the doctor. She lost her eye-brows, eyelashes and a lot of her hair. Although her back was badly bruised, she was not seriously hurt. I don't think I even received a ticking off!

Life was exceptionally good for us at this time, my father came home early one day, pulled my mother into his arms and danced round the floor with her shouting *"We've made it! We've made it! I've been given a rise to TEN POUNDS A WEEK!"* This was clearly a very substantial salary at a time when factory workers were getting less than £2.00 per week.

During this period of my childhood, I was often sick and lost weight; this had been put down to Acidosis, but by May 1928, I was losing weight and going down-hill rather rapidly. I was referred to a Consultant Physician and was diagnosed as having a Rheumatic Heart. This was a bad blow for my parents, not only did it cause them grave anxiety with Audrey's death still fresh in their minds, but it threw all their plans of moving into a larger house into jeopardy. However, I was soon installed in the front bedroom in Silver Street, where I was tempted with rich food and smothered in kindnesses. Minnie Mitten, from "The Rising Sun" sent over special titbits daily, whilst her daughter, Gracie, virtually lived in as a playmate. One day, Granny Bellamy, a very rare visitor, appeared with a jugged hare! This certainly caused a few raised eyebrows as it contained a lot of port! Anyway, my father enjoyed it! I did a lot of writing and drawing during this time and Granny Gale kept my crayon drawing of the "Mauretania", the great liner of that time, which I now have. Despite all the cossetting, I still failed to respond to treatment, so it was decided that I should be sent down to Torquay for a long convalescence, accompanied by my mother.

By this time we had another new car, this time a big four-door Austin with a fabric body, and we all set off with Granny Gale and me in the back. I can remember one incident on the journey. We reached Telegraph Hill just the other side of Exeter and with a struggle and in low gear managed to reach the top. There we saw a host of cars all with their bonnets up and the radiator caps removed, boiling and steaming merrily. We joined them and my father wrapped a duster round it and carefully unscrewed the cap of our radiator. Suddenly, there was a great gush of boiling water, which shot up into the air and if it had not been for his thick tweed jacket he would have been badly scalded. This was the age of punctures and boiling engines, so it was not unusual.

I remember little of my stay in Torquay except that it was very boring and I longed for my toys. We lodged in a hotel on the cliff tops above the "Palm Court" and it was a long descent to the beach - and an even longer climb back to the hotel! Quite soon however I started to gain weight and the local physician said that he didn't think that I had a rheumatic heart anyway! So after a couple of months we returned to Silver Street.

July 1928 was marked by being accompanied by Auntie Edna, Mary and Stuart on our annual holiday to Cliftonville. My mother loved Cliftonville and spent holidays there right up to the end of the war. We stayed in a Boarding House and spent very happy days on the beach. Mary and I seem to have shared bathing costumes, as in the many photographs that exist of this event she and I both appear in the famous zebra swimming costume. Stuart was not yet a year old at the time. It is fascinating to see the two mothers in their cotton frocks and cloche hats walking along with us in our bathing suits. When wearing a costume my mother always wore a swimming cap. Everyone was very discreetly covered.

On our return from Devon it was decided that I was ready to go to school and I was entered for Miss Woodward's Primary School, which was situated in the rooms adjacent to the Congregational Chapel, a stones throw from Granny Bellamy and "Kenilworth". I believe that Mary went to Hawthorn Road School at the same time

It was an unbreakable tradition in the family that, unless you were out of town, a daily statutory visit to "Mother" was essential. It was a ritual that my mother found very hard to cope with and the fact that my school was so close placed even greater pressures on her to comply. I think on the whole that she managed it, but relations between Silver Street and Kenilworth were often a little strained. I certainly loved going to school, I wasn't one of the world's great scholars, but I had a desire to learn and Miss Woodward was an excellent teacher. I can see her now as a patient, kindly but rather subservient type of woman who was most respectful to my parents. I think that Granny Bellamy had a strong hand in the management of the Chapel Rooms which might have had something to do with it! I had many little friends there, Woodcocks, Clarks, Seddons and others whose names I forget. I discovered a letter to Granny Gale for her birthday in 1930, in it I write *"I cleared the inkwells out the other day. A new little boy is at school his name is Clifford Wise he does not do his work and he has to do his sums on rainy days while we play indoors at games all day he must not"*. Actually we were a very happy crowd and I enjoyed all the children's parties which were generated automatically by birthdays and other festivities.

In the autumn, in common with most of my peers, I entered into Miss Pinkham's Dancing School. I remember little of it but I can see myself in sailor's uniform, thoroughly enjoying dancing the sailor's hornpipe at Miss Pinkham's Annual Christmas Exhibition of her students. This, a charity evening, took place in one of the local theatres and always played to a packed house. Together with five others I was on first, dancing the "Sailor's Hornpipe". This was rapturously received, (I'm sure that as nowadays all parents wanted their children to be applauded!) and at the end of it we were all presented with gifts. Uncle Harold from London, who was there, had prepared me for his present, which was a milkman's trolley with wooden bottles in it, very realistic but in miniature. This was wheeled on stage and I, as instructed by him, picked up a couple of bottles and yodelled *"MI- ILK"* at the top of my voice. During the ovation which this non-programmed action received, I was hustled off the stage with my cart and I don't think I was ever asked to perform again!

In the Spring of 1929 we left Silver Street. For some time my parents had been discussing the possibility of moving into a larger house and excitement rose as the options were discussed. My mother was a close friend of Mrs Seddon, who lived with her family at the top of Station Road and this contributed to their keenness to find a house in that area. I too, loved Mrs Seddon and she reciprocated. At one famous tea party I apparently turned to her and said! *"If I hadn't got a real Mummy, I would choose you as my Mummy"*! A real vote winner!

Eventually the parents settled for No 25 Station Road, which is at the bottom on the left hand side as you go down to the station. Nowadays, together with the adjacent house, it has been converted into a hotel. Granny Gale came to stay with us and altered or made all the curtains and loose covers. That was her profession, so they were very smart. There was a large garden at the back and my father brought in our one legged friend as gardener. Together at the weekends, they laid better lawns, pruned the fruit trees and finally, they built a low wall across the garden with steps from the lower level to the higher, thus creating a patio adjacent to the sitting room. A short mews lane at the end of the garden, debouching into Queensberry Road, led to our garage, a fact which brought him great pleasure as he still loved his motorcar! We loved our new house and the level of entertainment and general jollification grew apace. Mattie Wilson, my godfather, and a very close friend to them both, was as exuberant as they were and the group that grew around them really set a great pace, with dances, Farmers Hunt Balls, musical evenings, fancy dress parties and so on. I have a splendid photograph of them all in fancy dress on the back of which my mother has written the names but described the two of them as "Plain and Wholesome"!

1929 was memorable for the expedition mounted by my father, ably assisted by Uncle Harold, the Wales family, Mattie Wilson and another great favourite of mine Harry Palmer. Uncle Harry, a bachelor, was well over six feet tall and I worshipped him both for his size and the fact that he worked in Java, which I found very romantic. This motley crowd were loosed on an unsuspecting France during the August holidays, in the guise of playing Rugger matches, whilst my mother and I, joined by her great friend Phyllis, were dispatched to the "Bungalow", Cliftonville to await events. There were postcards and letters to keep us abreast of developments but I don't imagine she did more than guess the half of it! They visited the battlefields as a matter of course, and I think that at this stage things were more or less in control, but during the second week they felt less inhibited and starting with a monumental party in Paris, which seems to have got out of hand, as they eventually had to be poured back into their hotel after having caused some devastation! My father sent a collection of postcards from Paris to prove that they were there! I still have them.

They then progressed through the unsuspecting countryside of Normandy for five days before catching the ferry back to Dover from Boulogne. I believe that they did manage to play a few games of Rugger, but the French hospitality overwhelmed them! Apparently, at one point, there was some confusion as to the real purpose of a bidet and when after misuse the contents had to be transported to a more accommodating vessel, my father was chosen for the task and poured them down the well outside the back door of the hostelry! To make matters worse he was caught in the act and they had to drive off rather fast. Life was quieter at Cliftonville and I have a photograph of myself dressed in my sailor suit sitting on top of a stuffed elephant. My mother sent this to Granny Gale and on the back said " *Boy (Bless him) taken last Sunday after tea at the Bungalow, Cliftonville (Aug 1929)*". Some of us had to behave with propriety! Clearly Granny had sent a postcard to us because I sent one to her which reads *"Thankyou for your picture are you injoying yourself love and X's Boy"*.

There were other holidays and enjoyments around that time. We went down to Devon on a touring holiday taking Harry Palmer with us. Because he was such a tall man, he sat in the front of our car which had a canvas hood, and was considered to be very sporting. I think that it was a "Clino". We travelled without incident for much of the way, but then my father decided to put the car through its paces by climbing Cantisbury Hill in North Devon, a well known trials hill at that time. All went well until we were about two thirds of the way up, when he missed a gear and lost speed. At that point he shouted to Uncle Harry to bail out and push. Uncle Harry leapt to his feet and pushed his head straight through the canvas hood, becoming fixed there with his arms pinned to his sides. My father and mother became quite hysterical with laughter and the car finished up on the side of the road, whilst they tried to extricate him.

I believe that it was in 1929 that the Graf Zeppelin visited the airship station at Cardington near Bedford. My parents were both very excited as they had been invited to join an official party and go into the saloon of the Graf Zeppelin and inspect it. The idea was that the R101, which was due to make her maiden commercial voyage, was to arrive at the same time and exchange visits would be made. We arrived on the field at about 2 o'clock. The R101, which was the world's biggest airship and had been built at Cardington in one of the two huge hangars there, was already in the air by the mooring tower trying to tie up. It was rather like mooring a ship as a rope was thrown to secure it to the tower and then it was winched in, giving access to the platform etc (see photograph). It was a windy day and they were not being very successful. The tower was a steel pylon, with a bell top and presumably contained stairs etc to give access to the platform.

Suddenly, everyone was pointing south towards the Chiltern Hills where a silver cigar shaped object came into view. I recollect that it seemed to be very fast in its approach although I don't think it flew at more than about 75 mph. It swept over our heads very low, and landed with exquisite precision on the grass within the boundary ropes which were laid out ready. My parents were already in the enclosure whilst I had to wait outside with Gracie Mitten. The steps were then set up and there was a great amount of comings and goings around the Zeppelin, whilst all the time the unfortunate R101 was still struggling to get tied up! The wind was rising which, I believe, cut short the visit and after about three quarters of an hour, the Zeppelin just lifted off, almost noiselessly and disappeared southwards. The R101 was still struggling when we left for home.

A year later, in October 1930, the R101 crashed in the north of France killing 44 people. Apparently this was caused by a rain storm and it flew into a hillside. In 1936 I was with my father enjoying a few days holiday on the south coast. It was a very sunny day with clear skies and he pointed to the sky off Brighton and said *"Look there goes that blasted German spyship photographing all our south coast defences"*. It was high in the sky and again this lovely silver cigar shape. I believe that it flew just outside out Territorial Waters. His distrust of the Germans was very strong. In May 1937 the Graf Zeppelin exploded as it approached the mooring mast in New York and I believe that that was the effective end of airship travel.

1929 was marked by the beginning of major commercial difficulties throughout the world caused by the Wall Street crash in October. This did not have such an obvious effect on this country in that the impact on jobs was only just beginning, but then, suddenly, unemployment increased rapidly. My parents still continued to live the life of Reilly and enjoyed every social occasion that offered itself. They always seemed to me to be going out to dances or dinners. My father was so often in his evening dress that it ceased to be an unusual event calling for comment. Equally my mother, always a lover of clothes, enjoyed a growing wardrobe and kept in the height of fashion. Whilst we had lived in Silver Street she had formed a friendship with two women who had a Boutique of high fashion clothing in the Rockingham Road just opposite to Woodcocks Store. The only one that I can remember was Miss Waddell, thin, dark and long nosed. I was not attracted to her at all. My mother, unbeknown to my father, or so he told me when he tried to explain the situation to me in the summer of 1939, began to buy clothes on credit and the bills started to mount up; a recipe for disaster.

She was very involved in Charity activities at the time, especially Dr Barnados Home in Kettering. For my birthday in 1929, Uncle Mattie gave to me a very expensive cuddly toy, modelled exactly on his Fox Terrier, a Crufts Champion. It was really inappropriate for one so young but I valued it and carried it about with me everywhere. One morning we were going out to have coffee with some friends at Barlow's cafe and as we reached the top of Station Road my mother noticed some Barnardo children with their nurse in the small garden which used to be sited there and we crossed over the road to speak to them. I had a sudden sense of compassion for them, a sort of overwhelming desire to help them in some way and make up for their deprivation. Instinctively, I gave them all that I had with me which was the model terrier dog, and handed it over to the nearest child. The nurse thanked my mother profusely for her generosity and she in turn, felt unable to say that I had no right to give it away. I can remember the embarrassment of it and as we eventually walked away, my mother turning to me and saying *"Now look what you have done. How shall we ever tell Uncle Mattie?"* At that very moment he appeared out of the George Hotel, as if by magic and I ran up and told him what I had done. I always remember his reply which was to the effect that when you are given presents then they are yours to do what you want with, and that was the end of the matter.

At this time the Station Road was always busy with horses and carts collecting and delivering goods to the Railway station. I was fascinated by the horses and especially by the trace horses which were attached to the front of the shafts when particularly heavy loads were being moved, giving two horsepower up the hill. These were detached at the top of the hill where it joined the Northampton Road and then returned to the station with their drivers ready for the next load. I was well known to many of the drivers and often they allowed me to walk up with them and then ride back on their horses. I loved the very special smell which horses possess, especially those, like these, which were beautifully groomed with polished leather and shining brass. Our gardener used to watch as well and if a horse performed in the general area of our front gate he was out in a flash with his bucket to collect the droppings and put them on "Mr Ronald's peaches"! Always the reason!

Those peaches were the cause of a drama in the house when the gardener reported to my father that a small bite had been taken out of the back of all those growing at a height that a small boy could reach. I played the innocent, but eventually, and justly, I was convicted and threatened by my father with a smacked bottom but, mother intervening, was dispatched to bed as a punishment. It was lunch time I remember. After my father had left, my mother and her friend Dorothy came to my room. I remember them pulling the curtains and played games with me. Finally one of them went up to Barlows and bought my favourite cake for me for tea. My father, who was never home before about 6pm, returned unexpectedly, found out what had happened and the most appalling row ensued. It was quite frightening and I did not forget it. It was I think the first time that I realised that parents were not always nice to each other.

The garden at Station Road was on two levels and the top level contained a very nice croquet lawn. Both parents enjoyed croquet and my mother wore a very smart pair of long white bell-bottomed trousers when playing. Tea parties were very much in vogue and processions of gorgeously dressed ladies came during the afternoons. I found this rather a bore although many of them brought toys or sweets for me. Eventually my father decided that I needed a pet of my own as a companion, and we all went by car to his warehouse in the Arcade, just off the Market Square in Northampton, to choose something suitable. My eye fell on a blue-grey kitten and duly "Puss" joined the family. I loved her dearly but was fascinated by the fact, which I had been told, that cats always fell on their feet. One day, alone in the garden, I threw her up in the air as high as possible to see if this was true. Unfortunately in her case it wasn't and she damaged a leg on landing. This time both parents were furious and I got the smacking that I deserved. "Puss" recovered but avoided me at all costs!

During 1930 my mother had to go up to London for another operation. I remained in Kettering with my father and we spent a lot of time with my Granny Bellamy. On Sundays after chapel we all had to go out for a long walk. This almost seemed a part of the religious practice of the time and was purgatorial to young children like Mary and me. It was quite normal to leave Kenilworth by 10.30am and walk in what seemed to us to be baking sunshine for two to two and a half hours. We went as far afield as Warkton or Pytchley. We always went with my father who really tried hard to make it all good fun. Uncle Bernard always made a good and plausible excuse; Auntie Edna went up to help Granny prepare the Sunday lunch and looked after Stuart. Mary and I used to come home dry mouthed and panting for a drink of water. This was always refused and we were both sent to lie on the floor of the parlour until lunch was served.

At one o'clock we were summoned, sat at table, still no drink allowed as it reduced your appetite, and were served with a vast piece of Yorkshire pudding in salty gravy. This had to be eaten and was followed by beef, roast potatoes and two or three vegetables. Everything immersed in salty gravy. That consumed, we were both allowed a glass of water before the pudding. After this meal we were told to be quiet until tea-time so that the adults could have their "Sunday Afternoon Rest". Failing this, and perhaps worse, we were despatched to the Sunday School. At five o'clock an immense tea was served with sardines, meat-paste, cucumber, tomatoes, lashings of bread and butter with various jams. If one did well at all that then this was followed by fruit salad, tinned, with cream. This was ruined by the fact the Granny always insisted that we eat our fruit salad with bread and butter! Cakes followed if you still had room.

I was easily bored and of an inventive mind so I found things to do such as decapitating the hyacinth bulbs or, even more dramatic, cutting the fringe off Granny's orange velvet table cover with a pair of scissors. Mary was not only horrified at my daring but to be fair did try to stop my more aggressive activities. It was said that much of the blame for this wicked behaviour was because my mother spoilt me. This may well have been justified, as I loved both my mother and my father. I hated to hear him not refuting open or imputed criticisms of her. This was the period when the breakdown of the relationship between my parents began to accelerate and perhaps my behaviour added to this. Although I could not crystalise why, my instinct was to become even more difficult as a sort of antidote to the gulf between the "Bellamys" and my mother. In a way I suppose I was fighting her corner for her. Subconsciously I found myself to be in a minority of one, with all the powers that be, criticising my mother in her absence. I was acutely conscious that much was implied but not said and, in a way, this was even harder to accept.

During this time especially, my cousin Mary and I were inseparable. We walked for miles together and played all sorts of games of imagination very happily. It was at a time when there was virtually no danger in allowing two very young children to go out alone provided that they went within certain known bounds. We were both six years of age and well known in the town. Our preferred area was the cricket ground and the fields up towards the Cransley furnaces, both on the Northampton Road. One day we took our usual little cardboard suitcase full of toys and lost it. We both decided to "fib" and say that a big boy had taken it from us; this seemed to have been believed and consequently our outings were watched with more care! Another day we heard that a man had committed suicide in a certain house on the Northampton Road. It shows the ghoulish interest of the very young that we went there and had a good look at his house!

My mother returned after a few weeks and we were together again. She was not well, and I have vivid recollections of her running away one evening after a row with my father. To be fair he was absolutely distraught after her sudden departure and we drove around in the car trying to find her. It was a wet evening and eventually he found her on the Cransley Furnaces hill walking along the road to Northampton in the dark. Although there was this atmosphere of insecurity, my life was still very happy. Granny Gale was a frequent and concerned visitor and I kept up my correspondence with her. I have one of my letters before me now dated 3 February 1931 (Granny kept them all!). It is written in a clear and very neat round hand.

"Dear Grannie   *feb 3 1931*
I like your letter very much is uncle well I think your present is very nice indeed I often sit in your little chair. I love it I shall be coming to see you soon. mummie and Antie are knitting me some socks. for me to wear.arnt I a luckey boy. I am going to the panto this week it is nice cinderella I wish you could be hear to go with me. love Boy daddie is not coming home tomorrow to dinner love Boy give my love to little Granny XXXXXXXXXXXXX Mummie gives hers love"

The present was a diminutive wooden arm chair with a separate interior sprung seat. This survived the subsequent sale as it was mine and so was removed to London, returning when Granny Gale came to live with us in 1954. It is now in the possession of my eldest son, Simon.

I used to write a lot of stories as well and send them to her. I still have the tale of Willie Waddle who was taking his sister to visit the market when attacked by some cruel men, so he went to the police; they caught the men and that was the end!

Clearly at this time business had become exceptionally difficult. My father's earnings were being squeezed, the big house was a drain on his income and my mother's spending habits were having a dramatic impact on their lives. She had run up substantial debts in Miss Waddell's dress-shop and altogether they were living well beyond their means. He began to borrow to try to keep things together and this in turn of course snowballed as he had to repay people. Granny Gale did all she could but that was little as she was a widow on a small wage. Uncle Bernard was unable to help although I believe that Auntie Edna, always a wonderful sister to him, managed to give him the few pounds that she had saved. Uncle Leslie and Auntie Peggy were now in the new bungalow at Roundhill Road and had no surplus, especially as trade was in the doldrums. Eventually my parents sold their silver to Uncle Harold in London in return for a £5.00 I.O.U. in order to try to stave off a summons from Miss Waddell. Later this was redeemed by Granny Gale although to be fair, Uncle Harold never took the silver from them. That silver is in my possession now, and I found the original receipted copy of the IOU retained in Granny Gale's papers.

In the spring of 1931 they decided to cut their costs by trying to find a small bungalow nearer to my father's work in Northampton. I recollect visiting a number of wooden bungalows on the Kettering Road outside Northampton with them but without success. I was very aware of their lack of enthusiasm for this course. In fact I can still feel their lack of real interest and determination to make their marriage succeed. I retain a very unhappy memory of one of those visits where an argument spilled out in the rain as we stood on the veranda of one of these houses. Amongst my mother's possessions I found a brown envelope marked "made by Boy Bellamy for his mother May 25th 1931". In it was a card with a sailing ship on the front and a small dressing table cloth with the initials "OB" in one corner in big red stitches.

In July 1931 England tried to stop the run on the pound and eventually devalued it by 30% in September. The effect on our lives and that of millions of others was dramatic and immediate. My father's business collapsed and was bankrupted. In common with many leather merchants large orders were placed annually for goatskins and the like, from India and other overseas countries. These skins, in many cases, were already on the water. The devaluation meant that the price increased in pound sterling terms was too high for firms to meet and certainly too high to enable them to trade profitably, so they went under. Two million were unemployed by this time and the numbers were rising daily.

In the early summer my mother had fallen ill again and they decided that this was the moment when they should separate on the basis that when things had stabilised, they get together. My mother, having come out of hospital, stayed in London with Granny Gale, whilst my father moved in with his mother. It was planned as a temporary move which, as the months went by, became permanent. My father sold up everything we had, including all my toys. I have always resented the sale of a wonderful steam engine and the various gadgets which it drove. It was a gift from Uncle Mattie and represented a mine-head with moving buckets and a sieve which one could fill with real sand. However thanks to all this prompt action, he avoided going to Court and made arrangements with the creditors, which, eventually, he managed to meet in full.

I believe that Grandmother Bellamy was not willing to have a small, lively child living in the house and Auntie Edna was busy with two children, one of whom

Stuart, was under three years old. As nobody seemed very enthusiastic to have me, it was agreed between them, that I should go to Kirby Hall to stay with Alma and Joe Hawkes. They had become good friends of my parents. Joe was the caretaker for the Ministry of Works, whilst Alma was a very trustworthy motherly sort of person. They probably felt that I couldn't come to much harm out in the country anyway. The plan then was that once my mother had recovered, I was to join her in London and, subject only to her continued improved health, I would be sent to school there until the family could reunite.

On reflection this does seem a most curious and complicated solution but I imagine that with all the attendant problems surrounding them both at this time, any solution seemed acceptable provided that I was away, cared for and safe. So, after we had closed up the house and my mother had been put on the train to London, my father took me over to Kirby Hall.

He had always had a fascination for the wildness of this huge, empty Elizabethan ruin. Built by the Hatton family in the second half of the 16th century, it is situated in a shallow valley and concealed in trees just to the north of the Gretton-Deene road. Occupation had been sporadic throughout the centuries and by the latter half of the 19th century it had been totally abandoned and as rooves collapsed and chimneys toppled so the main structure had deteriorated in sympathy. The isolation of so splendid a building was in itself a curious factor and the nearest villages, Gretton, Weldon and Deene were all at least 3 miles distant. In the main building, three of the bay window rooms were still, relatively speaking intact, and my parents used to hold picnic parties there in the summer. In addition, with a group of their "Twenties" friends they held a rather wild New Year party there in the late 1920's. I understand that during this the fire was so blazing hot in the Library, where the Party was in full swing, that the wall above the fireplace began to burn! At the end of 1930 Kirby Hall was put into the care of the Office of Works and Joe Hawkes was appointed as the first caretaker with special responsibilities for the garden. Joe was an old soldier who with his wife, Alma, was well known to my parents. I had met them on several occasions, in Weldon I think. Alma had no children of her own and we had developed some affinity. I came to love her directness and her decisive manner and I felt very secure with her. I believe that in a strange way she loved my waywardness and my independent spirit. She may well have felt a bit sorry for me as well, but if she did, then she certainly didn't show it!

She was a small, agile woman with a wrinkled, nut-brown face. She was always cheerful and her clear blue eyes were full of love and laughter. A real country woman she knew about animals, birds, bees, plants and country life generally.

She didn't believe in "*them doctors and their fancy medicines*". Her cures were basically three; for cuts and grazes a strong application of iodine and then a handful of cobweb, which was in plentiful supply, for coughs, colds or throats, goose grease liberally applied on pieces of old blanket or towelling and NOT to be removed until she said so: for rheumatics, arthritis and other muscular pains or aches, either goose grease or a distillation of herbs which certainly included nettle, often applied as a poultice. She bustled everywhere, and whenever I seek a definition of that word then there is Alma! She wore boots but didn't lift her feet very high, her swift movement wasn't exactly a shuffle, but the very technique always added vigour to whatever she was doing. She was never still, bullied her adoring husband and had no truck with any of the men working on the place. She had a birdlike quickness of the eye which confounded one. The room was always full of wasps in the early autumn, as she had bowls of fruit from the wild plums and crab apples ready for jamming. She used to pick the wasps up by their wings and throw them directly into the fire, where their lives ended with a quiet terminal Pssst! I watched her do this many times but never had the courage to emulate her example. She wore a sackcloth apron except on Sundays and under it was a flowered dress which never seemed to change. Joe, her husband, a tall ruddy faced man, rather gaunt looking man, was already bent by the arthritis which bedevilled him all his life. He was an ex-soldier and I believe that this is how my father had met him initially. He was one of the most patient, gentle and kind man that I have ever met. I never heard him say anything untoward to or about another person. He worshipped Alma and it was always a source of wonder to him that she had agreed to marry him. She was, I believe, a few years older than him.

This was the couple to whom I was entrusted. Alma was to become both my nanny and my surrogate mother, although of course at that time it was not appreciated that this brief sojourn would in fact turn into a long term relationship. It is a great compliment to them both that in April 1950, when I became engaged to my wife, Ann, amongst the first people to whom I introduced her were Alma and Joe. Similarly when our first child, Simon, was born, we immediately hastened over to show him to them. Alma, I remember, placed a warm brown egg into his hand, a country custom guaranteeing happiness and prosperity in the years to come.

Entering by the garden door on the western front of the house, brought you into a small hallway. Immediately on the right was the door to the cellar, then on your left a sharp bend after which, on the right were the stairs to the upstairs rooms, and almost opposite, the door to the ante room and rest of the house. If one continued straight on, the corridor led to our living room. Just before entering the living room, to your right, lay a small scullery containing a stone sink and a drain. This was our only washing facility. Behind the sink, a window looked out over the "Great Gardens" which, at that time, were still a wilderness waiting to be restored.

The living room comprised one large room, the original house library, in which there was a typical standard cottage open fired iron grate with brass tap, water cylinder and oven. This was always kept alight. The major items in the room were two large kitchen tables on which everything happened and on each of which stood a paraffin lamp. Around the three walls were lines of bookshelves and cupboards containing food, china, linen and various possessions. The front end of this room looked out over the fields towards the Deene-Gretton road through a beautiful stone mullioned bay window. The bay was partially screened off from the big room, giving access on both sides of the screen so that the room itself acted as their small parlour. Around the windows were wooden sills on which stood orange trees which Alma grew from pips and which bore miniature fruit. Standing in the centre of this bay and adjacent to a small table and chairs was a lectern on which stood the family bible. The room was high-ceilinged and painted in white which was much stained with smoke from the lamp fumes.

The stairs to the bedroom were made of thick oak planking and led up into a large room above which was divided down the centre by a partition. This divided the bay window and, as in the downstairs living room, this window gave the only light. Around the wall was some old panelling, on top of which, and at bed-head height, was wainscoting. I was given a bed in the centre of the wall in the right hand half of this room, whilst Alma and Joe slept in the other half. The room was about forty feet long and twenty wide so my bed with no other furniture looked like a rather small pea in a large pod! This arrangement never changed in the subsequent eight years whenever I stayed with them.

My father had promised to remain with me for the first night but Alma felt that it was best that he should go as I might be unsettled by his presence. So he went and left me to her care. I can't remember experiencing any real fear or even a sense of being left unprotected. Kirby Hall was immense, full of interest; it was a sunny day, Alma had lunch ready for us and instinctively I trusted her and her husband. The culture shocks however soon commenced. Spending a penny for instance was allowed outside in the garden but not close to the front of the house. A chamber pot was supplied for the bedroom. More major matters were reserved for the family four holer earth closet situated at the back of the building and relatively speaking a long way away. It meant walking right round the front of the house, down a grassy hill or alternatively, right through the house via the Great Hall, out of the back door, down the flight of steps and across the grass. It was amazing how quickly one became well regulated and went once a day and at the same time! The E.C. was well supplied with newspaper on a wire hook to use as lavatory paper. It was rather smelly, always damp to sit on and not really conducive to long stays. I found out later that some of the effluent leached into the cellar beneath the house, thus creating marvellous conditions for the rhubarb which Joe forced there!

Having been used to running water in the bathroom, and hot water from a gas fired geyser over the bath, it took me time to understand that all water came out of the well which, containing delicious and crystal clear water, was sited at the bottom of the cellar steps. This meant that every drop of water came up in the galvanised buckets which were kept in the scullery. I learned that water was not a commodity to be wasted. Hot water came from kettles boiled up in the living room or from the small tank and the brass tap by the fire. The only place in which I could be bathed was the stone sink in the scullery. The rooms were unheated and a bath standing in the washbasin in that sink was an experience that I tried, without success I might say, to avoid in the years ahead. Joe washed and shaved every evening, in a metal basin on the living room table but I never knew whether or how they both bathed.

Lighting was only by paraffin lamps. There were two in the living room, with an additional one in the bay window which was only lit on Sunday evenings in the winter. As there were no side windows in the living room it was quite dark and the other two lamps were lit most evenings. One stood on the work table, (where it all happened!) just by the side of Alma's wicker chair, and to the right of the fire, whilst the other was moved as needed. Joe always smoked a pipe after his tea but I can't remember him reading more than the occasional paper. It was a matter of daily routine that after breakfast the lamps were filled with paraffin, the wicks trimmed and cleaned and, if there was any smoke on the glass, then the globes were wiped clean too. The lamps gave a very soft light and I found it pleasant to read by, but the room was large and much of it lay in shadow.

That first night, Alma, armed with a single small candlestick, took me up to bed and tucked me in. I have no recollection of being in any way frightened when she left me. Next night she gave me the candle stick, assured me that there was nothing to fear and I went up to bed on my own. I am sure that she checked that all was well but from that time forward I always went up without difficulty and alone. On reflection I am astonished at my confidence in her, the stairs were old, they turned through 180 degrees to the right, they cast shadows and the candle flickered. Upstairs must have seemed vast and it was really still a ruin hardly restored at all and certainly lacked plaster and paint. The stub corridor which led out of the bedroom, took you into unfinished roof-space. This proved to be a wonderful place for swallows' nests in the summer.

There were always lots of field mice around which Alma trapped both in the living room cupboards and in her main larder which was adjacent to the Great Hall. Occasionally bats flew in to the bedroom but none of this worried me. However, I was frightened of the rats which tended to come in during harvest time and often ran around the wainscoting above the bed head. They slithered. Even Joe drew the line at that and hurled things at them! I was never bitten and they never to my knowledge actually ran over the bed. I did have the sheepdog, Rover, sleeping in my room after a while and we became inseparable friends.

During those early days I stayed close to Joe or Alma. She kept hens, bantams, geese, ducks and guinea fowl and we had great fun collecting their eggs. Many of the hens laid wild out in the bed of reeds and nettles which adjoined the brook, so we used to watch out from the bay window, especially for the guinea fowl, or listen out for the tell tale cackle of a laying hen and then try to find the nest. The vegetable garden was on high ground overlooking the west side of the Great Gardens and Alma kept her bees there as well. She was a great bee keeper and looked wonderful in her hat with the net dangling one each side. She never wore gloves but opened up her hives talking continuously to the bees. As far as I am aware she never seemed to get stung. She sold her honey in the tea room which she opened for visitors in the summer. Thinking about it now, with all the regulations which exist on serving food, the authorities would have had a fit. There were more flies and wasps on the cakes and scones than currants!

Joe did the digging and the potatoes, whilst she sowed, hoed and garnered all the other crops. Fruit and vegetables were bottled, beans stored in salt and eggs preserved for the winter in isinglass. Apart from tea and sugar I don't remember them buying groceries. She bought meat I suppose, as there were usually a couple of small hams hanging from the ceiling above the fireplace. Once a fortnight we used to walk the three miles to Weldon and go to the Village Stores on the Green to do some shopping. Alma used to walk at a hundred miles an hour and I had to keep up with her or suffer her tongue, so, although she usually bought "two penn'orth" of sweets for me, I wasn't overkeen on the expedition, but then 2d in those days bought a quarter of a pound of Smart's Toffees!

Apart from Alma, the real power at Kirby Hall at that time was Mr Gale. He was the foreman of works and with a team of two labourers was working for the Ministry of Works to make Kirby Hall safe to visitors and as time permitted, to restore it. He was a very fine stone mason and much that he did stands today. Unfortunately as the years progressed my exploring, climbing about in the buildings and general disobedience to his restrictions proved too much for him and we became sworn enemies.

This was the period when Joe was starting, with the Ministry of Works, on the general plans for the re-creation of the gardens at Kirby Hall. The area in front of the building had at one time contained a formal garden, the plans for which still existed and his dream was to be allowed to copy them. Work had started at this stage and a posse of men were digging the front and levelling. I can really only remember piles of earth but I suppose that some sort of plan was gradually taking shape. I have some recollection of stone foundations being exposed towards the brook and talk of an old village which had been raised to the ground. Joe seemed more occupied with tending the new lawns in the Inner and Outer Courtyards. I was not allowed to play there nor was my presence encouraged in the old ante room and parlour where Mr Gale had his office and stores. So, when not clambering about in the old buildings, I spent time in the raised wild garden on the west side of the house exploring an area which was full of brambles and rabbit holes. This was part of the original West Terrace and I loved it. One day I tumbled down the edge of a steep bank with vicious brambles and the earth seemed to open up in front of me. I couldn't get out and my terrified shouts attracted the whole team. Eventually, hauling me out, they were surprised to see a top of a stone figure. Later they dug it out and found that it was a piece of a sculpture, "Rape of the Sabines", which must have stood there in Christopher Hatton's day. It was erected near the spot and no further pieces were ever found, but it brings back many memories.

My father visited me fairly frequently but he must have been trying desperately to sort out their affairs and to find another job. Living with his own mother must have been rather humiliating, especially when she had opposed his marriage in the first place. Luckily by the end of the summer, my mother had recovered sufficiently for me to join her at Granny's house in London. My father collected me, somewhat reluctant to leave Alma, so he told me, and I was despatched in the care of the guard from Kettering Station to go to St Pancras and a new life in the big city.

This "Care of the Guard" business was quite normal in those days. Guards with their red and green flags were standing by their trains on the platform and to be put in their charge was an accepted practice. A sixpence or sometimes even a shilling changed hands, my mother or father then seated me wherever indicated by the guard, which was usually in the restaurant car. After we had commenced the journey he would come along and see that I was all right or get me a glass of milk and a biscuit. At the other end he would personally hand me over to the nominated person. I always felt very safe and actually was often spoiled by other travellers who saw what was afoot and bought me a drink or perhaps shared some chocolate. I was always involved in conversation and used to spin terrific stories. I remember once telling a couple that I had just landed from the steamer, coming from New York and "weren't your English policemen wonderful"! I romanticised a life which at the time seemed very real to me. I wonder what they must have thought!

R101 on mooring tower

Station Road, Kettering

Bill 1928

Kirby Hall

Alma and Joe 1950

CHAPTER 5
Life in London - 1931-1932

My mother met me off the train at St Pancras Station and we travelled to my Grandmother's house at Wells Road (Shepherd's Bush) on a double-decker red bus. It was the first journey that I can actually remember on such a vehicle and I was fascinated. The staircase to the upper deck ran in a semi-circle at the rear of the bus and then, once you had reached the top, you sat on the upper floor which was open to the sky I was intrigued by the fact that we towered above the other vehicles and in future always tried to sit up there. It gave you a remarkable view, it was a great experience and you could see everything I remember that day especially as we had to change buses until finally we caught a Number 11. My mother was recognised by the conductor, who deposited us right outside our own house, which was very impressive to me! No 11 buses finished up in the bus station at the end of Wells road itself. All very convenient!

Wells Road was a short dead-end road which ran parallel with the Metropolitan Railway, the electric train service which served stations up to the City. On the corner of our side of the road was a public house and opposite that Goldhawk Road Station itself, where you bought tickets or drank tea in the dingy cafe inside, which incidentally, still exists. Under the railway arches facing us, were a series of workshops and almost directly opposite our house but slightly to the left, was a smithy manned by three working smiths and their apprentices. All the local horses were shoed here and I was to spend many a happy hour watching them. The row of houses came to an end at the entrance to the Bus Station. A foot-bridge crossed the railway line opposite this and led to Hammersmith Grove and to a small park or playing field. The space under this bridge was a haunt of the "Naughty boys and girls who smoked". I was banned from going there, which made it immediately doubly attractive! Later I discovered that my mother had gone there consistently as a child where she had smoked dried tea leaves in brown paper!

My grandmother's house was a three storey narrow brick and stone built Victorian building, second in the row of some twenty houses, which were built in pairs. It was rather drab and shaded by a large polled lime tree standing in the tiny front garden. There were two sets of stairs, one down to the basement entrance and one, much wider and more imposing, leading up to the first floor. The basement door opened into a small hall which led on to our daytime accommodation. A narrow corridor lead to the foot of the stairs and then jinking round to the right headed for the kitchen. On one's right was the living room, then, either up the stairs to the first floor or just past these and on the right, was the parlour. The corridor then continued on again into the narrow kitchen and the scullery; then a door from which the corridor led out into the back garden. This was about twenty yards long but narrow and ended at a wall. Behind that, a scrubby field which a little later, was built over to create an extension to the bus station, the huge brick wall of which then dominated the gardens of all the houses. None of the gardens was really tended and the land was sour, although ours contained an attractive laburnham tree which flowered copiously every year. The lavatory was outside under this tree; it backed on to the scullery and a paved path led to it from the back door.

Half way up the stairs was a small landing and leading off it was my mother's bedroom with a window overlooking the kitchen roof and the garden. From the landing, stairs continued up into the main entrance hall. Off this and to the immediate left, and over the parlour, was my grandmother's bedroom which she shared with my Great Grandmother. Next to that was the master bedroom looking out over Wells Road which was occupied by Uncle Harold Turnage. At the end of the corridor was the front door which was used only by Granny's tenants, Paddy and Bridie Mills and their daughter. They occupied the top floor of three small rooms. We saw little of them and they were very quiet in every way. There was no bathroom in the house, but I think there may have been an inside lavatory at the top of the stairs which connected with our own beneath.

The house was in no way strange to me as I had stayed there quite often when I went up with my mother for short visits, but this time, as my mother explained, it was for life. I adored my grandmother, Big Granny, who was all and more than a small boy could desire. She was patient, thoughtful, forgiving, kind and as generous as her circumstances permitted; she was always there. She represented security in my life and looking back I think this was probably the most important factor at that time. My mother was lovely too and I enjoyed being with her, although it was not so much fun without my father being with her. My great-grandmother, Granny Gigg, or Little Granny, was in her eighties and spent most of the day in bed, getting up in the evening to sit in the parlour by the fire and listen to her wireless. Then there was Uncle Harold, Uncle Tony, the man in the house. He left at 8.30 am and went to his job as a salesman for Cherry-Blossom Boot Polish. He returned each evening but went out to his club most nights after his tea. He was a fine tennis player as well as a leading light in the "Penguins", an elite swimming club.

The other member of the family was Hannah. Hannah had been Little Granny's maid of all work when they first moved to Shepherds Bush as a fairly wealthy young couple in 1885. At the time of which we are talking, she was certainly in her eighties although I never really learned her exact age. She had known Big Granny since she was six years old and called her "Nellie" despite the fact that all the orders were given and payments were made by her!. She was however, much more respectful to my mother, referred to as "Miss Olive" and Uncle Tony as "Mr Harold, Sir". I was "Boy" but still treated as a person from above stairs. Hannah looked after Little Granny, did the washing, cooked Uncle Tony's "Tea" for a prompt 5.30pm, washed up the breakfast, made the beds, except for my mothers, and cleaned the house. She had a remarkable old knife polishing machine which she used each week on a Friday; a large circular wooden structure with slots at the top into which one stuck the knives and then turned a handle. There must have been some form of abrasive in the wheels which cleaned the stains off the steel blades and polished them very effectively. She did all these things without complaint until she died in 1937 after 52 years of service during which time she would only take 10 shillings a week which was the amount that she needed to live on. There was nil inflation in those days. She had an incredible quavering voice and Uncle Tony's accurate but wicked imitation used to reduce us all to tears of laughter.

My mother and I shared a double bed in the little bedroom; there wasn't space for cupboards, only for a small dressing table and so our clothes were hung with my grandmothers in a wardrobe just inside the door of her room on the right. Granny's bed was opposite that door and a chest of drawers to the left shielded the end of Little Granny's bed. Uncle Tony's room was large and very masculine, with a huge gentleman's pantechnicon standing against the wall. This had been owned by my grandfather and had drawers and racks for everything that a man could need. When my grandmother moved out of London I took this to pieces and have made a lot of other furniture with the mahogany.

Downstairs the kitchen was long and narrow with cupboards and a table on the left and a long table on the right under the window. Through a narrow door at the end there was a gas stove and the Belfast type sink with a cold tap. As one entered the kitchen and on the right was the door to the outside lavatory. Whilst, under the parlour window, was a shelter for Pip, the Old English Sheepdog who had belonged to my grandfather. After tea in the evening, the kitchen became a bathroom and if the corridor door was closed then, so I soon learned, no man was allowed in!

There was no electricity in the house and all the lights were powered by gas. Gas mantles with small globes hung on the walls in strategic places and the pilot mantle glowed gently orange during the day. As they were never fully extinguished, at night one pulled the chain on the side of each mantle gently, until, with a pop, the gas lit and the light gradually grew. The mantles were very fragile and difficult to replace without damage. Incidentally, the street lamps in Wells Road and elsewhere were also gas, and a man used to come round with a long pole and pull down the chain to re-light them each evening. Shepherds Bush market was lit dimly by gas lamps but on each stall there were Tilley lamps which glowed brightly and emitted a hissing noise. It was really quite attractive to see each bathed in a pool of light with comparative darkness between stalls.

I was bathed each night in a metal basin filled with hot water placed on the end of the table in the kitchen and after that I went through to talk to Little Granny who would be sitting by the fire in the parlour. She often allowed me to play with her wireless, a "Cats whisker" which stood on the shelf by her chair; the earphones lying in an old metal washbasin for amplification. She twiddled the knob until the set was tuned in to the B.B.C., at Rugby, I believe. It was crackly and faint, but entertaining. On the other days I went through to the fire in the other living room where Big Granny read to me. She went to work at about 8.am each morning, followed shortly by Uncle Tony, but whereas he always returned at 5.15pm she was often delayed and came in late. Mummy and I always waited for her for our tea, usually eggs, herring, kippers or, occasionally, lamb chops or similar with vegetables which Granny cooked.

My mother was convalescing at this time so stayed in bed until Hannah carried up Little Granny's breakfast and then she and I dressed and went down to eat ours in the living room. I can't remember what we did to occupy our days but we did a great deal of visiting to various school friends of my mother. We were visited occasionally by Uncle Leslie, who always seemed to feel very guilty for coming. On one occasion Auntie Kathleen, Uncle Raymond's widow, came with her two sons, they travelled up especially by train from Rochester where she was living. It was a gesture of solidarity between two daughters in law who both felt that they had some cause for grievance.

Granny's sister, Alice, lived with her husband, Harry Whawell and family in Mitcham. The two sisters were very close friends and we often went over to Mitcham by tram on Saturdays. It was a most exciting journey. Trams ran on rails which were laid in the centre of the roads and took their power from parallel overhead electricity lines. They were like buses and had wooden slatted seats but made a great screeching noise as they cornered or crossed the points at junctions. They had a peculiar whine as they accelerated and always felt to be going faster than they actually were. The conductor used to get out at certain places and change the overhead connecting rails onto other lines so as to permit the tram to change direction, although there were points men at major junctions, such as at Hammersmith, who routed them down the correct tracks. I was fascinated. Sometimes we returned late at night. London was very rough in the area which we passed through and the conductors became involved in struggles as they evicted drunks or tried to prevent them from coming aboard. There was relatively little traffic but the streets were crowded with people. Most folks had to work until 5pm on Saturdays and shops remained open, and very busy, until ten or eleven o'clock at night.

I loved the Whawell family and they were always interested in me and all that I did. Aunt Alice was like Granny but softer faced. She had four daughters, Marie (by her first husband), Sylvie, Audrey and Phyllis and a son Jim. My pin up was Auntie Sylvie and she was always the one that I chose to bath me when they visited us. Uncle Harry was a large man with a huge, deep, rumbling voice. I both worshipped him and was terrified of him. He was the Kings Armourer, as were his father and grandfather before him, and he worked at Hampton Court. His word was law and if, for instance, he slept after lunch, then nobody dared to talk in more than a whisper until "Dad woke"; he epitomised "MANHOOD" to me. He never raised his voice, was courteous to all, but his word was there to be obeyed. Granny loved him and I felt later, when Aunt Alice died, that they would marry but it was all too late.

Very soon the day came when I had to go to school. My mother had gone to St Stephens Church of England School as a child, which was on the Uxbridge Road just beyond the Metropolitan Line Station.

The Inspector's Report for 19 February 1931 reads as follows (I was in the Boys' Section):-
"In the Boys' Section of the School the syllabus has been carefully worked out and presented. The result is that thoughtful answers were obtained from all classes, particularly the top ones. A good tone pervades the School and Religion is obviously a reality."

In order to get to school, I had to walk the full length of the famous Shepherds Bush Market and was fascinated by it. There were not only dozens of stalls but also a shopping arcade running along under the railway arches. They seemed to me to be selling everything in the world from food to toys, tools to jellied eels. The whole atmosphere was vigorous; everybody shouted and seemed to know everyone else. Everyone seemed to be in a hurry, and everywhere one heard good humoured banter. Good wishes were shouted at my mother by a number of the stallholders and she assured me that when I went to school they would all be on the look out to see that I behaved like a good boy. We then arrived at the school, I was registered as a pupil and put into Juniors Class 1; my mother pressed a halfpenny into my hand for a bottle of milk at break, said goodbye and then I was on my own, except for thirty or so ragged and noisy children.

Initially it was a bit of a culture shock. The language was pretty fierce and whereas I had been brought up to believe that only bad men said naughty words and ladies shouldn't even say "damn" I was soon disabused of this and learned a freedom of expression which would not have been acceptable in Kettering! The Cockney accent presented no problems, although again there were local market uses of phrases or words which were a bit alien. I have always been a bit of a chameleon which probably stemmed somewhat from this introduction, and most certainly I did not wish to stand out as somebody different. I was always a good mimic and quick to learn.

The great game at that time was "Flickers". Most children collected cigarette cards which were available in every packet of cigarettes. These came in sets, cricketers, footballers, countries of the world, birds and etc. There were hundreds of different sets to collect and, if you were lucky, special albums to stick them into. I think that they really achieved their objective of causing smokers to smoke more, as parents were pressed for certain cards by their children so they smoked those brands which contained the range of cards that their children wanted! The problem we all shared was how to create a fair method of swaps and "Flickers" dealt with that in a clever way. Players stood their swaps up against the wall of the school playground and Seekers came round, identified a particular card or set that they needed and proceeded to flick their own swap cards at it until eventually, if they were skilled, they knocked it down. The Player took all cards which failed to knock down one of those against the wall. It was a good idea but like all good ideas it was ruined by a few experts who could pick any card at five yards and with unerring aim knock it cold! I had taken a few of my specials to school, no self respecting boy would be seen without some, learned the game and was soon cleaned out. In this way I made my first friend. He took most of my cards, commiserated with me and we walked home from school together. His name was Colin and he lived in the next street, Wood Grove. At that time none of us knew what a tearaway he was! His mother lived alone. He did not know his father and they were very poor indeed, although he never seemed to lack anything.

The weeks up to Christmas passed happily. I was reasonably intelligent and became quite popular in the class as, being rather cheeky, I attracted trouble on myself. Such is fame! I could always be depended on to accept a challenge; rude word in chalk on the blackboard, flicking an ink bomb at the girls or passing notes. I wasn't a leader of trouble but an able team-mate.

I stayed in London that Christmas; strangely I remember with absolute clarity the moment in the night when Father Christmas, dressed in a red robe arrived in my bedroom. I don't know to this day whether it was my mother or one of the Uncles, but come he did and left me a very satisfactory selection of toys. I did not go to Kettering during the Christmas holiday, nor did I see my father. One day during the holidays I went up to Marble Arch in Uncle Syd Wales' car, shopping. We returned along the main road through Lancaster Gate, my mother sitting in the front seat of the car. Suddenly she saw a blind man striving to cross the road and it was clear that none of the, relatively speaking, light traffic was taking any notice. She told Syd to stop, leapt out of the car, held up all the traffic and then taking the blind man by the arm walked him slowly and deliberately across the road. I was impressed by her thoughtfulness, her courage and the kindness of her gesture. I have never forgotten this lesson.

Money was very tight at this time and after Christmas when Granny took Mummy and I to the "Empire" (Shepherds Bush Empire) to the music hall, I had no clean shirt and had to wear my pyjama jacket under a sweater! Granny had free seats at the front of the Dress Circle because she knew many of the Artistes. We ate oranges, I remember, and I got in to terrible trouble through dropping my peel onto the heads of those in the Stalls below - by mistake of course! After the performance we went back stage and met some friends of Granny; they always said nice things about me but didn't play with me or entertain me. Worst of all, they all seemed to drink a lot, and I didn't find it very interesting.

By this time every Saturday morning I went to the Lime Grove Baths with Uncle Tony. This was a ritual performance when he took both his weekly bath and swam. We took towels and carbolic soap and were issued with "Slips" on arrival, small triangles of cloth which you tied on at the hip. It was "Men Only" in the morning and, although nudity was not permitted, some people didn't bother to wear their slips. If seen, they were called out of the pool by the staff and not allowed to swim again that day. In the corner of the swimming area was a white tiled square bath, known as the "Hot-pot"; it was about fifteen feet square and perhaps two feet deep. This was filled with piping hot water and occupied by the "Residents", of which Uncle Tony was the doyen. They lay slowly cooking in this water for what seemed like hours, from time to time shouting to a member of the Staff to heat up the water. I was allowed in this bath as well, but the conversation was well above my head. When sufficiently boiled, one stood up, the carbolic soap was put to good use, a quick sluice down and then straight into the the pool for a cleansing swim. Shallow end for me as I only did the dog-paddle but Uncle Tony dived in like a seal. I felt immensely proud to have him as my uncle as he powered up the pool in an immaculate crawl, admired by all. Although I shared in his reflected glory, I cannot ever recollect that he tried to teach me to swim. I think that most of those present had to work it out for themselves.

The Easter Term began quite well. Our classroom was large and light containing about twenty five desks. I was in the back row against the wall. I remember getting on quite well with my form mistress as I was by far the best reader and liked both English and History which were her two favourite subjects. I have very few actual recollections of school but remember vividly the day when the School Inspectors came.

One of them presented our Class with the problem of the fox, the goose and the sack of wheat. Apparently, the owner had to take them over the river in his little boat. Unfortunately the boat would only take him and one of the three items. Bearing in mind that the fox would eat the goose and the goose would eat the corn, how did he do it? There was a most ghastly stunned silence throughout the room. We had never been faced with such a logical problem before! Then suddenly I got a sort of divine inspiration and produced the correct answer! I gained immense kudos from this!

It must have been towards the end of the Easter Term that I really began to enjoy and to understand the wickedness of Colin. He always seemed to have chocolate or sweets to eat and yet never had money. To begin with he persuaded me to spend my half-penny milk money on the way to school. *"Only f ---ing sissies drink milk"* was his cry. I understood that he spent his milk money on the way home so that when we got back to his street, we could share all sorts of delicacies "bought" by him. One day he showed me how he "bought". He knew all the stalls where sweets were on show in cardboard boxes laid out to the front. He would stand close to a selected group of customers, preferably a woman and her children, as they purchased sweets and whilst the stall holder was occupied in filling the paper bag with their selection, he quietly pocketed whatever was available, but remained standing there, looking innocent. He then calmly waited and walked away with them as they left. I was filled with admiration but, initially anyway, lacked the courage or the need to try it myself and to be fair he never tried to involve me.

A note from my mother to my father confirms that I was getting out of hand and difficult to control so it was arranged that I should spend the Easter holidays with my father in Kettering. As the time drew close, a further note states that my Grandmother Bellamy was ill. She eventually died on 18 April 1932, and my mother went up to Kettering for the funeral whilst I remained in London. Although I was unaware that my Grandmother had such a high standing in Kettering Society, I was always aware of the strong influence she exercised over her family. The notice which appeared in the Kettering Evening Telegraph was full of praise for what in anybody's terms was a remarkable life of service to the community. A paragraph from the Evening Telegraph summarises her life very well, headed "A Life that Will Long be Revered" it says: *"In many other good causes this gentle lady was a potent power, and the grief of her daughter, Mrs B. Shrive, and her two surviving sons, Mr H Leslie Bellamy and Mr Ronald V Bellamy, will be shared by a host who valued her friendship and admired her noble character."*

Although my mother was sad, I had sensed a certain relief and expression of hope in her reaction to her mother-in-law's death but this was dashed by her tearful return to Wells Road when it became clear that we were not going back to Kettering. She was still far from well, possibly over sensitive, but she certainly returned from her visit to Kettering badly hurt and shaken. I was only conscious of this through the snippets of conversation that I overheard; conversations which were terminated abruptly as my presence was noticed, as well as her sense of despair which was readily transmitted to me although I didn't fully understand the reasons. Many years later I talked about my mother and father to Uncle Bernard, Auntie Edna's husband. He told me that *"No family could exclude you as completely as the Bellamys!"* I suppose this was what my mother felt. She would still have liked to rebuild her marriage but my father, remembering his mother's opposition and getting little positive encouragement from his brother and sister, who mirrored her views, wasn't prepared to meet her to discuss the matter in a constructive fashion.

This was the time when I started to misbehave and become almost uncontrollable. I can't put a logical explanation on it except that it was a way of getting attention at any cost. I began by creeping into Little Granny's bedroom and stealing money out of her purse. I discovered that she always kept it in the left hand little drawer at the top of the chest of drawers as one entered her room. With care, this could be slid open without her hearing and there were always a few pennies in it which I felt that she wouldn't miss. I became a wealthy friend to many school mates in this way. Next I joined in the game of stealing from the front of the market stalls, not often, but frequently enough to give me a taste of the thrill. Our gang of seven to eight year olds became known in the market and we were both watched and then shouted at if, as a gang, we approached a stall. We were reported to the school mistress and ticked off, but there was no real evidence and the effect was to give me more status in class.

At the top of the market just across the road from us was a "Smoked Eel "stall. It was very popular and especially in the early summer evenings, when it was crowded with men, and occasionally women too, swallowing eels or eating winkles, whelks and other shell fish. I was forbidden to go near there as later in the evening there was often trouble. Colin thrived on it and often got a penny for fetching a jug of beer from the"Bush" from someone too idle to cross the road himself. There was a jug and bottle department at the side door of most pubs at that time where minors could go to get beer for their parents. One evening I joined him and we were caught red-handed by my grandmother. I was brought home and scolded but this and countless other small incidents were telling on my mother, the end of term was approaching and she was at her wits end.

I was allowed to go to one of the market stalls on my own if the occasion demanded it. Granny sometimes ran out of food and cash I suspect, usually about the middle of the week. The last stall in the market sold vegetables. it was run by a friend of Granny's called Alf. I was given a 1d or sometimes 3d and told to go to Alf and ask for a "penn'orth of pot herbs". I handed over the money and he used to put a great variety of vegetables into the brown paper bag and I would run home with it and within a very short time we seemed to have the most lovely meals! I am sure that a large number of locals had to use the same facility.

When the term ended, my mother was delighted to find that my report was quite good and that I had won the English prize, "The Mill on the Floss". Secretly, I was very pleased, but enjoying my rather dominant naughtiness somehow couldn't find it in my heart to conform and so I continued to get into trouble through my deliberate disobedience. My mother was quite unable to punish me and undoubtedly that goaded me on to misbehave with even greater enthusiasm as I sought to establish her breaking point.

One of my friends was Mary O'Brien who lived next door in No 3. She was at St Stephens, my age, in my Class and a goodie-goodie. We became friends in the sort of way that one could be with goodie-goodies, and I was constantly trying to impress her. One day we were playing with a ball and broke a pane of glass in her fathers shed. I boasted that I had a pen-knife with a blade on it which cut glass and we would repair the broken pane. She was thrilled as it might save her from having another thrashing, but the truth was that I had only seen a penknife containing such a blade and that, on a market stall. The penknife cost a shilling. I now had to deliver or lose face! I couldn't possibly raise a whole shilling, so the only way out was to steal the knife. The stall in question was up a small side alley half way down the market. So telling nobody, I went up there, luckily found that the penknife was near the front of the stall. I waited until the stall holder was not looking, removed it and then walked away. There was no hue and cry and I arrived at Mary's house displaying my new possession with pride. It totally failed to cut the bit of glass which was disappointing but the knife became the envy of the gang. Incidentally, Mary got her thrashing. Her father was a great believer in corporal punishment and I kept well clear of him!

As usual during the weekend, my mother and I went down the market to buy some vegetables. To my acute concern, the stallholder from whom I had stolen the knife, saw us and invited my mother to come to the back for a minute. Nothing further was said except that she looked very embarrassed. After we had been home for a few minutes Uncle Tony called me into the living room and asked if I had a new penknife. I denied it and he then produced it out of his pocket having found it under my pillow. I blustered, was given a much deserved beating and then he frogmarched me back to the stall and made me apologise. The shilling was duly paid and the penknife confiscated. It was lucky the stall holder was an old friend of my mothers; clearly, he had seen what happened but decided to play it in a friendly way.

I think that my mother was becoming ill again at this time and my wickedness must have made all this so much worse. Anyway she became very tearful and, rather dramatically, packed my few things into a small suitcase. Next day she took me up to St Pancras station and put me on the train to Kettering. Once again the guard was given instructions and I was set down at Kettering Station where to my surprise there was nobody to meet me. The guard told me to sit in the Waiting Room and wait for my father. This was not really an option for someone such as I imagined myself to be so, taking my suitcase I started to walk to "Kenilworth" as I believed that my father would be there.

It seemed a long way up Station Road, Bowling Green Road and then along the London Road by the Cattle Market to the Congregational Chapel. I saw nobody that I knew. It was a hot sunny day, my suitcase was a burden and I can well remember turning down Tennyson Road, deciding to walk on the right hand side, opposite "Kenilworth" to see if I could see my father through the front window. Inadvertently this caused me to pass in front of the house of the

Robinson family almost opposite to "Kenilworth", who were our cousins. Apparently my father was sitting in their front room talking to them and was astonished to see his small son walking past the house, apparently quite unconcernedly, carrying a suit case. He dashed out of the front door and taking me by the arm took me into them. Clearly they were disgusted with my mother for sending me off, apparently so callously, without even notifying my father. I was fussed over and made to feel really special! In fact, my mother had sent a telegram to Bowling Green Road to announce my departure and had assumed that this had been received.

Telegrams were the normal method of contacting people in the early Thirties and the telephone was a relatively rare object. I read recently that 274,000 new connections were made in the whole of 1933 and in 1932 673,000 international calls were made! This is less than in 12 hours today.

On the death of Granny Bellamy, the Shrive family had left Bowling Green Road and moved into "Kenilworth" and their old house was now occupied by Mr and Mrs Walter Sleath. My father rented a room there but he had left for "Kenilworth" before the telegram had arrived and they had no telephone. I have little doubt that this caused the situation between my parents to become even more distant. For some time after this, I was not encouraged to be in contact with her and I became rapidly more and more attached to my father who was much firmer with me and introduced me to a more structured sort of a life.

I went back with him to the Sleaths and we shared a double bed in their back room until he was able to sort things out. They were very kind to me, fed me well and they had a daughter, Muriel, who was about my age so I had a ready made playmate when I wasn't able to be with my father, which was frequent as, being a commercial traveller, he was away every day in the week. He had "digs" with them until going into the Army in 1938.

It was the summer holidays and schools were closed. During the next few weeks, he decided that I would go to Hawthorn Road School with my cousin Mary. This was not far from Uncle Leslie and Auntie Peggy in Roundhill Road, and somewhat to his surprise, they offered to let me live with them and offered their spare room. They had no children of their own, and the agreement was that they would look after me during term time.

My father, having failed to find employment in the shoe trade, had started a business of his own and was selling his own brand butter "Welland Vale," stocks of which he kept in a small rented warehouse near to Kettering Station. He had purchased a Ford 8 and called on all the small corner shops. He was an immediate favourite with all the lady shopkeepers as he was so gentlemanly towards everyone.

This question of employment was in itself interesting. My father always refused to become a mason, whilst Uncle Bernard was a great enthusiast and achieved high office in later years. I was present one day when Uncle Bernard said *"Well Ron, if only you would take my advice and become a mason you would find work back in the Leather Trade. Join my Lodge I would willingly help you"*. My father was furious and almost shouted back words to the effect, that *"If to get a job one had to join the bloody masons then he'd rather sweep the streets!"* I didn't understand his reasoning but was quite frightened to see anger between them and never forgot his attitude, to the extent that I have never been tempted to join this very worthy organisation myself. Despite this altercation they remained good friends and Uncle Bernard always welcomed his brother-in-law's presence in his house and at his table.

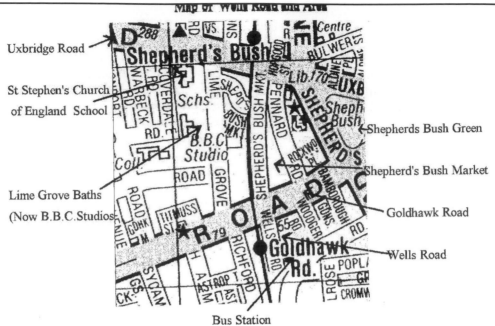

Uxbridge Road

St Stephen's Church
of England School

Lime Grove Baths
(Now B.B.C.Studios

Shepherds Bush Green

Shepherd's Bush Market

Goldhawk Road

Wells Road

Bus Station

Map Shepherds Bush – Wells Road

London 1920s

CHAPTER 6
Kettering 1932/33

Auntie Peggy and Uncle Leslie always went on their holidays to Lowestoft during August so they were away when I arrived from London. It was a hot summer and very difficult for my father and I to sleep in the double bed in the back room at the Sleath's house. I imagine too, that I was very restless and my father short of sleep! He decided that I should go to the seaside and found a lodging for me in Cliftonville where the landlady was happy to keep me and generally see that I was cared for. He took me there in his car and apparently I settled well. I was disconcerted because I had to sleep in her sitting room on a converted sofa bed. This was comfortable enough but it was a noisy room, next to her kitchen and entrance hall and I had difficulty in getting off to sleep. One night I semi-woke up wanting to spend a penny and automatically got up and knelt by the bed as if I was in London, where I had a chamber-pot. Unfortunately there wasn't a pot there at all and it all went into the sofa springs and stained her covers. I was semi-aware of what I was doing when I was actually doing it but felt too frightened to go out into the kitchen where she was talking to some friends. In the morning the stain was discovered. I denied that it was me and she was even more irritated because I lied to her. She telegraphed my father immediately. He dropped everything, came down and collected me, although he never blamed me for the event, which was a comfort.

I spent much of the ensuing month at Kirby Hall where Alma and Joe were as welcoming as ever. Although for most of the time I was on my own, I could always be with one of them if I wanted company and I always had Rover by my side. The roof adjacent to our bedroom was a constant source of attraction, especially as it was forbidden territory. To get onto it one had to clamber through the open rafters running above the ruined corridor beyond our bedroom. At the top there was a fairly wide ledge with a deep guttering running along the west face of the house and above the old ballroom. This was a haunt of swallows and there were dozens of fledglings there to watch.

In one of the rickety chimneys in the ruined East Lodgings, abutting the Inner Court, was a jackdaws nest and I tried without success to get hold of a young jackdaw, Mr Gale having told me that it would make a wonderful pet. The rather complex chimney structure plus their great height eventually defeated me. Perhaps he was inciting me to break my neck! He was certainly not pleased with me at the time, as, in the course of my clambering, I had brought down a great mass of brick and stone dust mixed with soot in one of the wide chimneys of the original kitchens. In fact this did him a good turn as it exposed the old spit

87

which was previously hidden and which stands there to this day. I was not thanked for my discoveries! Between 1932 and 1940, I nearly always spent some part of my holidays, especially summer and Easter at Kirby Hall.

Very soon August had gone and I was taken to Havencourt to stay with Auntie Peggy, Uncle Leslie and their beautifully brushed pedigree Airdale dog, called Peter. They had bought a very smart new bungalow on the corner of Roundhill Road. It was built on a large plot surrounded by a lap-fence which protected their immaculate garden. The bungalow itself was L shaped so going in through the front door which faced onto Roundhill Road, you went into a furnished hall. Turning right, through a door into the sitting room took you straight through the kitchen. The kitchen back door led out onto a patio/path running round the garden and, immediately on the right hand side, to the spacious garage where Uncle Leslie kept all his shoe cleaning kit as well as tools, hoses etc. His car was washed whenever it had any dirt on it at all! In fact we used to think that he washed it before it ever had any dirt on it!

Turning left in the hall led one to the master bedroom with, next to it, a second bedroom, both facing Argyll Street, whilst straight ahead was the small sewing room and to the right the bathroom. The rooms were furnished with great taste and the walls covered with the pictures which Uncle Leslie had received from the division of his parents' effects. I always loved one picture especially, a Frank Salisbury sketch for one of his paintings in the Houses of Parliament, with soldiers in helmets carrying halbards and pikes. My room was next to theirs, had a double bed in it and wardrobes containing Auntie Peggy's clothes. They were a very conservative couple and had regular habits. Meals were at the hour, sitting quietly reading in the sitting room after tea was mandatory although we occasionally played cards. Bed was at 8 o'clock and my father bathed me if he was in town, which was fairly frequent. Auntie Peggy never bathed me but Uncle Leslie ran the bath then left me to my own devices.

I soon settled to the routine and loved them both for their quiet competence. Uncle Leslie was proud of his wife, his house, of his appearance and his car. He dressed immaculately with highly polished boots and spats. After breakfast on Saturday mornings, he put all his shoes and boots out into the garage and cleaned them off with dubbin before polishing each one with loving care. He then blancoed his spats without which no self respecting commercial traveller would be seen! This was ritual and it would have needed an earthquake to change the habit. It is interesting to recall that "spats were an essential item of every gentleman's wardrobe". A spat is also an oyster and they looked rather like an oyster shell. They fitted over the top of shoes or boots and buttoned down the side, making a very tidy join between shoe and trouser. They must have gone out of fashion towards the end of the 1920's.

During the weekend, he always wore plus fours and cut a very imposing figure in them. He was a big man, his waist was generous and he looked to be a man not to be trifled with! His shoe polishing done, he polished his car. My task for the Saturday morning was a complete bore, pumping the water into the header tank! The water came from a well in the garden and there was a 500 gallon tank up in the roof. By the side of the kitchen door was a small wooden handled reciprocal pump. It took about 30 minutes of hard pumping to fill that tank and I did that each week under the watchful eye of Uncle Leslie whilst, in the adjacent garage, he cleaned his shoes.

He had at this time a splendid car with a dickey seat and I used to join Auntie Peggy in the dickey when he took us out for a spin on Sunday. This again was a ritual, she in a cloche hat with a huge scarf wrapped round her head, me in my best clothes and sporting a cap if Auntie Peggy could find it. I hated it and used to hide it whenever I suspected that the chance for having to wear it was looming up. Uncle Leslie wore a special cap, goggles if we drove fast, and usually had his pipe clenched between his teeth but then he nearly always had a pipe in his mouth anyway. The car had a wide running board on each side. The battery was fixed on one and the other the spare wheel.

In order to get into the dickey you clambered up on narrow metal steps let into the back nearside mud guard. It was breezy in there but surprisingly comfortable. I was always dreadfully car sick so to be outside like that was a great relief. We drove out to Brigstock and collected wool for Auntie Peggy's corns or cowslips for the cowslip wine which she made. Occasionally we went out later and stopped for a drink in Geddington or Warkton. Auntie Peggy had a sherry, Uncle Leslie half a pint of bitter and I had an orangeade. She loved Warkton and had her eye on a thatched cottage on the main road on the edge of the village.

Auntie Peggy was older than Uncle Leslie and their friends, on the whole, came from a yet older vintage. I didn't realise until much later, how clever she had been, but the comparison made her very much the young woman amongst these older ones. An excellent seamstress and cutter she was always well dressed and ran a small dressmaking business, although by this time, this was mainly for her close friends. She loved her games of cards and was out a great deal in the afternoon. I wasn't a "latch key child" but sometimes had to wait to get into the house. My father, who was very gregarious and knew everybody, had made friends with the people opposite, Mr and Mrs Corby and their son, Aubrey. They were elderly and Aubrey was their mainstay, having taken over his fathers business as a milkman. I was always welcome over there and learned a great deal about milk, cleanliness, the washing down of separators and other equipment, milk floats and even horse-care. On Saturdays I was allowed to join Aubrey in the dairy when he returned from his round and watch him clean up. Milk was served into jugs which each of his customers brought to the door. There was no such thing as a bottle. *"Revolting things "*said Aubrey *"much better drunk fresh out of a clean churn"*. He sold wonderful creamy milk and I was spoiled by being given a great glass with gobbets of cream on top. His measures were beautiful and were made of polished steel with hooked brass handles so as to hang over the side of the burnished churns. He rode around in a dark blue, two wheeled milk cart drawn by "Mutton", his old horse, who knew as much about the round as even he did. She never had to be told to stop or move on. Habit had shown where each of their customers lived and she moved automatically from door to door; something that todays electric cars cannot manage!

Aubrey had been wounded in the War and had a badly deformed right arm which was twisted from the elbow and his right hand was turned into what was almost a claw. He would hold things by pressing them against his side. He was not at all bitter about this, never complained and just got on with his work. He was a devoted son, did not consider marriage until both his parents had died and he spent all his free time with them. He was about the same age as my father and went out of his way to be kind to everyone. I just accepted him, but in truth if I was in trouble with my father for disobedience or something of that nature, he was a refuge, and was sympathetic towards me, although he never interfered.

At the beginning of September I was taken to Hawthorn Road Primary School which was only two streets away from the house. I was put in to a class run by Miss Jarvis who I discovered from Cousin Mary had taught my Aunt Edna. She was a thin tall lady with dark hair which had a tendency to escape from whatever style she adopted. She was deeply caring, a good teacher and I respected her. Happily for me I was in the same class as Mary and soon made a lot of friends. They all had bicycles and my father bought one for me so that I could join Michael Swain and various others on cycling expeditions.

I had developed a great interest in trains and one of my longed for treats was to go down to the railway bridge over the main L.M.S. line at the end of the Headlands down the track which led to the Kettering Golf Course and see the trains at night. During the day I used to sit on the fence there for hours, noting train numbers and counting the carriages on the passenger trains or trucks on the goods. This was something that went on for years and I got to know the faces of many of the stokers and the engine drivers, many of whom waved as they went past. There were the famous trains such as the "Thames Forth" and the "Thames Clyde" with sign boards on them. These usually flashed past at high speed, rattling through the points as they passed the Kettering marshalling yards and did not stop at the station. Occasionally, however, they stopped at the junction signals and shouted "Good day" to me or wished me well. They always appeared to be friendly. All the engines and the coaches were immaculately clean and if they stopped, even for a short time, they spent their time wiping some part of their engines over with oily rags. They took great pride in everything about their profession.

The shunting engines were a constant source of interest as they assembled the goods trains on the far tracks. There was always something to see. Goods trains had dozens of trucks behind them and made the most wonderful noise as they started off. Each buffer banging the ones of the truck behind and then banging on to the one in front as the engine took up the strain. They didn't have quite the appeal of a fast moving passenger train but there were other compensations as there was a Guard at the back in a little truck with a stove in it. He used to stand out on his observation platform as the train went through the marshalling area and often waved or shouted as he went past.

This was the year when I started to have some treatment for my teeth. I don't think that orthodontists, specialising in straightening out children's teeth, had been invented then and major adjustments to irregular or deformed teeth were rarely made. My father took me along to meet the redoubtable Mr Clenaghan, a Scottish dentist, whose surgery was on the Market Place in Kettering. It was made quite clear from the very beginning that patients, especially small boys, didn't complain! My first appointment dealt with two small fillings and I was not offered any form of pain killer. I don't think that anaesthetics, apart from gas, were widely used then. He told me to open my mouth wide and with a foot-operated treadle drill commenced to grind out the bad bits ready for a filling. I found it extremely painful and shrank away from him. He stopped, gave me a stern lecture and started again. The drill ground very slowly and very coarsely and tears flowed down my cheeks. He was unmoved and continued inexorably. Eventually came the bliss of the taste of cloves, which went in with some sort of a base mix, prior to the filling itself. At the end of this anguish he told my father that I was *"Quite a brave lad!"*. I have never taken any injection for fillings since that date. I can feel him there, long since dead, standing in front of me and growling *"Keep your mouth open boy and stop caterwauling!"*

During that first term at school I was still somewhat coloured by my London experience. I think that I worked reasonably hard but I still had difficulty in seeing that stealing from shops would be wrong. I can only remember it happening once, but I do have a very clear recollection of stealing a bar of chocolate from the corner shop near the school and sharing it with a friend. Although he ate it, he was obviously unhappy about doing so, told his mother and I was beaten by my father; not very hard, but hard enough and I never did it again!

Having no house of his own, my father celebrated Christmas with all sorts of families or friends who invited him out. It was not practical to share this with me, so I was sent up to London, where I had a lovely time and was thoroughly spoiled. It was strange but I had no desire to meet my old friends again and in my spare time, whilst everyone was working, I played about in the kitchen cooking. My speciality was sponge cakes. I used to cook one (with about six eggs!), eat all of it except for two slices and give those to my Mother and Grandmother on their return from work! I used up dozens of eggs, but it kept me occupied during the day whilst Little Granny was in bed and Hannah was in the house.

I have a letter written in very neat round hand dated Wednesday 29 March 1933 which reads:-
"Dear Mummy
I hope you are very well and happy. On sunday the 26th Daddy and I went to Kirby Hall where there is a lot of flood water here we sailed our lovely boat "Brittania" and to my dissapointment it could not float because the water was too shallow. Then we had tea and went home, only before we reached saw the swamp, we caught some tadpoles and some frog spawn.
Next day we went to school and went out to play rounders with "Peter Hudson" (son of the Grammar School headmaster). *Next day I went to school and we had "Country Dancing" in which my partner was Hilda Knight Ahem, Ahem, Atishoo. Ah thats much better I can write better now.*
After that event we had arithmet -ic and had "Ten mentel" questions. Oh Daddy is giving me the sign to come to bed.   *Love to all "boy" X*

At this time I was still in close touch with my mother. Letters were full of childish news, drawings and were fairly frequent. She was ill in hospital again during April and May and then was sent off to Clacton for convalescence. My father did not keep such things from me, but I remember that I was beginning to feel that she wasn't really so ill and that it was all a question of her not pulling herself together. I don't believe that my father deliberately put such thoughts into my mind but that was the general attitude of the rest of the Kettering family. It was infectious. I found a further two letters both dated 31 May 1933. The first was from my cousin, Mary Shrive from "Kenilworth":-

"Dear Auntie
Yesterday we held our school sports, it was a glorious day. The lines were marked out in lime. lionel got second in the Relay-race, and had a blue ribbon. Norma Hulett was in six races and she was first in four races and second in two. Norma(Gotch) was head-girl and had more ribbons than any of the boys. Gorden King was the headboy and he and Norma won a fountain pen each. I hope you will soon be better. best love   Mary XXXXX"

and then from me, written from Havencourt:-

"Dear Mummy
I do so hope your illness is over and you soon will go to the convalescent home. Yesterday was the school sports and we had a lovely time. We had to be there at two fifteen and at about half past two the games commenced and the girls had several races and then came the boys potatoe race where I got fourth it was a shame for I would have had a pink ribbon if I had been third. The ribbons were in this order, white 1st, blue 2nd, and red third. next came the other races and then came the relay race. I with 2nd Munds, Alesbrook, English, and myself 3rd Ambrose, Keeper, Halmer and Erving. I got a blue. yours faithfully   Lionel"

I don't think that the "Yours faithfully" would have worried her! but she would not have been very enthusiastic about the "Lionel" which was very "Bellamy", every one else calling me "Boy" including, it must be said, my father. My mother was still in touch with friends in Kettering and I found a letter from Mrs Henson, who lived in St Peters Avenue close to "Kenilworth". Her husband had just died and she was thanking my mother for her flowers and saying *"Well dear I had sonny* (me!) *down to see me the other day. He had a nice new bike and this morning he came down again. I asked him if he had written you a nice little letter. he said no I am not good at letter writing. He told me yesterday at the school sports he won a badge. He was wearing it. He looks well so you need not worry about how he is."* My mother must have improved after the visit to Clacton as I went up to London for the summer holidays in July.

During the Christmas break, although I have no recollection of this, I had been taken up to Christ's Hospital, the "Blue Coats School", by my mother and Syd Wales. The Wales brothers had all been educated there. I took and passed the entrance examination and early in the summer was offered a place there on scholarship. This came through when I was in London and my mother got in touch with my father about this opportunity. Apparently she had omitted to tell him that I was sitting the exam and whether he resented her friendship with the Wales family, especially Syd, or whether he felt that if I went there he would lose me I don't know but he flatly refused to let me take up the offer. I was totally unaware of all this but shortly afterwards he insisted on my return to Kettering. In the meantime he had contacted Blackfriars School, Laxton, a Catholic boarding school run by the Dominican Order. He had managed to arrange a place for me there on generous payment terms, £25 per term I believe, and I was entered for the Winter Term 1933. I was then nine years old and was going to be ten on 1 December. The situation between my parents was cool at this time and I think that the point of no return had definitely been reached although neither of them sought a divorce. I know that I was continuously torn in my loyalty and although I loved my mother and her "Troop" (the Wales brothers, Uncle Tony and others with whom she went around) I was happier in Kettering with my new found friends where there was so much more contact with people of my own age. I found a letter to her dated Wednesday 6 September which reads:-

"Dear Mummy

I hope you are well. I am going to School on Friday and have had a tusk out and have got the toothache and am waiting for daddy to come home from somewhere I don't nowhere I do wish he would hurry up I want a game of cards. hurry up Pop. How is Pip well I hope. Am having some new clothes and have got some new suits. how are the "Troops" well I hope. Is it nice in London now beastly and wet here and mud is everywhere. Love to Everyone

Boy XXXXXX"

At the bottom of this in my fathers writing:-

"P.S. A very badly written letter. He had to be caned before we would write at all"

Somehow this does not ring true as I suspect that he really was away!

I was still living at "Havencourt" at that time and my trunk, purchased from the left luggage office, was duly packed with my school clothes. I don't think that I was very aware of what "going away to school" really meant in terms of the separation from all that was familiar. I certainly didn't understand the "Catholic" aspect which filled my Low Church Aunt with horror although she could see the financial sense of the proposal. I don't think that I gave it much thought. In fact, reflecting on it now, I suppose that I was so used to being moved from pillar to post without much ceremony that this seemed to be just some other move, probably temporary. Little did I think that this would change my whole attitude to life and that it would be my home for eight months of the year for the next eight years. Although the school collected on Kettering station to catch the branch line train to Wakerley and Barrowden, the nearest station to Laxton, my father decided to take me there by car, as it was my first term.

CHAPTER 7
School Years 1933-36

We left "Havencourt" in the car after lunch and took the Stamford road which I knew so well, as it was the road, which we took when driving to Kirby Hall. We passed through Weldon with its old church and the lantern in the tower, which, my father told me, was to help the worshippers find it in the fastness of the Rockingham Forest. Then on to Deene and through Bulwick before after a couple of miles, we turned off the Stamford road, wound our way up three-quarters of a mile of stony track and finally stopped in front of an enormous, stone, Georgian building. There were other parents outside with their children whilst two imposing looking white-robed figures with a long string of rosary beads hanging from their belts, were welcoming and talking to them. My father and I carried my trunk into the front hall and were directed by a senior boy to take it down some winding stairs into the cellar area. This was vaulted, very dimly lit and was filled with boys, some very noisy, others looking rather out of place, sad and clearly wondering what they should do. Then back upstairs and one of the priests, actually Fr Jerome, the Bursar, took us through the Great Hall and showed me into the library before disappearing upstairs with my father.

I entered through a pair of central doors. Directly in front of me was a large bow window which looked out over two croquet lawns, beyond which was a large cricket pitch. The central part of this room was furnished by a round table on which lay a pile of newspapers. The room extended on either side, with several alcoves off it, fronted with a large deep window, each of which housed refectory tables. The walls were filled with bookshelves and bore, what seemed to me to be, thousands of books. I was mesmerised and wandered down to the right to look at some of the book titles. Suddenly I became aware of a stocky, white robed figure standing near me, he had very aquiline features, was almost bald and yet somehow very appealing. *"What's your name, boy"* he said in a deep nasal voice". I was uncertain as to how to reply, but happily said *"Bellamy"*. *"Ah"* he said *" You are a new boy aren't you and the youngest boy in the school. I have put you in Form 1. I am the Headmaster, - Father Henry. When you talk to me or indeed any of the priests you call us Father."* I said *"Can I read these books, Father"* and he replied *"The First Form table is here in this alcove and you can always sit here when you are not in class or in prep. I suggest that you start reading at the bottom left hand corner of the shelving THERE and by the time you leave you will reached THERE"*, pointing to the bookcase on the other side of the alcove *"and will have read them all!"* said with a little chuckle, which in the years ahead I came to love so much. (Reflecting on my reading which, as he indicated to me, became very diverse, I appreciate that to some extent he meant what he had said and I read an enormous diversity of books, appropriate or inappropriate, becoming a speed reader. Although the latter has some advantage, it has a major disadvantage that if, whilst reading, you come across description as opposed to action, you tend to move on quickly because you want the "story line". It should also be said that with boys of my age we spent a lot of our time reading comics. The key boys' papers which I enjoyed included *The Wizard, The Rover, Hotspur, Boys Own* etc. These were relatively sophisticated stories and certainly ensured that you read them by torchlight under the bedclothes. When I was much younger, I enjoyed *Rainbow* and *Tiger Tim,* but there were not so many cowboys in them! I think somehow that the habit of reading comics went out when *The Beano* and *Dandy* came on the scene, beautifully produced, but not quite to my liking.

Then my father came in and Fr Henry took both of us to the refectory where a simple meal of tea and brown bread was available. After which my father and I returned to the car. Without further delay he kissed me goodbye and left. I think that that was probably one of the loneliest moments of my life. I knew nobody, nothing of the geography of the place and nothing of the structure. I was totally at a loose end, felt very sorry for myself and went away to have a good cry in the cellars.

After a short time I found myself next to another tearful boy, we exchanged names, his was Peter Dutton, and he told me that his two elder brothers had been at Laxton. Then Matron, Miss Hoskins, appeared and told us all to unpack out trunks. We had to put our clothes, sheets etc into a series of numbered lockers in the linen room. I was given the number 65. There were 65 boys in the school I discovered later. After this we were all taken into the library where Fr Henry talked to us about the school and the routine that we were to follow, after which we were taken up to see our dormitories. The Lower School dormitories were in the main part of the building near to the Fathers Common Room whilst the Upper School were housed in the East Wing. My dormitory was called the "Big Indian" and on the walls were extraordinary pictures of Indian scenes with tigers and various hunting or domestic activities. These, I believe were very valuable and unique having been installed by Lord Carbury in the early 19th century. The two huge windows were curtain-less but fitted with wooden shutters, although I discovered that these were only closed in the worst of the winter. Each boy had a metal bed, already made up, a small bedside table and a chamber pot. Washing facilities, rather basic, were three floors down. We descended by a series of stone stairs winding round a wooden-goods lift shaft, arriving in a rather chilly room adjacent to the cellars. Each boy was allotted a small locker for soap, tooth brush etc. There was no hot water, bath day was each Saturday and 15 minutes were allocated to each boy for their bath-time.

There were some showers with hottish water but they were only available if one had played games.

There were eleven new boys, all of them in Class 1. I was the youngest by almost twelve months. By this time we were becoming bonded together by our isolation, so that when the warning bell rang for supper at 6.55 pm, we all felt more at ease. The whole school had to line up around the Great Hall before all meals and then the head boy called them into the refectory. We then filed in table by table. Form 1 was on the Lower Middle Table. I did not understand the significance of this naming of tables until next day. If there was any food left over then the Head boy or one of the prefects stood by the serving table and called out the name of one of the tables - Lower or Upper Middle, Right Side, Left Side or End table. Then there was a concerted rush from those on the nominated table to get a second helping! It was not a very consistent method, and favouritism - true or alleged! - was a source for constant discussion. In addition, two boys were appointed as bread cutters each term. This was a sinecure which carried great favours such as giving the hot new bread to one's own table or special crusts to ones cronies etc. I had a lot to learn!

After supper we hung about rather silently until five minutes to eight, when we lined up in the cloakroom and then, forming a crocodile, went over to Chapel for Compline. This service was totally alien to me, I was used to short, very short, "God bless Mummy and Daddy and all those I love" type of prayers at night. Dutton, who was next to me in the pew, was very helpful and showed me how to use the prayer book. Compline, which was sung, was followed, for the Lower School, by bed, although after that first night, we always had half an hour of noisy "let off steam" recreation in the Lower Common Room before going to bed. The drill then was to change into pyjamas, grab your towel, descend the stairs to the wash room, supervised tooth clean and face wash, up to bed, prayers then lights out and silence. This silence was mandatory and disobedience carried a heavy penalty, certainly a caning of three or four strokes I was told, often given by Fr Henry personally. His beatings, although just, were apparently very solid and painful, and should be avoided at all costs. I remained silent and, in common with many of my companions, snivelled quietly until I eventually slept.

Promptly at 6.50 next morning a prefect appeared in our dorm clapping his hands and exhorting us to get out of bed. My bed was by the window and as it was broad daylight by about 5.30am I had been awake for some time and restless. A peremptory cold wash was followed by the inevitable crocodile over to the chapel and Mass at 7.15. This again was totally strange to me. I was used to singing, blood and thunder sermons and a rather stark and boring service. This was really something else and I was fascinated. It must be said that I was also completely defeated by the language, Latin, and had to be restrained from going up to Holy Communion by Dutton. Apparently he had been told that I was not a Catholic. I was very impressed by the apparent devotion of everyone, the solemnity of the occasion and the candles, shining silver and the coloured vestments. I think that my conversion to Catholicism started from that moment! Breakfast followed with porridge, bread and a small pat of margarine and coffee. We had an egg and jam on Feast Days, jam on Sundays, and, occasionally, corn flakes, bacon or some other delicacy.

It was Saturday morning and at nine o'clock we were taken round the class rooms and interviewed by some of the priests. I had never met a Catholic priest and I don't know quite what I had expected but I know that I was most surprised to find that they were ordinary people who talked and laughed just like normal human beings. Unfortunately, my form master, Fr Clement Feely, was perhaps the least humorous of them all. He was a tall, angular, rather bent, elderly man with sparse long black hair thinly combed over his head. His face was long and with his large nose he appeared rather lugubrious. I was not very impressed, giggled too much out of embarrassment and we got off to a bad start. He made it very clear that he did not tolerate any lack of attention or misdemeanour in class. He then explained the discipline structure. Prefects could award Lines, Penance Walks or Whackings. Lines were easy to understand and in the months ahead I wrote a number of them. The penance walk was awarded in slots of fifteen minutes. This entailed you walking up and down the wide path running between the house and the cricket pitch with your hands behind your back. No talking, no slouching, shoulders back and don't dare to try to do less than the time appointed or the next one will be doubled. The ultimate was a whacking, usually three or four strokes of the cane, given by Fr Aelwin Tindal-Atkinson. We were then issued with the necessary school books and allotted a desk in the big study. It was here that we were to do all our preparation, write our letters and do general work. Otherwise everything took place in our class-room.

Lunch then followed. This was the main meal of the day and always included meat or fish and vegetables, followed by rice puddings or some good stodgy pudding like "Dead Babies Arm", called as such because it was white, soggy and rolled up in pieces of cloth for cooking. Food was brought up from the kitchens by the girl servant staff, nearly all of whom came from Newcastle. They cleaned the house, made the beds, emptied the chamber-pots, kept table and washed up. We called them "Skivvies", not of course to their faces, and they did many kindnesses for us. The senior girl "Betty Malpas" became very fond of me and made me her special care whenever possible. This lasted right through my time at Blackfriars. I thought that she was very old. She was probably about 25 at the time! It was a long way from kitchen to refectory and it must have been a very hard job. There was an antique wooden hand lift from the cellar level up to the refectory level but it was very small, rope operated and rarely used by them.

One of the worst tasks allocated to small boys was the stocking up of the wood chest in the Father's Common Room. This entailed reporting to the prefects in the wood shed outside, holding out your arms to make a cradle and then being loaded up with huge logs. You then staggered up the six flights of stone stairs and dumped the logs in the wood baskets. It was very hard work and really a strain for small boys. If the prefects didn't like you, then they gave you more to carry. I often dropped some off on the way up the stairs as it was quite dark, but if you were caught doing this then you had to carry extra loads later.

After lunch we were free to go out for a walk or to play compulsory games. We were not allowed to remain inside the house unless we were ill and could not enter until 3.30pm even if it was raining. We walked in the school grounds which were extensive. Then we went around the Wakerley Woods or across the park to Laxton, where we could buy bread, sweets and biscuits. We did not wander far in the early days but gradually as we got our bearings, we enjoyed the freedom and walked quite long distances. Dutton and I were still very much together; he was very shy and slow but very open. His parents were Catholics and owned a big shop in Stone, Staffordshire. There was a Dominican Convent in the town and because of this and his brothers having been at the school, he knew some of the Blackfriars priests already. Tea at four o'clock comprised the usual plain bread and cups of tea. It was voluntary and at 4.45pm we were marshalled together and told to sit at our desks and write letters or read. At six o'clock we were dismissed and had an hour's recreation in our common rooms.

This formula was very much the pattern of my life for the next eight years. It was very structured and it was perhaps a bit restricting but it gave one a sense of absolute security once you became used to it. The school had been founded in Douai, Belgium in the mid-17th century to educate the children of Catholic gentry from England, known as recusants, and had a fine record. The essence of the Dominican educational policy was to have small classes, not more than eight boys to a master if possible, and to have top flight teachers. All the priests were highly educated men although naturally, their teaching abilities or their appeal to individual pupils varied. They set out to discipline the body, but to give free reign to the mind by promoting an almost university attitude to learning. They encouraged all forms of reading on almost any subject and involved the boys in theatre and debate; The Aquinas Society for theological debate for instance. All this was available from the youngest to the oldest. It did mean that the idle could ride the system, whilst those who were natural workers advanced rapidly.

Initially I was well advanced, as my reading was ahead of my age group and my writing reasonably mature. For instance, I despised Dutton for his slowness and said so. I must have hurt him by my jibes. Despite these, we remained close friends until he was killed when his destroyer was sunk during the battles off Algiers in 1942. As the years progressed, it was the thorough and careful students such as him who made the academic mark whilst the quicker minds got by on a superficial knowledge of the subjects. I fell into the latter category, was first or second in my class for the first three years, then middle to tail end and only really stretched myself at the very end. A great pity as there was much to be gained there.

The days passed quickly but I revolted against authority and soon found myself in trouble. Petty rules always grated on me and if I could see no logical reason for silence for instance, then I talked. The same with petty restrictions on bounds and I became a centre for any trouble in the dormitory as well. Eventually, the prefects, having exhausted their patience with lines or the penance walk sent me up for a whacking. This was a painful experience but gained me some kudos and if anything I behaved more badly as a result. I had a total of forty-three strokes of the cane in my first term. I believe this was a school record and, happily, I never matched it in the years ahead. The whacking system was primeval. On being awarded a whacking you had to pluck up courage and heart in mouth you knocked on Fr Aelwins door, hoping that he would be out. *"Come in"*. *"Father can I have a whacking please -- three"*   He questioned you and if satisfied that it was just, then *"Fetch me the steps"*. These were a set of library steps three high which stood behind the door in his room. *"Kneel on the bottom step, bend over and grasp the other step"* Your trousers were as tight as a drum across your bottom as you touched the step on the other side. Then a sense of awful anticipation as he threw his scapular over his left shoulder and having flexed the cane, raised his arm and there followed the exquisite pain as the cane struck. It was a matter of honour that one didn't cry out. In a few seconds it was over, *"Thank you father"* choking back a sob and then outside. In the meantime horrid small boys, hearing that there was a whacking afoot, assembled on the stairs outside to kick your backside as you went back down the stairs. Despite all this I still disobeyed, although after the first term, serious or persistent individual disobedience gradually ceased. I think that I had to show that I was a somebody, although I was the youngest in my class. Cocking a snoop at authority was a powerful way of demonstrating this "couldn't care less" attitude. The priests were well aware of the domestic situation vis-a-vis my parents. Looking back on things, there must have been other problem children and they were helpful in the extreme.

I have few letters from this period and probably didn't write to anybody very often. It was not, (and is not!) a virtue shared by many small boys. However, my first letter to my mother from Blackfriars is quite informative:

"Dear Mother
How are you I hope you are well I am. It is lovely at school and I know the college every where. I have not time for a long letter for I have to go out in 2 minutes time but still I will try to write as long as I can. I am number sixty five in my bedroom and my napkin ring. There is Dutton just coming up he is a poor thing he can't do latin, french or arithmetic and is ever such a dunce at games. We have pillow fights here and all sorts of things with games of rugby we played two colleges already and have one both. Love to all   Boy

and another: written towards the end of my first term:-

"Dear Mummy
I am a very happy boy Daddy came on Saturday thank everyone for their lovely presents and as for yours they were lovely.   Love Boy"

This referred to my birthday in December 1933 and shortly after this we broke up for the Christmas holidays.

Once again I went up to stay with my Mother in London. I was taken out with "The Troops" at the weekend, swam with Uncle Tony on Saturdays and walked Pip along the embankment at Hammersmith Bridge. The River Thames was filled with barges and floating debris. It was a muddy, oily, black, and slow moving cesspool! When Pip went in after pieces of driftwood, he came out stinking. It was nevertheless a fascinating highway and we spent hours just watching the river traffic. I loved this part of my holidays. Apart from occasions like this, there was little excitement. I went up with my Mother to visit her dress design workshop near Moorgate and, otherwise, stayed at Wells Road cooking. It was not great fun for a ten year old boy to be on his own with two old ladies every day, Great Granny and Hannah. I longed for my bicycle, the freedom of Kettering, the space at "Havencourt" and the fact of being in the country. Granny Gale told me that I once said to her *"I am a country boy, Granny"* and that really says it all. I loved my mother but I was too young or perhaps too selfish to want to put up with difficulties in order to demonstrate my love. It would be wrong to say that I was conscious of all this at the time but this was the last

Christmas that I spent in London until 1942 and, after that, I suspect that I was a reluctant visitor to London except for short stays. I found a note, for instance, in a letter of December 1935 in which it says *"I am sorry I said I was coming up after Christmas but we have not made any definite arrangements"*

During the Easter term I wrote to her saying :-
"Dear mummy,
How are you well I hope are you feeling better yet I hope so I am except for a headache I haven't had a whacking this term I am behaving so well this term how is Grannie getting over it I hope.   *Love   Boy"*

Shortly after this on 29 April 1934, Little Granny, Olivia Gigg, died at Wells Road. She had been frail for a long time and had been ill during the previous two months, she was 87 years old. I wrote a letter of sympathy to my mother and it is interesting to see the impact of the Catholic practice on my thinking, even after so short a time at school.
"Dear Mummy
sorry I couldn't write to you before but I was so busy. I am terribly sorry for you up there tell big granny that the first form and Father Henry saying prayers for her soul to reach Heaven and we are all very sorry especially me as granny was so good to me what a terrible difference it must have made to granny added years onto her life I dare say well I must go now but I really truthfully wish I could afford to have a high mass said for her soul.   Love   Boy
P.S. Don't worry too much because she is sure to reach heaven"

After Granny Gale had died in 1976, I had to go through all her papers, which included death notices, her singing programmes, my mother's 21st birthday cards and all my letters. Amongst the miscellaneous items I found notes in Little Granny's writing recording her spiritual thoughts and snippets of prayers. She was a deeply devout lady, always seemed to be close to God in every way and surely her influence continues to this day. There was also a rather nice note from a friend which read:-

14 May 1873 (Her Birthday)
A Happy New Year, to all who, Are dear, May hope love and joy now, Possess them, And the battle of life be to them void, Of strife, Here's a health to our friends, And God Bless them signed: *L.Otley for Olivia*

In the same envelope, but I suspect from a much later date in the 1890's, I found a silk woven bookmark, presumably from one of her children, which is headed "To my mother". It is decorated with roses:- *"Dear Mother Let thy tender care be graven on my heart. May God for years thy life yet spare, averting deaths rude dart.*

How gratefully I feel thy worth, Oh Mother! How I love thee! May joy await thee here on earth, and heaven smile above thee". Although it would not be true to say that I missed Little Granny very deeply, I loved her and she was another link in the chain between my mother, Granny Gale, London and myself which her passing weakened still more.

My father was very well aware of the fact that I was keen to become a Catholic. He had discussed this with Fr Henry and they had decided that it was purely because of the desire to be like the others and should be played down. However I persisted in my desire and attended mass each Sunday during the holidays at the hutted church at the back of Bowling Green Road. There was a family there called Langley, who, seeing that I was alone, began to keep an eye on me. Shortly after we had met, Mrs Langley invited me down for tea with her children. They lived at 91, London Road in a large semi-detached house. It was my first exposure to a really good catholic family and I was bowled over by their happiness, their togetherness, their sense of fun and their charity to others. I know now of course that this is not the prerogative of catholic families but at that time to find such an outpouring of love was overwhelming to me. It was the antithesis of the undemonstrative attitude adopted by my own family in Kettering. I began to spend as much time there as possible. The mother was called "Gerts" and their father "Uncle George". Their sons, Basil, an apprentice aircraft fitter usually in Coventry, Gerard, a seminarian at Oscott and the baby, John, aged about 6. Jos (Joscelyn) was the eldest girl aged 17, Aggie (Agnes) next, then Mags (Margaret) and finally "Tich"(Mary) who was 4 years old. We had a glorious time together, playing in their garden on our bicycles, singing around the piano, board games, eating, and meeting priests and nuns from all over the world. They kept open house and were involved in every aspect of Parish and Diocesan life. They became, and remained, my role model for a family, and I owe them a great deal.

Early in 1935 I asked Fr Henry and my father whether they would now let me become a catholic and to my great pleasure, it was accepted by both of them. My father was not present but on 6 March 1935 I was conditionally baptised by Fr Henry, in the sacristy, with Brother Rupert Groves, an old boy, as my godfather. Then on 7 March, which was the great feast day of St Thomas Aquinas (" Tommy Acq's Day ") I made my first Holy Communion. I was uplifted by it all and felt quite different for a few days but then like everything in life I began to get used to it and it became more of a routine. In 1936, the Bishop of Northampton visited the school and I was confirmed, taking the name Dominic. I have never lost the sense of faith which I gained in those early years and, apart from a period in 1946/1947, I have persisted in the practice of that Faith despite the doubts and difficulties that have presented themselves. It has undoubtedly been one of the mainstays of my life.

One of the many joys of Blackfriars School was its location. It stood in substantial grounds, some 40 acres, and these were set at the edge of the park belonging to Lady Bandon, who lived at the Laxton end of the road through the park. We were allowed to wander in the park and the surrounding woodland provided that we did no damage. Every day when we were not engaged in sports we spent at least two hours outside walking and as a keen naturalist I got to know every inch of the surrounding land. The local gamekeeper was a Mr Hercock, and initially we were very friendly. However with a weather eye on Mr Hercock's game tree, my friend Peter Dutton and I recorded such a host of murdered creatures that we were appalled. This tree was situated outside his store hut on the north side of the park bounded by a belt of woodland on a ridge overlooking the Stamford road. It was hung with badger, stoat, weasel, occasional rats, carrion crows, magpies, jays, hawk, and other creatures too many to mention. Nothing was spared if it could be said to disturb his pheasants, especially during the breeding season. We became so incensed, not only with the tree but also the host of maimed and dying animals we found, that we began to seek out his "gins" and set them off with sticks. These steel jawed traps were usually sited in drains, but also in runs in thick undergrowth and they contained many of the occupants of his "Tree", as well as rabbits and occasionally hares. Wild life was everywhere and, with hindsight, I don't suppose his activities denuded the area of any individual species but it was all so cruel. I think he suspected I was to blame, on several occasions warning me out of his woods, but we were very careful and he could never actually prove that it was us who did it.

Another item which we destroyed with regularity was the snare. These were set in rabbit runs and comprised a brass wire loop bound on to a thin but strong green cord. This cord was pegged into the ground and then the wire was formed into a running noose, balanced on a thin split stick and hidden in the grass across the run. Rabbits were the target but we found a fox cub one day with its leg skinned right to the bone. We collected two or three of these snares one afternoon and coming round a corner in the ride met one of the men from the village face to face. *"So you're the two little buggars stealing my snares"* he said and he looked so angry that I thought that he was going to hit us. *"Don't you realise that I rely on these bloody rabbits for a meal"* he added. I muttered something about it being cruel and snatching the snares from my hand he almost shouted *"Don't you bloody lecture me on cruel. You kids at the school were born with a silver spoon. If I catch you with one again or if I lose one again I shall sort you out personally so watch it."* We were very chastened by this and later found out that he lived in the village, had a large family, had lost his job and lived by poaching and odd jobs.

We were very keen on butterfly collecting. On the south and east side of the park were the famous Wakerley Woods which were filled with the most wonderful selection of butterflies; these ranged from the common to the very rare. We were armed with big nets, bottles with cotton wool soaked in ammonia and a tin for the dead ones. Once caught, they were killed in the bottle, transferred to the tin and then on return, set up on cork boards on which they were pinned whilst their wings were stretched out so as to display their wonderful colouring. In its way it was as brutal as Mr Hercock or the poacher but then like fish, butterflies don't scream when hurt, just flutter helplessly.

Our other "must" was a visit to Laxton to the back of the White's house, where we could buy bread, cakes, biscuits and a small selection of sweets. Mr White was the village baker and provided the school with long wholemeal loaves of delicious bread. He was a tall, lean man, rather saturnine with longish black hair and aquiline looks. He brought the bread to school in a high wheeled cart pulled by a very lively high-stepping black horse. He drove across on the park road at a spanking pace and drew up under the stable clock with a flourish. The maids queued to come and help him with the bread baskets and we all suspected that he had many conquests amongst them. He didn't have much time for the school boys but on one occasion allowed me into his bake-house. He showed me how he filled the brick oven with wood in the evening, fired it, got up in the early hours, raked out and then set the bread tins in to bake. He had a long pole with a small piece set at right angles with which he manoeuvred the tins in and out. His wife was as quiet and domestic as he was awesome and she supervised all sales. Her two young daughters never left her side and watched us, big-eyed as if we had come from another world, which I suppose in some ways we had. My favourite purchase was a "Buzz" Bar which was made by Lyons and cost 1d. It was the precursor of "Kit-Kat". I would often buy a 2d loaf and eat the hot bread and white crusts on my way back through the park. My other favourite choice was Sharps Toffee at 2d per quarter. It was amazing how full you could feel for 3d!

The next two years saw me settling in at school, enjoying the sporting aspects and still working quite hard. I was often in trouble and couldn't distance myself from becoming involved in silly pranks. I strongly denied any involvement in one dormitory feast and was caught red handed a few days later carrying food from one dormitory to another for a dare. I endured "Four" from Fr Henry. He had a heavier, less flexible cane and was renowned for following through, so that you were really heavily marked. He was probably unaware of this fact but it certainly wasn't an experience that one wanted to renew! On another occasion, I found the inside of a golf ball which, rather like the incredible high bouncing balls that one can buy nowadays, bounced beautifully on the stone floors. We were forbidden to play in the Great Hall but I couldn't resist trying once or twice. The ball soared up into the air, but when it bounced, it went off at a tangent and straight through a valuable oil painting of Saint Jerome. I was seen by one of the priests and set to kneel in the hall until my fate was decided. About half an hour later I was allowed up and nothing more was said about it. I was surprised and relieved. However, on Saturday we all queued outside the Bursars Office to collect our pocket money. 6d-1/- per week was the regulation level. The Bursar said *" Ah ----Bellamy ---, no pocket money"* When I assured him that my father had left 10/- with him at the beginning of term, he replied that I would need about twenty years without any pocket money in order to pay for the repair to the oil painting. I was dumbstruck and walked out in total despair. As I reached the door he called me back *" I will pay for the repair and give you pocket money if you promise never to play ball there again.If you do, you will not only have to pay for the repair but also repay all the pocket money that I have given to you"*. A very relieved little boy never played ball in there again!

I was happy at school during this time and enjoyed the "Month days" when twice a term our parents could come and take us out or we could go out with a friend. My letters are filled with *"Walked five miles to Kirby Hall met Daddy had a fine time"* or on another occasion *"Said Goodbye to Mrs Dutton my friends Mother after a hearty dinner"*. My father was very good on these occasions and we often took out three or four boys and played cricket. For example at Whitsun 1935 *"3 o'clock met Daddy how lovely two bottles of fizz and a glass of milk - yo ho ho and a bottle of rum.*[He took] *Old Rhodes, Irving, Clarke and myself for a game of cricket"* My father was very good in giving me support in this way. He was very poor at this period and told me later that he was having to borrow money from Mr Corby the dairyman, in order to keep up with my school fees.

 The school did not possess a swimming pool but we used to walk about a mile across "Mussons Field" through the old entrance gates, across the Stamford Road and swim in the lake there. It was clear water and one had to dive in from a wooden platform. I had been boasting of my prowess as a swimmer and was somewhat taken aback to find that there was no shallow end! I realised that I had to brazen it out and, having never ever dived before, jumped headfirst into water. I was relieved when I actually floated to the surface and then managed to dog paddle back to the bank. There was no tuition for swimming, it was definitely sink or swim and I gained the rudiments by watching the others. I have never been a stylish swimmer but despite that can stay afloat for long periods.

Christmas and Easter holidays presented a mixed experience as I stayed for much of them at "Havencourt" but quite often I stayed with my father in his "Digs" in Bowling Green Road. We sometimes ate with Auntie Edna but as meals were provided in the "Digs" we went there most of the time. My summer holidays obviously presented my father with greater problems. We broke up at the end of July and did not return to school until the middle of September. This meant that he had to find some occupation for me for 8-9 weeks and at the same time earn his keep. In this first long holiday the plans got off to a disastrous start as his arrangements for me to go to London fell through, my mother being in hospital unexpectedly The end result, however, was that I spent most of the eight weeks at Kirby Hall.

It was during that holiday that I experienced the presence of a ghost there, an experience which I have never forgotten. I used to jump the missing stair tread in the Great Staircase which enabled one to get up onto the second floor and walk through the old Great Chamber into what we called "Queen Elizabeth's bedroom", above the old billiard room. This room had a number of false wooden pillars running up each side and you walked down the centre of them to get through into the adjacent rooms. Incidentally it was strictly out of bounds at the time, as the stair jump was considered to be too dangerous. Any way, just after lunch and on the most lovely sunny day, Rover and I wandered into the old Parlour where Mr Gale was working. He asked me what I was doing and I replied that I was going out to the 40 acre, the big field at the back. He apparently took no further notice and as I came out of his workshop to go out through the Great Hall into the air I had a sudden thought to go upstairs. I did not know that he was watching me. We ran up the stairs, took the three foot jump, dog as well, and sauntered through into the Great Chamber, which was bathed in sunshine, without a care in the world. Suddenly I felt a great fear and a sort of iciness around me; I looked down at Rover who was lying on his stomach with his ears back, his hair on end and his teeth bared, not moving. I wanted to run but couldn't move and had a feeling that a "something" was coming close to me. At this point I must have screamed and then fainted. The next thing that I knew was Mr Gale carrying me and then a few moments later, Alma, who had been in the larder, and had heard the rumpus came along too. She was furious as she thought that Mr Gale had hit me! There was nothing wrong with me and I was soon outside again after getting an unusually strong telling off for going up there when it was forbidden; that's what happens to wicked boys and so-on! I have no explanation for this at all; I had no repetition of it there or indeed anywhere else in Kirby and I remained unafraid when I was alone, even at night.

During this long period at Kirby I spent a lot of my time with Ronnie Hart, Joe's cousin's son. He was slightly older than I was and certainly more streetwise. We played in the old buildings, explored, spent hours collecting butterflies from the adjacent woodland and went swimming in the old mine workings, long since worked out, on the way to Weldon. Sometimes we wandered as far as Gretton where there was a shop and bought sweets. We often got up to mischief and waged a desultory form of war with Mr Gale. This really took the form of disobeying his dictums on entering places forbidden to us rather than doing any harm but he used to be satisfactorily annoyed and we were always delighted by his explosions of wrath. I am sure that the restrictions were for our own safety more than for any more esoteric reason. One of the forbidden places was the tower building adjacent to the old kitchens on the east side of the building. This contained a stone staircase which had a substantial piece missing. The upper area provided a nesting site for a number of pigeons. One day Ronnie dared me to jump the gap in the staircase and after considerable doubts were expressed as to my courage I jumped and just scrambled home. He wouldn't follow, *"Rotten coward"*, so I gained on points, however there was only one way back and this was to jump downhill onto a descending staircase. I couldn't bring myself to do it and we were discovered by Mr Gale himself. Ronnie got a real lathering for that. Being a village lad, whose father was a friend of Mr Gale, he could be dealt with. I was left there from the late morning until they went home at 4.30pm when one of the men came with a ladder. A painful episode!

Later that summer, I went over to watch the three of them recovering stone from an area at the end of the west terrace where the bank was covered in trees and ran down to the stream. There were dozens of little white lilies there. They were actually eating their lunch sitting in the sunshine and when I approached, one of them handed me a piece of bread with a white slice of a root in it, saying that it was a special tasty thing. I ate it and immediately my mouth became absolutely dry with no saliva; it was a horrible feeling as if I had taken a huge mouthful of aloes. It was some form of wild root but I have never been able to identify it. I ran away at their laughter and tried washing my mouth out, drinking and eating, but nothing would make it better. Alma was furious with them and then, out of the blue, my father arrived and he had a row with Mr Gale accusing him of trying to poison me. I kept clear of them after that but the storm soon blew over!

I imagine that it was this incident which decided him to send me to Joyce Garton, a school teacher at Cranford, and I spent the remainder of the holidays on the farm. For some years, my father had been friendly with George Garton and his family who farmed at Cranford near Kettering. We visited them quite often and I had stayed there for the occasional day. He loved his sport and he went there each year for rough shooting, and for the annual rook cull. The latter was a barbaric day designed to thin out the young rooks before they left the nest. Mrs Garton and her daughters then had the task of plucking the squabs and making them into rook pie. Not my favourite meal! At this time my father was seeing a lot of Joy their daughter. She was a very sweet young woman and very nice indeed to me, always giving me time for reading or talking.

It was harvest time and after a little training I was put in charge of the empty wagons as they returned from unloading the sheaves of corn in the rick yard. My job, with the two Shire horses, was to return the wagons to the fields as quickly as possible so that they could be reloaded. It was an enjoyable task and I suppose that the horses could have done it without me! I learned what remarkable creatures they are and remember one instance demonstrating this very clearly. The track along the side of the brook had developed deep cart ruts. I was walking alongside the left hand horse holding loosely onto its reins when my foot slipped in to the runnel and the horses hoof came down on top of it. I instinctively winced as I waited for the pain that must surely follow. The horse put no weight on that hoof at all and I withdrew my foot without damage! How could it have felt my foot through a metal shoe and a horn hoof? It was an enjoyable task for a small boy and I was deeply happy.

I spent a lot of time at the smithy which was on the corner just down the road from the farm, waiting with the horses whilst they were shod. I loved the smell of the burning horn as, holding the horses hoof bent backwards against his leather apron which was resting across his knee, the blacksmith fitted the shoe. It was almost miraculous to see the strip of metal heated up and hammered into a curve which identified so readily with the individual hoof.

Each morning, if we were awake early enough, we brought in the cattle for milking. There were about thirty cows to milk and in the cold of early morning, the men used to snuggle up against their sides and coax as much milk out as they could. "Stripping" they called it as they got the last drops out. Every milker had his own specials and the cows knew exactly which stall to occupy. Some were absolute devils and had a habit of kicking forward with their hind leg and catching the bucket or the unfortunate man. The language at those times was fierce! The farm cats used to come in for a drink and the men would squirt a jet of milk direct from the teat into their open mouths. They did this once to me, but warm fresh cows' milk tastes very different to that which has been cooled and separated and I didn't repeat the experience. Mr Garton's son, George, and I became good friends and after this, I nearly always managed to spend some time with the family during the summer holidays.

At the beginning of 1936, King George the Vth died. The country went into mourning for him and we all returned to school wearing black armbands. The sadness was shared by the whole country and was very genuine. Even at my age I had a deep sense of loss. It was about this time that I first became aware of Mussolini and Hitler. The former was the subject of jokes at school, but clearly, the grown-ups around me were filled with concern and although I didn't fully understand why, I knew that both my father and his old soldier friends were unhappy about events in Germany.

I had always possessed a good clear treble voice and loved singing. I was already in the Choir and the Glee Club. We were trained by Fr Gerald Vann, an excellent organist and I was soon appointed as leading treble and soloist. Singing in church was enjoyable but my heart was really in the folk songs which we sang as part of the Glee Club. One of our priests was Fr Ceolfrid Heron, member of a family which included a number of well known singers and actors. His three sisters, who sang professionally as the "Heron Sisters" used to come down to the school and I fell in love with one of them (aged about 25!). They used to invite me to sing with them and I have their autograph. I was very keen on the school plays but at this time only landed women's roles. I was the Queen of Hearts in Alice in Wonderland, Lady Macbeth, an old woman in the chorus of Murder in the Cathedral and so-on.

I have a very long eight page letter written to my mother dated 2 July. It refers to my pleasure in writing poetry and essays and says that I am to have one of each published in the "Howardian", our school magazine. The poem was called the "Prioresses Tale". I had written a book containing 41 pages of poems and essays and I asked her whether it was worth getting them published. Conceit of the boy! Incidentally I still have the original! It is full of poems and stories and written neatly in a round hand.

In my letter, I noted that I usually received about 4/6d for my birthday and wondered whether 5 shillings would be a fair price for such a publication. The letter then goes on to express my interest in autographs as my mother was a scorer at club cricket matches and met many famous sportsmen such as Hammond, Sutcliffe, Verity, Leyland, Wooley and the like. Rather munificently I *"would be prepared to give 2d for Wooley's or Obelenskys autograph"*! I enjoyed my cricket and reported a batting average of 5.5 runs in eight innings and a bowling of 12 overs, 8 wickets for 30 runs.

The letter gives an insight into my life at school and that of my peers. *"Melius just got four for hitting a chap on the arm in the dormitory, but he has been let off. Stapely had two this morning he cried, I suppose they hurt. Now there is a cats concert outside our dormitory window, the Upper Common room chaps are making a horrible row. Macnamara is dabbing some horrible white lotion on his gnat bites. Clarke is asking for papers and no one has any to lend for him to read. Repton is charging around the dormitory hitting people who call him the 'Mother Prioress'. My holidays start on 25 July 1936 I am looking forward to them."* I then asked whether my friend Sebastian Rhodes and I could cycle up to London as I would like to stay with his family at their house in Cricksea near Burnham on Crouch that summer.

The book also contains a diary describing our Easter holiday tour of the south of England. This marked the start of my father's new job. He had been appointed sales manager to Dudson Brothers, a firm who made pottery in Staffordshire and was beginning his role which was to cover the whole of England and Scotland. I travelled with him a great deal and gained a first class knowledge of the highways and byways of the whole country. We always shared a room in the commercial hotels in which we stayed, so I imagine that it was an economic way of holidaying me as well. He was both knowledgeable and interesting to be with. We never passed a famous spot without at least a brief visit. I learned a lot during the next three years. Evidently, I had been invited to stay with Seb Rhodes for the summer holidays again as I record that *"We then went on to Burnham on Crouch where we stayed at the Anchor Inn. We went over to Mr Rhodes house where we talked and looked at photographs and paintings until about 9 o'clock. At 9 o'clock I went to bed and got up early and went out to look at the boats by our window which overlooked the harbour."*

One morning during that summer term I looked out of the dormitory window and saw three green and yellow caravans parked in the old stone quarry just outside the school grounds, in what we called Musson's Field. After breakfast we all rushed over to see who it was. They were horse drawn caravans and each contained a heavily bearded man, his dirndl dressed wife and, in one case, several small children equally quaintly dressed. I was fascinated and went up to one of them, who later I knew as Dunstan. He was a short stocky man and his wife, Rosamund, was blonde, tall and dressed in a beautiful blue gown, rather Madonna-like. He told me that they were Distributists and were looking for a place to set up a colony. They did not accept all the modern equipment, shared everything and were "Back to the Land" pacifists. Their leader was John Hawkeswell and he and his wife already had three little children in the caravan. The third member was a Heron, one of the same family that visited the school and sang. They were all Catholics and attended mass at the school. They stayed there for some time before moving on to a permanent site on the Laxton edge of the Wakerley Woods, and were most hospitable. The land they then acquired was very poor and they had great difficulty trying to live off their produce. The women suffered most, they not only existed in primitive conditions, bore children and tried to keep house but also they spun and wove their own cloth, buying nothing. As the years passed, I remained very friendly with them and helped physically where I could. They were almost communist in their attitude to politics, certainly very left wing, and I found their political views increasingly attractive. At one point I seriously considered becoming a card carrying communist and they supported me in this attitude provided that it was "Christian Communism" which as Fr Gerard patiently explained was an oxymoron! Hawkeswell's wife died eventually through too many children and over work, or so the other men said, whilst another wife had a mental breakdown and went into an asylum. Dunstan and Rosamund survived, surrounded by their children and grandchildren. I was told this by one of their grand daughters, who was so like her grandmother to look at that when we met her in a public house in Harringworth, I recognised her at once!

We returned home for the summer holidays, on 25 July 1936 and immediately afterwards my father took me by car to stay with the Rhodes family. This was my first time that I actually stayed with school friends and in this instance, as they were totally impecuneous; I suspect that he had already arranged to contribute towards my upkeep. From then onwards I nearly always went to stay with friends' families for at least a part of the holidays. Mr Rhodes was a struggling artist, who worked as a cowman in the nearby milking parlour in order to provide for his family. The eldest son, Francis Cecil, named after their famous cousin in Rhodesia, was at sea. The second, Sebastian, was one of my friends at Laxton and the daughter, Mary, was 12 years old, the same age as me. Their mother, a sweet woman, lived in the tiny cottage with a younger daughter, whilst their father lived next door in the wreck of a barn which he called his studio. He said to all and sundry including me, that he did this because he couldn't afford to sleep with his wife she was too fertile! It was domestic chaos, with few facilities but thoroughly enjoyable. We ate al fresco in or out of the house, and lived outside all day, every day. We walked for miles along the river, in the river or elsewhere and slept like logs. Each night we sang to his guitar. He had spent a lot of time in Spain and taught me to sing a lot of Spanish songs with the semi-tones and the arab airs. I loved singing with them and in our enthusiasm we often went on until we all virtually fell asleep. We said evening prayers, very liturgical, around the altar in the studio. Strictly men only. After which we drank glasses of milk, whilst he searched our hair for fleas and found many, which he popped in a candle flame or pressed into the hot wax. There was no electricity and reading by candlelight was hopeless as there were only two candle holders. We slept more or less where we wanted on palliasses covered by a blanket.

Just next to the track which wheeled round to the cottage was an old ships bell on a post. Travellers could sound this bell and a man who lived in a hovel on the other side of the river would row over and collect them; I believe that the fee was 1d. He was not a particularly friendly person but he knew the family and occasionally we would get a lift over in his boat and then back later when there was space. I believe that this was the last ferry of such a nature in England. If you were on foot and the ferry was not operating, then in order to cross the river, you had to walk up to South Woodham or Fambridge where there was a bridge.

Despite his poverty, Mr Rhodes owned a beautiful old clinker built 16 foot lobster boat, "Pride of the Crouch". She was well known on the river and I believe was about 70 years old, one of a class which had ceased to exist. She was gaff rigged and very easy to sail. He had contracted a dreadful sort of carbuncle on his right hand that summer, it was a complaint caught from cows udders, was very infectious and it prevented him from milking. Accordingly we spent a lot of time sailing and always did the shopping by going down to Burnham by boat, a long job as he had no engine. One of our main delights was to pack up a huge bread and cheese lunch and go round Holliwell Point towards the Blackwater; on one occasion going up river as far as Maldon and spending the night under the stars. The Blackwater was filled with cargo ships moored in mid stream and idle because of the shipping slump. I wonder how many of those were sunk five years later when the battle of the Atlantic was in full swing.

As you enter the Blackwater, on the port side and under the sea, we were told, lies the remains of an old Roman town, Othena. We used to moor over this at low tide and dive down into the seaweed to try to find the old houses or discover some antiquities. We never made any discoveries but it was great fun. I recollect that there was a chapel on the adjacent sea wall called St Peters on the Wall. It was thought to have been built by St Cedd in 654 AD, largely from old Roman buildings, tiles etc.

One of Mr Rhodes' close friends owned a working barge which plied between Burnham and the Thames. We spent many happy hours on her and one glorious day, Seb and I were taken on as cabin boys and sailed through the Cut which ran between Foulness Island and the mainland, coming back on the bus. Many barges took this, it was too shallow except for them and thus they avoided the sea lane to Shoeburyness. It gave them direct access to the industrial area at the back of Rayleigh, where there were many wood yards. We spent much of the voyage running up and down the mast, nearly to the mast-head, on the huge wooden rings which carried the main-sail and when there was a light wind we slid down the curve this formed in the main by swinging down off the Gaff. I drew pictures of his boat and used to sit astonished as we watched the barges taking the Cut. They appeared, from our side of the river, to be sailing over the land. That part of Essex was totally flat with no landmarks. To me, it was mystical, and I can see it in my mind's eye very clearly.

Lying on the edge of the water about two miles upstream from us was a large fishing smack, sunk and left to rot. It lay between an island and the shore. This was a great place for us and we spent hours at low and mid-tide "sailing" her to incredible destinations. Her ballast was still intact and that represented the gold which we carried. Mary, being "only a girl" was the cook and cabin boy. She never protested! The sea wall and the edge of the water were covered with sea spinach and we took great bundles of this back to Mrs Rhodes to cook. I wasn't enamoured of it, but then we were always famished and ate whatever we could lay our hands on without argument. Also found along the sea wall were hundreds of tiny lizards and Mary and I rarely went out without one in our hands. They were tricky to catch and if you didn't get them by the front end, they bit off their tails which destroyed their value in our eyes. The tails, incidentally, grew again very quickly but one could tell if it was a replacement by a ribbing mark across their back. I had a special one which I called Dominic. He was always in my hand and seemed quite at ease. At night he was placed in a small box with grass in it.

After four weeks of this remarkable freedom my father came and collected me and I went up to see my mother before returning and travelling with him for the last few weeks. The Olympic Games were on in Berlin at this time and all the boys were "Jessie Owens", the American who broke five world records there. I was a fast runner and I used to rush about saying that I was running as fast as he had! My other hero was "Hyperion", the horse which won the Derby that year.

During this summer, the Sleath family had moved from Bowling Green Road and purchased a house on a new development, at 1, Larch Road, Kettering. It was a pleasant modern house and stood in a small garden with a good view across towards Warkton Mill. We used to walk along a track through allotments there when I was younger. It is now at the rear of the Technical College and in the middle of Kettering housing developments. Once again my father and I shared a room at the back of the house but this time it was next door to the bathroom.

When my father went off on a special sales trip, I wasn't always welcome to spend the day at the Sleaths and in some cases was invited to go up to my Aunt's house in Tennyson Road. I always had a wonderful lunch there, as she was a really good cook and knew exactly the sort of nursery fare that children liked. We had stews and mashed potatoes, peas, greens and carrots. Puddings were usually fruit pies, jam tarts with loads of jam and custard in a great jug. I tried to avoid Mondays if I could as it was cold meat and leftovers but that was not always possible worst luck! Monday was Wash-Day and it was the day when all hell was let loose. Auntie Edna rose at about 5-00a.m. and lit the fire under the copper which stood in the corner of the scullery just by the back door. It was filled with water from the pump by the sink and by 7-00a.m. the water was boiling and ready for the first load. I believe that this was the whites which were followed in sequence by gradually increasing "colours" or dirtier items. The atmosphere was awful, with clouds of hot steam, wet floors, and interminable baskets of washing going out onto the line or coming in wrapped together so as to keep them damp for ironing. I was young, and was a general dogsbody at this stage, but as I became more experienced, so I gained stature and was entrusted with "Hanging things out on the line". Again a high risk business, as it was difficult to balance them well and keep the props in place. My Aunt's eagle eye never missed a mark on her whites if you dropped something on the gravel! The really bad moment however, was when the sheets had to be stretched and folded. Auntie Edna was a big woman and powerful; when you were at the other end of a pair of sheets holding the corners neatly together as instructed, the ends gathered in your two hands ready for the pull, there came a moment of pure terror! It was no gentle pull, more of a snatch and you felt your raw finger ends begin to lose their grip. You hung on desperately as a dropped sheet at this stage meant a re-wash and ignominy for the failed puller! I can still feel the strength of her pull and the very real horror that this time you really would let go. The final matter was the starching of smaller items such as Uncle Bernard's collars and cuffs, a separate mystique into which I did not enquire. Tuesday was ironing day and airing clothes over the fire guard in the dining room. The house always smelt lovely on Tuesday, the fresh washing scenting the warm air. My two cousins bore the brunt of all this but as I always had longer holidays, I took over when they went back to school.

Most of my free time when I was in Kettering was spent riding around on my bicycle. My father had purchased a really sturdy (and heavy!) "James" for me. It had no three speed or any complex additions but sported a bell, a battery lamp, a very strong roomy saddle bag and carrier at the back. It was second hand and had cost him 18 shillings. I was immensely proud of it and during the next five years it carried me all over England. I was reluctant to part with it in 1941 when I went into the army.

I had several good local friends at this time but spent much of many of my days with Michael Swain who lived in Hawthorn Road and shared my love of trains as well as of cycling. There was so little traffic that apart from obvious precautions we were quite safe to go anywhere, town or country. One of the penalties of my freedom was that I was responsible for having my own hair cut. This was done every month in a men's hairdressers just off the Hawthorn Road. If you were under sixteen it cost threepence, but they didn't spend too long over it and you certainly came out well shorn. There was still a great deal of poverty in the country and I well remember one day being on my bicycle in a side road off Roundhill Road and seeing an out of work miner standing in the middle of the empty road singing for pennies. This was not an uncommon event but this time, I watched, listened and noted that people did not rush out with gifts. I had a banana in my saddle bag which my aunt had given me for my lunch. I rode up to him, thanked him for his singing and rather shyly offered him my banana which he took with great grace and smiling thanks. His gratitude remains with me as a lesson in good manners. He could have been offhand or refused but he didn't, he took it graciously and consequently, I felt very rewarded.

We returned to school in September and I have no record of letters until the following May when we had two days of celebrations for the coronation of King George the VIth. There was a High Mass and those interested, were allowed to listen to the actual broadcast by joining the priests in the Fathers Common Room. There followed a special lunch and we were free all the next day. That year, I was thrilled to be chosen as a member of the chorus in the School play "Murder in the Cathedral" by T.S. Elliot. Sebastian Rhodes took the part of St Thomas and apparently quite brilliant, so much so, that Robert Speaight who was playing the part in the Theatre in London at the time, came up to watch. I was thrilled to talk with so famous an actor, and I have his autograph. We had a lectern on stage during our production which he thought to be an excellent idea and he amended the London production accordingly! This initiation cemented my great interest in acting and I acted in every school play from thence forward.

The summer term seemed to inspire me to write better letters and in July 1937 I wrote a long letter to my mother saying that *"I will be very glad to come up for a week or two in the hols."* I then went on *"As for me, I am 5 foot high and weigh 7 stone 4 lbs. I am not under size and I grow very quickly."* I concluded by listing my Form placings for the year which were out of 8 boys, so not very impressive:- Latin. 6. Arithmetic. 6. Algebra. 5. Geometry. 5. Scripture. 7. English. 9. Geography. 8. French. 5. and History. 8. and I close *"When do you think Seb and I can see you. Seb is the boy I am going to stay with."* Once again my father took me down to Creeksea and although we did not cycle to London, I did spend two weeks in London after my stay with the Rhodes family and the balance of my holiday was spent travelling with my father.

The holiday in Essex was as enjoyable as ever. Mary, I think, was especially delighted to see me, as we played rather as equals, whilst Seb was more mature and distant. Nothing had changed except that Mr Rhodes was better and able to milk again. The holiday followed much the same pattern of freedom, singing each evening and sailing, as in 1935. There was however one incident when we were out with him in "Pride of the Crouch" which was unforgettable. Mr Rhodes and I set off together one day to sail out to the navigational buoy some miles out from the mouth of the Crouch. It was a lovely sunny day with a light wind. We called in at Burnham and picked up a lady whom he knew and who sailed with us from time to time. She was one legged, having lost her left leg in an accident. The usual "Sharpie" Races were in full flow and they were streaking about us in the estuary as we went on our rather more staid way. Sharpies and Crouch One Design were the "In" boats of their day and very fast. Clear of them the wind freshened but was patchy although we made good progress clearing the Dengie Flats by lunch time. We lunched aboard whilst we sailed on a broad reach with a gentle northerly wind. It was beautiful sunny day with clear blue skies and we seemed to have all the sea to ourselves

We were about a mile from the buoy and perhaps four miles off shore, when there was a sudden huge gust of wind which just seemed to appear from nowhere. We were caught full on the beam and she rolled straight over and turned upside down with all three of us struggling from under the sail as she went. It was devastating, but perhaps because I did not understand the seriousness of the situation, I was not frightened. The bottom of the hull was slightly below the waves and going further under from time to time. Mr Rhodes shouted that she was sinking and then burst into tears, at the thought of losing his boat I suppose, anyway, he became quite hysterical, finally shouting that if she sank that he would go down with her. Our companion was more pragmatic and told me to swim alongside her and we would strike out for the shore, which was a good four miles away. We set off and swam for a long time. After several minutes, she unstrapped her leg which was made of cork, shoved it under my chest and told me to hold on and paddle with my legs. We made some progress, perhaps the tide was with us, I don't know, but quite suddenly a large fishing smack was close to us. Interesting enough, although the sea was calm we didn't see her until she was almost on top of us, so the swell must have been stronger than we thought, greatly restricting our vision. They hove to, threw out ropes and hauled us shivering onto the deck. We were wrapped in blankets and plied with hot soup. They then sailed on turning back towards Burnham and must have alerted the life boat, as we passed it on it's way out to rescue Mr Rhodes.

Our rescuers turned out to be a group of young people who were on their way to spend a weekend in Holland and had spotted us in the water quite by chance as they had not seen the incident. They also had no engine, so the return took a couple of hours and during this time we tried to express our gratitude. On arrival my companion invited them all to her house but they declined and continued on their voyage. I had supper with her and stayed until Mary arrived and then we walked back together. Mr Rhodes was standing by his boat which had been towed back, *"Under water and too fast"* he said, and they had left her on the hard by the house, so as to drain out. It was Spring tide and as she settled, he saw with despair that she was astride the groyne which ran down the mud bank into the Crouch. It was old and ineffective but still contained some strong upright stakes. Several of these had penetrated her hull and he had not been able to push her off before this had happened.

The next spring tide happened a little later and he mobilised the whole family. We all stood around her, waist deep in water, waiting for the critical moment when we might be able to lift her the fraction of an inch required to move her off the piles. As the time of top of the tide approached we were instructed to start saying the "Hail Mary" together. We all chanted this and every so often we lifted as best as we could. We struggled for about fifteen minutes during which we failed to move her at all.

Despair was setting in when, quite suddenly, there was a slight wave, again we lifted, she scraped free, and began to settle on the mud by the groyne. *"Shows the power of prayer"* shouted a delighted Mr Rhodes. *"Wake from that motorboat"* said a more pragmatic and long suffering Mrs Rhodes!

On my return to Northampton, I discovered that a well-known pilot called Cobb was running an Air Circus in one of the fields on Pytchley Hill. I cycled there and watched his biplanes carrying out various hair-raising manoeuvres above our heads and then an announcement said that any ticket holder could hazard a guess at the height at which a nominated aeroplane would be flying and those closest to the right answer would have a free flight. As I had a ticket, I remember saying 3500 feet, never imagining that I could possibly win. In point of fact, another onlooker and I, having discussed the matter, both plumped for 3500 and won! We then had a splendid flight in an open-air cockpit in one of his biplanes, which flew over Kettering and I saw with great clarity my Aunt's old house in Bowling Green Road and their current house in Tennyson Road and, even more thrilling perhaps, the house where I was staying with my Uncle and Aunt in Roundhill Road. It was an unforgettable experience; very clear in the sunshine and although only lasted about fifteen minutes, it was a huge thrill. All in all, it was a memorable holiday.

New boy off to school at Blackfriars School, Laxton 1933

Sketch Blackfriars School stable & chapel from Vth Form study by Bill

Blackfriars School Summer Term 1934

CHAPTER 8
Blackfriars School 1937-1940

When I returned to school for the Christmas Term in September 1937, I was delighted to find that I had been made Captain of the under 14 Rugby Football team. I was a keen player and had enjoyed some success in the previous season but this was an honour that I had not envisaged and it did my morale a lot of good. In the event we had an excellent season only losing one match and that to Uppingham, which was a very much larger school than Blackfriars. Sport began to dominate my thinking and my performance in class slipped as I concentrated on hockey and athletics in the Easter Term and then of course cricket. I was now in Class IV, which is middle school and always something of a water-shed. Life was enjoyable and I had staunch friends; work and the possibility of exams seemed light years away. I only did enough work to stay in the middle segment of the class and avoid major trouble.

I had a very close friendship with one of the younger priests, Fr Gerard Meath. He had come to the school in 1934, just after his ordination, and he had been very supportive and generally helpful to me. Then he went off to Cambridge where he gained a double first in English and History, returning in 1938 to teach. He was very friendly with Peter Dutton too, and together, we used to spend a lot of time in his room. We were both keen on fish and water-life generally and established a small aquarium on his window sill, where we studied insects and dragon fly larvae. It was rewarding and led us on to study other forms of wildlife especially birds. I began to keep a nature diary.

There was another wonderful and saintly priest in a room on the same corridor called Sebastian Bullough. He was one of the church's leading professors of Bible Study and could speak and write in all the bible tongues. He taught us Religious Knowledge and made it so interesting and live, that I retained my exercise books for fifteen years after school when, to my chagrin, my wife destroyed them through a misunderstanding. However he produced several books relating to teaching Religious Knowledge which I have read subsequently and found to be excellent. Although so erudite, he was a man of the very greatest humility and we all loved him for it. He used to begin his classes by saying "our exegesis for today is --". He was a very tall man yet travelled everywhere on an ancient motorbike with a sidecar. He was a living St Francis, and whatever we discovered that was sick or injured, was taken straight up to his room. His room was tiny, perhaps ten feet by fifteen and contained his bed, desk, walls filled with bookcases and inevitably some ailing creature in a box or on a perch, often liberally fouling his room! I had managed to get up onto the school roof one day and collected a young jackdaw which I called Chaktek (very Henry Williamson - my long-standing literary hero). I kept him on a perch in the woodwork building and he became very tame. Unfortunately shortly after getting him one of his fellow nestlings flew down and joined him and wouldn't be dissuaded from staying. Eventually, I took him up to Fr Seb's room, whose firm friend he became, but where he created havoc not least by all the lime on the floor and furniture. However, despite this, he stayed and spent a great deal of his life perched on Fr Seb's shoulder. His greatest trick was to fly above Fr Seb's motorcycle as he went on his rounds serving the local churches. One day Fr Seb had to go to Cambridge and the jackdaw flew with him. When the spires of Cambridge came into sight "*he soared off to join his brethren*" or so Fr Seb told us! Chaktek survived for the whole of the summer term before leaving me. He returned to me when we came back from the holidays and was quite tame but ultimately he became independent. I still have photographs of him.

I was always very keen on writing stories or poetry and usually had some item in the school magazine. I liked to sign these with a flourish as "LB". I submitted one exam paper to Fr Ralph Hodsoll, my history teacher, which I signed like that. It was returned marked - "*I imagine the LB stands for Lousy Bloody which the paper submitted certainly is!*".

This was at a time in a boy's life when the questions of sexuality were becoming the foremost of ones problems. There was a great deal of self abuse as well as a general exploration of sexuality going on. I was a very attractive boy and had experienced some difficulties with older boys. I had been greatly helped with these problems by Fr Gerard who had my total confidence. The junior school had been interviewed and physically examined for the past two or three years by an eminent psychiatrist, who was conducting a series of tests on adolescence in a number of schools. The physical tests were all carried out in the presence of the Matron. When it was my turn I entered the room for my interview and the doctor said to Matron that she wouldn't be required. I was unconcerned, supposing that this meant that no physical examination would take place. He had always been kind to me, had even signed my autograph book, and I felt at ease with him. He often spent longish times over our sessions and seemed to be interested in my chatter which was flattering. This particular Easter Term the doctor questioned me deeply on these highly personal aspects of relationships with other boys and masturbation generally. I found it difficult to reply to him, I suppose basically that this was through natural diffidence but I remember a sense that I was being threatened by him as well. I was embarrassed and felt thoroughly awkward. He then commenced a physical examination which left me standing before him on a table naked. At that moment Fr Henry came into the room, told me to get dressed and return to my class room. We never saw the psychiatrist again.

The Aquinas Society used to meet each month and discussions were held on a wide range of subjects. I didn't understand everything of course, but always carried away something of general value. On one occasion we were visited by a hypnotist and after an interesting talk on uses and possible uses of this technique in medicine he asked for volunteers. Fr Cedric Burton, who had a glass eye, and who was not a very popular master, volunteered and we were all delighted to see him put into a trance. The hypnotist then suggested that he did a variety of simple things like passing him his glasses or turning the chair round etc. He did all these and we were satisfied with the demonstration. However at the end of the talk when Fr Cedric was acting perfectly normally having been released from the hypnosis, the hypnotist told us that he had left him with an instruction to do another action later but he wouldn't tell us what it was. We were all agog. Later, I heard that the priests returned with the hypnotist for a drink in the Fathers Common Room and whilst they were seated, Fr Cedric came in, stood on one leg and sang "God save the King" to an enthralled audience. I don't think the other priests liked him much either!

My voice was still good, and I was leading treble, although I was beginning to take Alto parts. We were still visited by singing groups and that summer it was the "Westwood Singers" who came. We had a great evening singing all the old favourite folk songs, at the end of which, they too signed my autograph book.

We had been joined by a new priest that year, Fr Dominic Sire. He was French and his twin brother was a Jesuit priest at Stoneyhurst. His parents were very wealthy and he brought some marvellous trains to the school which enabled us to form a train club over the woodwork shop in the Stables. I was a train buff anyway, and became a complete addict, spending as much time up there as possible. Amongst the items was a splendid 4-6-2 steam engine which fairly hurtled along the track. This gave me the ambition to see the new L.N.E.R. train which was to try for the world speed record and I persecuted my father until he agreed to take me to see it. That summer we went to the Whissendine Straight, near Huntingdon and saw the "Mallard" at speed. It was a fantastic sight as she was travelling well over 100mph. Her record was 126mph which I believe still stands. The train she was pulling was called the "East Coast Limited"

I went to bed one evening with a painful stomach ache which still persisted in the morning, despite all the potions which Matron poured down me. Fr Dominic was a failed doctor and took a great interest in medicine. He came up to the dormitory and ran the end of a bakelite fountain pen over my stomach asking me to tell him if there was any difference from one side to the other. It positively grated on the left middle side. He rang the doctor immediately – diagnosis - Acute Appendicitis. Our doctor didn't bother to visit but called me straight into the Stamford Cottage Hospital. I was seen at once and operated on that afternoon by Mr Debruyn, a South African surgeon, who told my worried father that if it hadn't been for Fr Dominic's prompt and accurate diagnosis, I would have had a burst appendix. This interest cemented a relationship between Fr Dominic and my father and later he was to become my legal guardian. After this I spent a few days convalescence with my father down in Bournemouth. I played so energetically on the beach there that I twisted the stitches round and developed a poisoned area which was slow to respond to treatment. No antibiotics in 1937!

The summer holidays were varied again as my father was still a representative for a pottery firm from Stoke and he covered the whole of the UK. I did enjoy marvellous and interesting car journeys around England, Wales and Scotland. Scotland had a special fascination as we used to go as far north as Oban and on several occasions saw golden eagles and the very attractive red squirrels, which, even then, were quite a rarity in England. We also spent a night in Glasgow and I remember my father taking me to Browns Shipyard where the Queen Mary was back under construction. I believe that they stopped building her in 1934. She was launched by Her Majesty The Queen in 1938 and I remember she escaped down the slipway and Her Majesty, who was quick witted, still managed to break a bottle over her bows.

My father always seemed to make friends everywhere and on the Horseshoe Pass, for instance, where the Carlisle Road meets the A1, he had a farmer and his wife as contacts. They were very kind to us and we used to eat enormous plates of ham and eggs fresh from the farm – one shilling for him and sixpence for me. We were not very fastidious in other eating places as I had a passion for Heinz baked beans and I either had a normal portion for sixpence or ninepence for a whole tin on toast. Delicious! *"Gutsy Baines"*, said my father with a broad grin on his face, but I never found out who that was.

As far as Wales was concerned, North Wales held huge attractions and quite often he would leave me for a day in Llandudno and I would spend the day on the Great Orme watching the peregrine falcons there and as an added bonus visiting the cave. I learnt a great deal, but that year especially I spent time in London and thoroughly enjoyed myself there as well. My mother was suffering from a worsening of her myasthenia gravis and as a result could not continue to follow her career in dress designing. "The Troops" had persuaded her to take a tiny shop in the Goldhawk Road, some 100 yards from the house, and just through the station entrance. She sold leather goods for dogs, baggage straps, ladies and men's belts, and so-forth. It was a pleasant relaxing occupation and she did not have to adhere to a strict timetable so we were able to enjoy outings together; Kew Gardens was a favourite. Having always been interested in the theatre, she had found a niche for herself in the Kew Theatre. She was appointed as a costumes consultant and eventually by the 1940's was heavily involved in casting as well. Richard Attenborough was one of her younger discoveries, and on several occasions during the war, I met him with her after a performance there.

On return to Kettering my father took me straight up to Stone to stay with the Duttons. They were a wonderful family, extremely kind to me and treated me as if I was one of their own children. They owned a large general store, selling everything from papers to toys. Peter and I spent our lives cycling around the area. I was introduced to trout fishing and caught my first trout on a "Bloody Butcher" taken out of the shop stock of trout flies. I was inordinately proud of that fish! The balance of the long holiday was spent travelling with my father who was finding life financially very hard. I remember very clearly when he left me at the Duttons he handed me a 10 shilling note saying ruefully *"Look after it, that is my last"* and I really believe that it was. He was always a generous and kind hearted man.

On my return, I discovered that I had a new cousin, John Bellamy Shrive, born in the August a week before my return. I was not used to tiny babies, so I wasn't terribly impressed but my Aunt seemed pleased so I was quite happy about it all. Auntie Edna had told me that she was expecting a baby and had said that having babies was uncomfortable but didn't elaborate! Clearly, Kettering was not the place to be in at such a time, so my father took me over to stay with the Garton family at Cranford.

There was one memorable moment when I was there that year; it occurred just as we came towards the end of the harvest. In those days the field was opened up by cutting a swathe round the edge with scythes so as to make enough room for the horse or tractor drawn binder to get in. Then, starting at the outside, the binder proceeded round the field in circles until at the end, there were perhaps two or three swathes left to cut in the middle of the field. Of course, during the cutting, a lot of game emerged but at the end, there were sometimes dozens of rabbits, pheasants, hares, and even foxes which had to run for it. We surrounded the field, farm workers, wives, and children, some armed with guns and some with sticks. My father was there this day with his 12 bore gun. Joy Garton who was on school holidays was driving the Garton's only tractor, a Fordson, and as the last swathe was cut, so game poured out in all directions. It was always a dangerous moment, but this field was by some woods and expectations were high, so excitement by this time was at a fever pitch. My father swung his gun, following a running hare and - "Bang" - shot Joy right in the bottom! Luckily she was wearing whip cord breeches and was far enough away for it to have done little more than sting but I noticed that he seemed unduly solicitous and keen to help!

I found harvest terribly exciting. I was there in the late autumn or winter when they were actually threshing the corn. Early in the morning I was woken by the "Dub-dub-dub" of the great traction engine pulling the threshing machine as it passed through the yard to the barns. These were packed tight with sheaves of corn which had been stooked in the fields after the harvest, then loaded on to the wagons and brought back to the rickyard for stacking. The threshing machine was lined up by the side of first of the stacks to be broached, whilst the traction engine with its great driving wheel was connected up to it by a long, floppy, endless leather belt. There were two men up on the top of the stack, one on the engine who was the general mechanic as well and several other men by the end of the elevator which was to carry the straw away for restacking in an outside rick on the other side of the yard. George and I were told to keep out of the way, but later we were given the filthy task of clearing the husks from under the thresher; a job which ensured that every orifice was filled with itchy particles of straw and dust. It was a hot day, we were all sweating and it all clung to your body. At the signal the engine started to turn and great gusts of steam puffed out of it smelling like my beloved trains as they passed under a bridge. When sufficient speed was reached, the driver threw a lever and the threshing machine burst into action.

It rattled and shook, the driving strap slapped about and it all looked very dangerous. However no one seemed to notice and then things really began to happen. The rick men took a sheaf of corn, cut the binder thread and then one of them spread the sheaf over the shaker box. As the stack opened, so the second man fed the first with sheaves. The machine transferred the sheaf into its bowels and a few moments later, corn started to flow out of the spouts at the back of the machine and chaff from a grille under the machine itself. Higher up at the rear end, straw poured out onto the baler, which then packed it tightly into oblong blocks, bound it and it was either fed onto an elevator or taken up a ladder to the attendant rick makers. Mr Garton kept coming to the corn sacks and taking handfuls of the wheat to see if it measured up to his standards; he never seemed very pleased, but then this was normal! Apart from brief moments for meals this exhausting work went on throughout the hours of daylight and took two or three days to complete. The moment it was over the machines moved on to the next farm without a minutes delay.

As in all farming activities there was fun to be had. One of the regular farm labourers was slightly mentally backward. He was a giant of a man and usually very good humoured. Late one day they started gradually lengthening the straw bales as they came off the baler. Joe was carrying these up the ladder almost to the top of a completed rick. He noticed nothing but sweated and complained a bit more as the bales grew heavier. Then he saw what was happening, grabbed a nearby hay-knife and shouting at the top of his voice chased the two culprits. I have never seen two men run so fast in my life! I think that they were right; if he had caught them he would have done them a grave injury. Luckily he soon calmed and the machine was adjusted back again.

It was Mr Garton's practice to empty the barn but to leave a few sheaves in the open space in the middle, well salted with tailings of wheat. This was left for a couple of days and became the residence of dozens of yard rats. Then, usually on the Saturday morning after harvest everyone arrived with dogs and sticks. The doors were shut tight, an expectant circle was formed and the youngest boy, on one occasion me, was given a pitch fork and made to go and lift the corn and throw it about. As I did so, rats appeared in their hundreds, or so it seemed. It was incredibly exciting as dogs and people chased them all over the barn. Dozens were killed but dozens escaped too. At the end, the victims were laid out for inspection. I was astonished to see how big some of them were.

My return to school in September was marred by the fact that I was to be kept in the IVth Form, as I had not done well in the preceding year. I was nearly 15 and found it hard to cope with all this. During the summer holidays the old Matron had left and had been replaced by a new lady called Miss Yvonne Coxon. She was tall, willowy, gracious, slightly vague, whimsical even, and I loved her dearly from the first moment we met. She must have been in her late forties or fifties. Her greying hair was done up in a bun which never quite stayed together and one of her endearing actions was her continual preoccupation with the whisks of hair which fell about her neck. To our surprise despite her gentleness she was a good manager and the school staff really worked hard for her. She quickly developed a special affection for me and from then on I had found my first surrogate "mother" to whom I was able to tell all. She counselled me and looking back, quietly taught me how to behave as a gentleman should.

She never talked down to the boys, but listened and then responded in a mature and constructive way.

Yvonne, I learned, was the daughter of a famous water colourist, had been educated as a gentlewoman, and lived much of her life in France. She brought a palpable social distinction to the school which hitherto, a masculine preserve with a matron devoid of social graces, it had definitely lacked. Her femininity meant flowers about the place, the staff laid tables with greater care, the house looked more cared for and so forth. She held tea parties during which we ate small delicacies and drank tea out of good china. Her practice of Catholicism was not only by her graciousness and her devotion to all at the school, but also in mass attendance and prayer without making any fuss about it. I owe a great debt of gratitude to her. A skilled painter, Yvonne taught me a lot about drawing and painting and I was quite competent by the time I left school at the end of 1941.

I think that in this relationship with Yvonne, which lasted until her death in the 1980's, young as I was, I instinctively tried to emulate my father's example. He was immensely popular with women, never sexually aggressive, always thoughtful and perhaps even excessively well mannered towards them, but genuinely loved their company. He had numerous girl friends, but was always courteous and attentive to older women. I remember many of the older ones and two of the special girl friends. Fergie, who lasted for several years, and was a sister at the hospital, and Joanna, with whom he remained close until after the war. He was happy in their company and always included me in their activities. I never took second place to or felt threatened by his lady friends, and this made them readily acceptable to me. He was always very masculine as well and I think that this appealed to them.

When I went back to school in September 1938, he told me that, unless I was away, future holidays would have to be spent in digs with him, as Uncle Leslie felt that it was too much for Auntie Peggy to have me to live there any more. He then went on to tell me that he felt that another war with Germany was inevitable, that he had been offered a commission in the Royal Army Service Corps, in which he had served in 1914-18, and had decided to accept. I was proud of him but felt concerned about my future.

My father visited school on my birthday, resplendent in his new uniform and decorated with his 1914-18 war medals. I felt very proud of him and the visit did much to lift me and my personal *"kudos"*. We both spent Christmas at Clacton which was fun although I would have preferred to be with a family. However he was talking about the probability of war and that if it was declared he had no doubt that he would be in France immediately. There was a certain finality about it and I wanted to share this all with him. I did go up to London and again there was talk of war. I remember an air raid shelter kit being delivered to Wells Road for erection in the garden, should war be declared.

Returning to school in January 1939, I wrote a long letter to my mother dated the 22 February. I talked of photography and the camera that I was saving up to buy. I had joined the camera club under the guidance of Fr Dominic. The letter included a relic of my disobedience *"Before I wrote this I went out into the bushes and had a cigarette. It is pouring with rain. I wish Pop would let me smoke because I only have to do it on the quiet which I do not like doing."* I used to spend twopence a week on five Red Label Woodbines. (Green Label had gone up to 2.5d!). I went on to say that I was top in history, this *"after losing five weeks for the operation in the summer term in 1938"*. Five pages of school, rugger and so-forth then *"I hope the business is beginning to improve again. What is your usual taking for the week? £14 ?"* I then picked some primroses and violets and sent them off to my mother in a small package. She responded by sending me 10 shillings, a fortune when you are on 1 shilling per week pocket money! I wrote back on 3 March
"Dear Mummy and Granny
On the safe arrival of that 10/- note I went up to Fr Dominics room and found that I had 52/6d so I was advised to buy a better camera which would last all the longer, so I have done thanks to you".
 Note: I bought a tropical wooden cased Zeiss plate camera with a Compur Shutter - 250th second and an F 3.8 lens. I used this up until 1942 with great success.
"I am so glad that you liked the flowers. I hope that they arrived in respectable condition, because the packing I admit was not very expert. ------- I appreciate your little lecture on smoking very much, and I hasten to assure you that I am usually very moderate. well it is nearly bedtime.   Goodbye Lots of Love to you both   Lionel"

My father was near Dorking at this time and with the Divisional Headquarters of the 1st Armoured Division, where he was Camp Commandant. He was unable to meet me at Easter so sent me down to the Apsley Hotel in Torquay for the Easter break. I was lonely but very happy there and met all sorts of interesting people. I had ceased to be shy in approaching people and always seemed to find someone who would talk and occupy the day. The son of the owners was in the Territorial Army and played Rugger for Devon 2nd Fifteen. Although older than me he was very kind and took me out quite often to watch cricket or to go swimming. Somehow one day, I managed to infiltrate onto the private beach of the Imperial Hotel and I met a charming family who were staying there. They had two girls of my age and they adopted me for much of the holiday. This was typical of my good fortune that I always seemed to find people who were happy to let me tag along with them.

In 1939, I played in the First Fifteen for Rugger, in the first Eleven for Hockey and the Second Eleven for cricket. I ran the 100 and 220 yards in the Inter Schools and did well, also winning the throwing the cricket ball competition with a throw of over 80 yards. I had been appointed Patrol Leader designate in the Owl Patrol of the Scouts and generally my position in the school hierarchy was becoming more established. However my school work remained moderate and I found it hard to make much effort. I saw my father occasionally but missed his presence in the holidays. I spent part of the Easter holidays in London again but also went to the Duttons for a week. The summer was spent partly at Kirby Hall, three weeks at Gartons farm in Cranford, and two weeks at the Apsley hotel in Torquay. The balance was with the Leach family in Chorley. The two sons, Eric and Arthur, were contemporaries of mine at Laxton and made me very welcome. I had my bicycle with me and we spent most of our time cycling around the lovely countryside near to them. They had two sisters, Eileen was my age but Margaret was much younger. We all got on very well together.

I cycled back from Chorley via the Duttons but, on the way, spent one night with another family between Warrington and Wigan arriving there late in the evening. I was awoken next morning by an incredible noise in the street outside. It was unlike anything that I had ever heard before and leaping out of bed I threw open the curtains and saw thousands of men and women on their way to the mills all wearing wooden clogs. The noise that they made on the cobbled road was quite unforgettable; a symphony of clattering if one could have such a thing. It went on for about half an hour until 7 o'clock. My friend told me that this was normal and that there were old men and women called "Knockers" who went round with a long pole knocking on windows until the person came to the window and told them to shut up. They were paid a penny a day for this wake-up service.

I arrived at the Apsley Hotel in late August 1939. War by this time seemed inevitable and was the talk of the hotel. I don't think that I was especially worried by it and it certainly did not spoil my holiday. Eventually on 3 September, we all assembled in the hotel lounge and at 11 o'clock, we heard Mr Chamberlain tell us that we were at war with Germany. I was elated in a funny way as I thought that if I was lucky enough and it wasn't all over, I would be able to join the forces like my father. It would be a chance to shine and to make a mark on life. It was planned that I should spend some time in London at the end of the holidays, but my father decided that this was an unnecessary risk, there had already been an air raid alarm there, and sent me back to school a few days early.

I think that I sensed that my parent's marriage was at a crossroads during this time. There was no specific reason except that my father seemed keen to keep me away from my mother and out of London. It may have been the threat of war but I became more and more concerned about my feelings towards them, to the extent that I discussed the matter with Yvonne and then with Fr Henry. He evidently contacted my father because shortly afterwards, he visited me and took me out alone. (Note: Normally we took out several friends when he came to the school) Anyway this time, we went to "The George" in Stamford for what turned out to be a man to man talk; I was nearly sixteen at the time. We both found the whole thing rather embarrassing as we had successfully avoided any form of discussion about it since it had all happened some seven years ago. However, he told me that they had both fallen in love at their first meeting and that they had married as soon as possible despite Granny Bellamy's gloomy predictions. All had gone well until after my sister, Audrey, had died and he had been promoted. After that, he said, my mother had become extravagant and they had got into debt. Then she became seriously ill and his firm had gone bankrupt so, taking me, she went to live with her mother in London, whilst he went back to live with his in Tennyson Road. Neither of them wanted to divorce or to marry again but nor did they want to live together. It was all very bewildering, too much for me to understand. I was relieved when he asked me if I understood, and I said yes, then we started to talk about other things This was the only formal talk that I ever had with him on this subject.

My mother was equally reticent although much later I became well aware that she had never ceased to love him. I had been in London again in the summer holidays and I enjoyed myself with all her friends. They always accepted me, took me with them for tennis, to the cricket matches, where my mother was still the scorer for the Old Blues, and teas and suppers out on the Thames. My mother, like my father, was charming and good company with no signs of any close attachment, yet from now on I watched her through slightly different eyes. My father had shared confidence with me and I was a bit more aware that the separation was not with a view to re-marrying. She had plenty of suitors, and I am sure that Uncle Tony was ready to marry her the moment that she decided to get divorced. Syd Wales clearly adored her. He would turn up at any time of her bidding with his ghastly canary coloured Ford 8, known as "The Fever Van"

131

and take us anywhere. I think that she was flattered by his devotion. She loved them all but in a detached sort of way. It was interesting to find that both Uncle Tony and Syd married within three years of her death.

Just before the end of term my father visited me again, he was on embarkation leave for France and we had two days together. He told me that he had just lost three men in a hand grenade accident and was clearly upset by it. They were priming the grenades ready for range practice. This entailed pushing a fuse into the priming hole. A second grenade had exploded before he could stop the men from doing it. The batch was then examined and they discovered that a small ball bearing had been inserted into the firing hole so that you had to use pressure to insert the fuse. This caused the capsule to break and the grenade went off. *"Fifth Column work"* he said and it was obvious that he was shocked and worried by the event. He left for France in December 1940, leaving instructions that I was not to go to London unless it was absolutely necessary. He increased my allowance to 10 shillings per week, left cash for clothing etc with Fr Dominic, made him co-signatory on his bank account and told me that Fr Dominic was now in charge of my affairs and would direct where I went for holidays until he returned. I spent the Christmas holidays at the Apsley Hotel, returning to school early.

My mother, isolated in London and not knowing Fr Dominic personally, was not at all pleased by my father's, in her view, high handed actions and I received a fairly sharp letter from her on my return to school. I replied to her on 5 February 1940 saying:
"Dear Mummy
Thank you very much for your letter. The whole tone of it was not a little embittered against Daddy and myself. Please don't take it that way. Anyway just forget it. I heard all about the fire raid and am so glad that you escaped. They shot a Jerry down near Kettering on Tuesday night. we heard the machine guns going.
I am joining the army next November if all goes well and hope to get a commission by the end of the year. I hate the idea of the R.A.F. unless I am on the ground staff. I hope to get my matric this July. get the marks in September." Note: This was clearly not possible as I was too young
I went on to talk about the snow and ice and skating then:
"My patrol, the Owl Patrol, is the Troops crack patrol now and I was congratulated by the Scout master. I had to organise the afternoons entertainment for the whole Troop this afternoon. Well; goodbye Love to Granny and yourself. Lionel"

Not a word about my father who was in France or really much comment on the war except that I was impatient to be in it.

Obviously there were major changes in life due to the onset of the war in 1939. However, as an individual who was not yet ready for enlistment and who, in any event, was well occupied, the changes were not so obvious. Other people fed me, rationing did not affect me particularly and, all in all, I was very fortunate. There were a number of physical factors noticeable. Firstly, reduction in the amount of transport, most of which were khaki coloured and belonged to the Army. All around Corby area, which was not far from School, were big oil drums which were often lit, presumably to create smoke screens for the furnaces there. Over the years I had become used to the beauty of the furnaces at Cransley, Wellingborough and Kettering, where, when the furnaces emitted the liquid iron ore at night, a brilliant red glow appeared in the sky. It was very beautiful and in a way always something that I loved to see and somehow brought home to me our need to protect ourselves from potential bombing by enemy aircraft.

I was now trying hard to become an adult. This was partially because of my father's absence and thus a feeling of controlling my own destiny, partially the stabilising effect of Yvonne Coxon, and also, of course my age and the war. I was strong in my faith and from this time on always rose at 6 am and served the 6.30 am mass. Then I went out for a run, showered, (cold shower!) and then took my normal part in the school day. I was a Vth Former but not yet a Prefect. I had gained my colours for rugger in November 1939, which was good for me and for hockey in the Spring of 1940. I was very keen on my Scout Patrol and hoped to use this as a means of getting into the L.D.V.(Local Defence Volunteers), which had been formed but was about to become the Home Guard. We camped in the School grounds in 1940 and then had an excellent summer camp, together with members of the Charlton family in 1941. A brilliant sunny two weeks which we all enjoyed to the full and which taught me a great deal about the problems of camping.

June 1940 was the month when the German Army was dashing across The Low Countries and France and we were about to evacuate everyone at Dunkirk. I had heard from my father on several occasions, all his letters were cheerful and included things such as *"We are ready to tackle them when the time is right"*. There had really been no fighting as yet and although complacency would perhaps be untrue, there must have been a sense of unreality about it all. I had received one letter which included a photograph of him with three prisoners, German airmen shot down near the headquarters. He was dressed in his pyjamas with a dressing gown! Apparently, the Germans escaped from their crashed aeroplane and ran off. My father was informed, got up and went over to the bath house to shave, luckily carrying his revolver, and was somewhat surprised when he discovered the Germans hiding there. He took them prisoner and was very pleased with himself. The Germans were equally happy and told him that they were not worried as Hitler would release them within the month, which he did.

I wrote to my mother on 1 June and the letter begins by telling her at what time she could best telephone me at school, so she was evidently worried by what was happening. It then deals with matters concerning some drawings which I had posted to her then, and only then, on page two -
"I am sorry that daddy is having a hard time of it. If the war lasts another year I am going into the navy. I could get a midshipmans position on the strength of my schooling and my way of talking." My father always adjured me to go into the navy.

We then got onto the vexed subject of the summer holidays -
"re the holidays before daddy went we arranged with Fr Dominic that I should spend 2 weeks at scout camp at Stoneyhurst on the Pennines. 4 weeks with Peter Dutton on a cycling tour of Devon and Cornwall which is already worked out, kit bought etc. 2 weeks in London unless there are air raids and 1 week at school. If the air raids start I shall have 8 weeks at school. That is what daddy wanted me to do. Please do not alter it because I am quite responsible and am a scout which means that I shall receive help from all the farmers and people.
Well goodbye will write again soon Love   Lionel
P.S. I think cigarettes are a dreadful price you are lucky to have been given so many"

My father returned home in late June having been cut off from his unit and having driven, with a small element of his Headquarters team, right across France to Brest. He spoke only "soldiers french", remembered some of the roads from his visit back in the early 1930's and had commandeered fuel to keep them going. He made light of it all, but said that the roads were thick with refugees to start with but later were quite empty although they were subjected to occasional air attacks. On arrival at Brest he found the British Troops busy smashing thousands of bottles of alcohol, burning cigarettes and destroying all the stores before being evacuated. He was allotted a section which included hundreds of vehicles for destruction and, that completed, was called forward onto one of the last transports, packed with soldiers, and returned to Plymouth. He then went by train to Salisbury Plain and rejoined the remainder of the Division. *"No arms, no transport"* he said.

Significantly, on arrival home, he telephoned Auntie Edna, not my mother or me, to announce the good news. His first instincts always turned him towards his family in Kettering. My first personal news was a week later when a fellow officer telephoned the school to say that he was in hospital and undergoing an operation. Fr Ralph took the message and immediately we thought that he had been wounded. and as a consequence, the whole school was put on a prayer alert. Imagine our faces, especially mine, when Fr Ralph again took a call which reported that he was doing well and that it was an operation for in-growing toenails. It took some time to live that down! I had written a poem about the war in France which was published:

Weary, slouching desperate men, thin columns on the dusty roads,
Stumble, fall, and rise again, crouching under bulky loads
Of precious rifles, burnished blue, shapeless packs, all grit and dust,
Tin pannikins once shining new, now coated thick with filth and rust.
Field boots muddy, clotted grey with Belgian soil so thickly spread
with flowers of hate not flowers of May and the bodies of the dead.

Heady stuff for a sixteen year old!

The Division in which my father served was desperately attempting to re-equip and there was to be no leave, so I stayed at school for the first part of the holiday. I cycled a lot, spent time with Yvonne, eating with her in her room, and from time to time went off with Fr Henry to visit people or places. I had been with him once or twice to visit the Charlton family at Woodford near Cranford and serve mass for him. He went there on most Sundays. Subsequent to this, I was invited to go over to see them when staying at the Gartons and had done so becoming most especially friendly with the youngest daughter, Frances (Franny). We really enjoyed each others company and I sought any opportunity to go and visit them. They were a wonderful family and although I did not come up to their fathers, George Charlton, standards as a shot, I was accepted by him as a countryman. He was the Land Agent for Woodford House and The Estate. The eldest daughter, Eleanor, worked as her fathers assistant, the second, Ann was in the FANYS, Joan, very glamorous, the WAAF and Dorothy, again a very close friend, was waiting to go into the FANYS or the ATS. Franny was too young for such prospects. Their mother, Mrs Charlton, whose sister was Lady Vaux of Harrowden, was a charming gracious lady and again I was fortunate in that she became very fond of me. I never stayed with them for the night, but was there from early morning until after supper. We did nothing very special. I helped Mr Charlton with setting up hides for pigeon shooting and I went out with him in the evening rough shooting. Franny, Dorothy and I walked in the woods or sometimes swam in the Estate lake. We talked a lot, helped Mrs Charlton and generally were well occupied.

After two weeks I went down to the Apsley Hotel again and to my surprise found that it was full of Prudential girls who had been evacuated from London in anticipation of the bombing and were now at work in Torquay. They were a splendid gang, there was a distinct shortage of men and they needed partners for the local dances. I was cajoled into going with them although I had never learned any ballroom dancing before. Two of them especially, Freda and Diana, I remember with particular affection. They treated me as if I was their favourite brother. After the Christmas holidays when we repeated the experience I wrote to my mother and said *"I can now do every dance except the rumba, not very well of course but well enough to pass on the floor"* I then returned directly to school as the Blitz had started and my mother warned me to keep clear.

Train journeys were always difficult during the war, the carriages were crammed with service personnel and there was never any room. I travelled via London to Stamford and if this was typical of my general experience I would have stood in the corridor all the way. I remember doing this once, when down the corridor came the news that the ticket inspector was in the next carriage. Immediately, one of the A.T.S. girls slipped into the lavatory and seemingly dozens of soldiers followed her. I was aghast! When the inspector arrived, he rattled the door and it opened a fraction and out popped a girl's hand bearing her Rail Warrant. He clipped it and moved on! Once he had passed they all came out again like rabbits! When nearing London, especially at night, the trains tended to stop and start as raids permitted. I had to change stations, taking the tube. That was an experience, as the platforms were used as air raid shelters and people were already beginning to select their places, children being put to bed and so forth. I believe that tubes stopped at midnight and the current was turned off. On arrival at Peterborough I stayed the night with a school friend, the son of jeweller there, and next day caught the bus for Stamford and then on to the school.

A few days later, as planned, I went up to Stoneyhurst for the scout camp. I cycled up to Stone with a huge suitcase strapped precariously onto my luggage rack, spending the night there before cycling on with Peter up to the Hodder, the river which ran through the grounds of the Stoneyhurst Prep school. We set up camp on the banks of the river with the remainder of the Troop. It was a wonderful summer, brilliant sunshine, clear skies and perfect for those who could enjoy it, terrible however for those involved in air war which was about to begin in earnest. I thoroughly enjoyed my week there. The activities were fun, I liked camp cooking and the outdoor life was ideal for my temperament. My nature diary came on in leaps and bounds with new experiences:

September the 4th - I could hear the young otters squealing but couldn't locate them
September the 6th - Whilst I was walking along the edge of the River Hodder I saw a huge
eel and tried to pierce it with my scout pole but it pivotted round on its tail and shot off down
the river.

I was drawing a lot at this time and my nature diary contains many pictures of animals and fish. I was also writing a lot of poetry. The highlight of the scout camp for me occurred towards the end of it when a scout chopping wood, missed with the axe and cut the artery in his leg. I was alone in the camp and, having just gained my first aid badge, I found the pressure point, stemmed the bleeding and managed to bind up his wound, before applying a tourniquet made out of an old rabbit snare. This then enabled me to leave him, run up to the Prep School and fetch the Matron. I received a Scout Commendation for that.

When the scout camp finished, I cycled back through Chorley with raging toothache. Arthur Leach took me along to their local dentist where I was told that I had to have the tooth extracted. The girl then asked *"Did I want the half a crown or the five bob"*. Naturally I said the half a crown. A few minutes later I had an injection and then, almost immediately, the tooth was pulled out. It was painful and my feet practically hit the roof! As I handed over my half crown, Arthur asked what the difference was between the two prices as far as the treatment was concerned. The girl said that they waited for about a quarter of an hour for the five bob to let the anaesthetic work and, afterwards gave you a cup of tea in the waiting room so as to take the pain away! As it was, I cycled down to Stone with no feeling in my face at all. I must have gone directly from Stone to Cranford, as I see from my diary that I was back in Woodford with the Charltons by 9 September where I reported seeing a green woodpecker.

My father came up to see me during the Christmas Term and told me about the camp that they were in on the Plain. He recounted the story of his friend, the artist, Simon Elwes, also on 1st Armoured Divisional staff, who had asked him one Sunday if he would like to accompany him out to tea with an old lady. My father agreed willingly, and after lunch an old Rolls Royce turned up, chauffeur driven, and took them to The Duke of Beauforts house. They were then ushered into the presence of the Queen Mother who served them tea. He was taken aback to start with but thoroughly enjoyed the afternoon and had been invited to go back with Simon Elwes later in the month.

I was now a prefect and a member of the rugger First Fifteen and to cap it all had been accepted as a member of the Wakerley and Barrowden Company of the local Home Guard. I took my duties as a prefect seriously and tried very hard to help to run a good disciplined school; I think with some success. It did mean that my work suffered in a critical year when I was to take my School Certificate. I practised with the rugger team three times a week and, nearly always, we had a match at home or away on a Saturday. I was shown a book kept by Eric Leach, front row forward, in which he recorded the results of all the rugger matches and commented on individual performances. His comment on me for 1940 was *"Bellamy gained his colours after the Stamford match. Played very well this season, very good tackler and quite fast. He deserved his colours. Is developing a good swerve."* Praise indeed! I see that we played seven matches, won four and lost three. It was difficult to arrange matches because of petrol rationing and all the attendant problems created by the war.

I attended High Mass on Sunday at 9 am and then cycled off to Harringworth for Home Guard Training. Very occasionally we went out on exercise. I led a very active life, was very healthy but my timetable lacked the academic aspect for which schooling is intended.

Meanwhile the bombing in London was terrible and Wells Road had been covered with incendiary bombs some of which had landed on the roof of No 5. They were all convinced that they were "after the bus station" but in truth, I believe the bombing was random. Uncle Tony and Fred, an old gentleman whom Granny had taken in to give shelter after he was bombed out and who stayed with her until his death many years later, managed to push the incendiaries out of the gutters into the garden and cover them with sand. A sort of flat ended hoe was issued to each house.

Early in November a land mine on a parachute was found hanging from the lime tree in the front garden. This was discovered during the blitz itself and everyone was evacuated immediately to a nearby shelter whilst it was defused. This was too much for Granny and she decided to leave Wells Road, finding a very nice house about a mile west of Shepherds Bush in Chiswick. The new address was 45 Fairfax Road. The house had a studio attached to it which was let to an artist and his lady. He was Tony del Renzio, who designed and painted scenery for opera and ballet and she, Eithel Colqhoun, a Modernist. I wrote to my mother at the new address on 11 November 1940.

Meanwhile at school I was busy producing and taking the lead in a production of "High Gang" at the time. It was my last female role and I was "Bebe Daniels". I tell her about the rugger and the revue then: -

"Last night, at least this morning, they bombed a place three miles from the school. It was 1 o'clock in the morning and I was lying awake listening to the sound of bombs and guns at Leicester when suddenly I heard a whine right over our heads, then another, then another etc. Suddenly they burst one after another, it was rather amusing. They made the Welland into a river about as wide as the English Channel. they machine gun around here a lot but that is all. We saw Coventry getting mucked up on Monday night and Leicester on Tuesday night. Last night it was Leicester again. Poor devils in Coventry. It was flattened in places. How is London? Any bad bombing?"

I quote this letter not for its historical accuracy as I feel that I was trying, in a way, not to show that I was "in the war" but to show how ignorant people could be about what was going on in the country generally and perhaps how insular we were. The London bombing was at its peak at this time. A German bomber did crash under the Harringworth viaduct whilst it was being chased by fighter planes from nearby Wittering. We also saw the Beaufighters equipped with a search light in their nose, which were being tried out as night fighters. In the main however we just heard the German bombers droning over on their way to the Midland cities. They made a very specific noise, and as nowadays, people who lived through the war can identify a Spitfire or a Hurricane by the engine noise, so could we with the German bombers.

At the end of the Christmas term my great friend and supporter on the rugger field, Jacques Remlinger, joined the R.A.F. and was sent to train as a pilot at Luffenham, 8 miles away. That Easter, he began flying solo in a bi-plane, a Hawker Hart I believe. One day he telephoned to say he would fly over the school after lunch to salute his brother, Pierre. Duly, he appeared, did several turns and then swooped low over us as we stood by the rugger pitch waving goodbye. Unfortunately, he misjudged, took the top of a pair of rugger posts and did a terrible belly landing, finishing up ignominiously in the rough grass. To our relief he was unhurt, and as we rushed over to the plane, he scrambled out of the cockpit as if he had done this all on purpose. He was collected, the plane quickly dismantled and taken away on a lorry. I believe that he was admonished. He passed out as a fighter pilot with flying colours and fought as such for the remainder of the war.

Rugby Team Winter 1940/41

Ronald Bellamy recalled
to the colours 1940

CHAPTER 9
School to Army 1940-44

The last two letters which I wrote in 1940 and posted on 2 December were written to my mother and my grandmother. I thanked them for their birthday presents, gave a detailed run down on the rugger and then, to my grandmother went on to say:

"I am wondering whether to join the army. Daddy can get me into the cadets from which I can get a commission in less than a year. I might get an examination to Sandhurst. How would you like your grandson to be a Lieutenant? I would like it very much."

Then to my mother I wrote:

"I am an inch smaller than Daddy in height when my hair is flattened but as it never is, I am his size. I weigh 11 stone, am 32" round the waist. have a 3.5" chest expansion and have legs like a horse. My nails are very long because I don't bite them."

By all this, I seemed to be pretty unsettled in my ambitions and hopes. I think that all boys at my age and at that time, grasped each fresh idea about "joining up", as the new gospel and that became our current driving ambition until something else was offered. The motivation was to get into the war by any means as quickly as possible.

Apparently the Bebe Daniels Revue at school was a success and I comment modestly:

"I was a wonderful Bebe Daniels looking rather like a cross between a 100 ton tank and H.M.S.Nelson. I was laughed at anyway".

I wrote again from the Apsley Hotel after Christmas having obviously enjoyed myself

"I had a good Christmas and made real whoopee. There are about 25 girls here. I have great fun with 14 of them. You would like Pat she's cute.Then there are the Brookes twins they are awfully good sports. Their names are Vivian and Olive. Pat is one of two very unlike twins Pat and Joan Just. Beryl is a good sport also Katie, Freda and all the rest. I am running short of cash it is expensive living. I hope my allowance comes soon. Love Lionel"

The girls were very kind to me, treated me like a younger brother, paid their way, even on occasion treating me. Freda, who was somewhat older, spent hours with me walking and talking. Unfortunately one of the girls contracted measles and we were all put into quarantine. I returned to school late, travelled all night and eventually got back at 12.35am on 21 January 1941.

This was the last letter in Grannys file and, from this time onwards, apart from the diary in my nature book, which shows that I was very active in watching and recording the activities of a wide variety of animals, plus a handful of some poems and drawings, I have no contemporary documents written by me on which I can draw. However the events of 1941 are quite fresh in my mind.

I found it difficult to concentrate on working to pass my School Certificate. Distractions were everywhere with all the extra-mural activities, the Home Guard, and of course sport. Anyway, the upshot was that Fr Henry interviewed me and told me that he would virtually guarantee me a place at Peterhouse, his old College, if I worked. I had great ability (his words) in both History and English, and should have no problem, but I had to get over this examination hurdle first. I even visited Cambridge and the College and was interviewed by one of his friends, a professor of History and I was deeply impressed. Personally, I thought that I was working hard, but subsequent events proved me to be wrong.

I saw little of my father who was at Dorking with the Divisional Headquarters. I now know that he had met Irene Mitchell, a Red Cross nurse, at the Dorking Hospital. She was the youngest of three unmarried daughters of Mrs Mitchell, the rich widow of a Scottish entrepreneur who had made his fortune in the Argentine. The Mitchells lived in a large house just outside the town. Both the mother and the daughters were very much taken with this courteous man and he was a welcome guest. Irene made no secret of the fact that she was in love, but my father played the "already married" card, with great tact, much to Mrs Mitchell's admiration. He told me later that Irene *"presented little temptation"*. He still had a very close relationship with Joanna, who I thought was very attractive when I finally met her in 1943. At this time she had just joined the W.A.A.F.

There was a different morality abroad at this period of the war. Things were bad, the future was very uncertain, life itself was constantly under threat and pre-war conventions were becoming relaxed. The prevalent thinking was that there may not be a tomorrow so take what you can today. I was totally innocent and ignorant as far as women were concerned. My sole talk on sex had been given by Fr Aelwin when I was sixteen. He showed us a diagram purporting to show how things worked, but he wasn't at all convincing. I remember rather cheekily asking him how he knew and he said that his sister had told him! I gathered that babies came from a point somewhere in the area of a womans throat and between her breasts. I had nothing of the actual sexual act explained to me, although I knew that in some way it was "down below" and was highly enjoyable. Some of my friends told lurid tales of fumbles in cinemas and so-on, but nobody that I knew had actually "done it" whatever "it" was. We didn't even find it engrossing as a subject of conversation, preferring sport. I did however love girls' company but not with any directed sort of passion, yet I was aware from the snatches of conversation overheard at the Apsley Hotel that many of the girls there were fairly uninhibited when they went out with the service personnel in Torquay. I thought that this was more to do with kissing and cuddling than anything else and, to be fair, with the majority of them, it probably was. Having said that, I don't think that our attitude to sex in any way compared to the apparent freedom practised since the 1960's. The girls that I met were as innocent as I was, but better informed on the mechanics. They obviously understood their personal risks, valued their virginity and didn't do much to encourage chaps to find out more. As in all things there were exceptions, but I certainly didn't meet one until I was much older.

I went on holiday at Easter, firstly to London and then stayed for a few days with Auntie Peggy and Uncle Leslie at Havencourt. London was a shambles, the bombing went on every night and the whole City appeared to be ruined. By this time my mother had been given her war job. She had been appointed as an assistant to the man responsible for the distribution of meat to the ships on the Thames! She was to work out of an office adjacent to Smithfield Market. A fitting role for a dress designer! To be fair, I think that this was organised by the Wales family whose father was a power at Smithfield. The job, which was hard work, entailed her visiting the ships and she was very well received. She told me once that they nearly always asked her up onto the bridge. This meant that she had to climb up a companion ladder with open treads. She had good legs and she said she always saw to it that her underclothes were neat and pretty!

This visit to London was exceptional as I saw some of the devastation which had been caused already. It was early April, just prior to the great fire bomb attacks of mid-April but it was still an extraordinary experience. We travelled up in the Metropolitan Underground, got out at Faringdon Street Station and then emerged onto the shattered streets. My mother obviously knew what to expect, but to me the broken fronts of buildings, the glass, and the rubble presented my first in-depth view of reality and war. It was far from romantic, and as we walked into the back streets behind Charterhouse, it seemed to become worse. I wasn't frightened, but I was shocked that this could have happened. I remember that in one street they were still moving rubble and searching for survivors. There was a little knot of spectators, like at any building site. Nobody seemed particularily disturbed and people were not rushing about. In fact my lasting impression was one of calm and normality under shambolic conditions. We visited her new office, I was shown off to her chief and then we went down to the local for a sandwich with somebody from the Wales firm. Her local was "The Cock" in the market itself and as we arrived at the bar someone said *"Here comes our mascot, our Ollie"* and lifted her straight up onto the bar where she sat laughing and talking to all and sundry, clearly they all loved her. Afterwards we walked over to Barts Hospital which I don't think at that time had been bombed and of course walked through Smithfield itself. The market was clean, swept and almost empty as in peacetime. Little did I imagine that one day she would be killed there.

We travelled back to Goldhawk Road Station and went to visit some friends, Mr and Mrs Bird, who lived nearby but in the direction of Chiswick. Unfortunately the air raid sirens sounded earlier than usual and we were caught out away from home. It was about 7.30 pm, just as we were preparing to leave them and return to Fairfax Road, which was about twenty minutes hard walk away. The Birds persuaded us to stay with them, at least until the pattern of bombing became more clear. By about 9 pm, the bombs all seemed to be miles away and up in the East End, so we slipped out of their house and headed for home. It was a clear evening and nothing untoward happened, except the *"Get on home, girl"* of an occasional Air Raid Warden. As we passed the pub at the junction of the Goldhawk and Stamford Brook Roads, almost home in fact, there was a devastating "Whoosh" and a bomb, followed by several others, landed much closer and in the general direction of Shepherds Bush. We ran on and I became aware of a fluttering noise all around us although nothing touched us. It was shrapnel falling from the sky as the Ack-Ack guns maintained their barrage over our heads. Actually it was rather an attractive noise and I didn't realise how much damage it could do to you. Once home, we sat up talking until the noises ceased and then went up to bed.

My mother thought it best if I returned to Kettering next day as she felt that it was stupid to take unnecessary risks. It was established that when in Kettering I stayed at Havencourt where they were both very welcoming to me. I visited the Charltons at Woodford, riding there on my bicycle. My cousin Stuart was very excited as a bomber had been shot down near Grafton Underwood and so we went out and spent the morning looking for gruesome remains. We found bits of the plane scattered over two or three fields and Stuart reckoned that he had a piece of hair from the skull of one of the pilots. I thought that it was rabbit fur, so wasn't very popular. I spent a lot of time with the Langleys that holiday, especially Mags (Margaret) who was my age. She was another very good companion and I became as fond of her as I was of Franny Charlton.

Back to school and the final term, with my examination looming ahead fast. I had left it too late really and despite my efforts didn't feel very confident about my performance. I had a splendid Home Guard experience that term. Our Battalion was called out one Sunday morning on a real exercise and told to defend the railway line across the Stamford road near to Duddington. I was acting as Lance Corporal with a fairly dull section under command. I was told to defend the railway bridge which runs over the main road itself, with my section of six men with rifles and hand grenades (not live of course). The remainder of the Platoon, under Lieutenant Singlehurst, were in enfilade positions on my right and left. I had decided to liven things up and had managed to get a pot of old paint out of the school maintenance shop. We then prepared four splendid paint bombs in old cigarette tins, the round sort with tin lids. My idea was to locate my riflemen above the bridge, whilst another chap and I lay on top of the arch and "Bombed" their tanks as they arrived. It seemed to me to be a more positive way of knowing if we had knocked them out during the ensuing battle!

We took up our positions at about mid-morning and laid about in the sunshine for what seemed to be hours. Then an umpire appeared so we knew that action was imminent. We lay concealed and waited. Sure enough, after about twenty minutes, two armoured cars appeared followed by other transport. One of them approached the bridge and I told everyone to lay still and do nothing. This worked well; the first armoured car approached slowly with great caution, covered by his twin. Eventually it drove under the bridge and then returned to signal to the rest of them that the way was clear. The lorries then came along in convoy with the two armoured cars at the front and, I believe, other armoured cars at the rear. At the critical moment we threw our four bombs at the front two cars. Three burst on the road, but one very satisfactorily burst in a profusion of greyish paint all over the front of the first vehicle. The convoy came to an abrupt halt as the front car driver couldn't see! Infantry poured out of the lorries and charged up the embankment, we fired our five rounds of blanks and the umpire called a halt.

There followed a fairly amicable discussion between the chiefs and the umpires before the column moved on. Meanwhile we "fraternised" with the enemy. I was told that the armoured car driver was apoplectic, he was personally very well painted and his car a spotted mess. He wanted blood, and I was very grateful to my section who remained discreet and did not disclose the culprit. Afterwards I was told by my Platoon Officer not to use this sort of initiative again without his prior approval. I think that deep down the "Brass" was delighted and my section bought me a pint at the pub in Wakerley; they were all highly amused. Unfortunately this was my only exercise involving regular troops and normal Sunday parades were always very boring with rifle drill and marching.

The term came to an end and, because things were not going well for the British at this stage of the war, it was decided that the Scout Camp should be held in the grounds of the School. The weather was remarkable, brilliant sunny days and warm nights. Camping conditions were perfect and we had a marvellous time. I had "almost" left school and felt very liberated, the exams were now behind me and I felt that life was about to open up.

Several of us stayed on in the tents after the end of camp and I was delighted to find that Franny was able to come over and visit us. Her sister, Eleanor, had become very friendly with the Heron family, one of the Distributists at Laxton and she brought her over with her. This also delighted Yvonne, who I realise now, was busy matchmaking! We had a wonderful time wandering all around the area. One memorable day we went to Kirby Hall and spent the day with the Hawkes whilst on another occasion Eleanor took us over to Deene and tea with Brudenells. That was an experience. Mrs Brudenell was a remarkable lady, an American. She insisted on "doing her bit", and was working in foul conditions in an ammunition factory in Kettering. Mr Brudenell was a character out of a Georgian history book. I only met him once at that time, although I saw him quite often when I returned to Northamptonshire later in the 1950's. He came in to tea wearing a hat, his tea was served in a cup with a deep saucer and then in true Georgian fashion, he poured his tea into the saucer and drank it. I was mesmerised! Edmund, the son, was younger than us and rather boring as he was only interested in playing the piano. Young people can be very unfair in their judgements!

Franny and I were enjoying a very innocent calf love at this time and I was very reluctant to leave for Torquay. However Fr Dominic insisted and I went down to the Apsley Hotel during late August. My examination results were due towards the end of the month and one day I received a telegram from Fr Henry. The wording is engrained on my mind *"Examination abysmal failure. Return to School at once. Father St John"* I was mortified, ashamed, frightened and anxious as to what would now happen. All my plans depended on getting a positive result and this failure promised to scupper my aims vis á vis getting into the services.

I caught the first train to London and after the usual 24 hour struggle arrived back at the school on foot. First I visited Yvonne, but she was not at all helpful, just saying *"You must see Fr Henry at once."* Next I went to Fr Dominic and Fr Gerard's rooms, but they were away so there was no alternative but to pluck up courage and knock on Fr Henry door. I knocked. *"Wait"* said his unmistakeable voice. I waited. It seemed to me to be about an hour later but was probably only five minutes *"Come in"*. I went in. *"Ah, Bellamy"* he said but he didn't invite me to sit down which was unusual, so I stood in front of his desk. It was hot in his room, I remember, and the sun was streaming in on me, whilst he was sitting at his desk in the shade, wearing an immaculate white habit. *"You have failed in every subject except English. I have entered you for the retake in December. None of the Fathers is prepared to give you any teaching time. It is up to you. Good afternoon"* I was stunned at his tone and at his summary dismissal. *"Thankyou, Father"* I said and turned away in silent tears and went out of the door. As I closed it, he said *"You can collect what books you require but you will not stay talking to any of the staff, we are all too busy. Go straight back now and finish your holiday."* This last sentence was said perhaps a little more gently but it was no comfort. I collected my books, didn't dare to visit Yvonne and slunk back down the school drive to the Stamford main road and hitched a lift to Peterborough. It was probably the lowest point of my life.

Back in Torquay, I tried to work but was quite miserable. Freda was my support and I was treated to elder sister advice. I worked at my books for much of the day, and she took me out each evening. One day my father appeared unexpectedly, he was on embarcation leave for the Middle East. He stayed for a couple of days before driving back to Kettering. We had a few beers together and he said that he knew I would pass next time if I really worked. He was good fun with the girls and we had dinner out with some of them on his last night. They were bombing Plymouth at the time and we could see the reflection of the fires and hear the sound of bombs, from where we were on the hill above Torquay. As we said goodbye, he suggested again that I went into the Navy, told me to keep out of London whilst the bombing was on, not to overspend my allowance as there was no more to be had and to consult Fr Dominic on all matters. I didn't hear of him again until I received the news in January 1942 that he was "Missing".

I returned early to school, and found that I had been appointed as Head Prefect, and Captain of the First Fifteen. Normally I would have been thrilled, but immediately, it became abundantly clear that none of the fathers were going to help me with my examination work. In fact they almost ostracised me and I realised that I really was on my own. After a rather unsteady start, I found my full pace and really got down to things. I was determined to "show them" I suppose.

However, sometime during October, Fr Gerald Vann, one of my tutors, asked to see some essays that I had done as well as some of my practice papers. A little later on, other masters did the same, and by early November, I was, effectively, being crammed and receiving a great deal of quality personal tuition. I was not over confident, but my work was taking shape at last which was satisfying.

On returning to school I had written to the Recruiting Office in Northampton and asked for an interview. This came through in October and I caught the bus for Kettering and then Northampton. I quote from "Troop Leader" page 2

"I reported to the Recruiting Office in Northampton and volunteered for the R.A.F. The newspapers at that time were full of heartwarming stories about heroic pilots and I was impatient to become one of them. In the event it appeared that everyone else had the same desire and there were no vacancies. I was very downcast, but remembering my father's words, I went along to the Royal Navy stand. At this stage of the war one still had, to some degree anyway, the opportunity to choose in which arm of the Service you wished to serve. For some inexplicable reason when I got there, I was not attracted to the Royal Navy and wandered on past the other recruiting stands; one, with pictures of the tanks in the Desert War, caught my eye. I hesitated there and immediately a very smart Sergeant buttonholed me and asked me if I was interested in the Royal Armoured Corps. I told him about my father and asked if I would be allowed to join him in the 1st Armoured Division."Very easy Laddie" said the Sergeant. "As you have a father in the Tanks (which he wasn't) you can go straight to the Armoured Training Regiment and in six months you'll be able to go out to Egypt. On that promise, forgetting the Royal Navy, I signed up."

At the end of November I received a telephone call from my mother to say that my father had written to her and was in South Africa. She sounded very thrilled and I was very happy too. Just before Christmas I too received a card from Durban. At about the same time I received my call up papers and was ordered to report to the 58th Training Regiment (RAC) at Bovington Camp on 1 December 1941. A rail warrant to Wool was included. Fr Henry contacted the recruiting office explaining about the forthcoming examination and as a result I was deferred until 1 January 1942. I duly took the examination, School Certificate Joint Board and by the time the results came in January, I was already in the army and it didn't really matter! However for the record, I obtained Credits in both of the English papers and History with Passes in French, Geography and Mathemetics.

The last few days at school were very enjoyable and I was sad in many ways to be leaving although impatient to get into the Army. Despite all the pressures of work, I had decided to take part in the School Play "Ambrose Applejohn" and I played the lead as Ambrose Applejohn himself, my first male role since joining the theatre group in 1936. During that last term Fr Henry introduced me to a charming couple called Stephen and Joan Rittner; he was the uncle of one of my friends. They heard that I had nowhere to go for Christmas, my mother was anxious to keep me out of London, I hadn't enough money for a hotel and I had no other "offers" on the table. They lived at Mayfield and I spent a very happy few days with them and their family befor catching the train at Paddington Station and starting on the next phase of my life. This is covered in my book "Troop Leader". I shall only refer to aspects of my family life which were not covered in that book because they were not germane to that other story.

During the third week of my training down in Bovington, I received notification from Kettering that my father was missing. Once again I was irritated that this went first to my aunt in Kettering and not to my mother or me. However, later my father explained that, at that time, he was unable to give a permanent address for me. At the end of the month I had my first weekend pass, I went to London and discussed this with my mother. She was a little sad too, as she had not been nominated as his next of kin, but I think that she had been resigned to it. I nurtured a secret hope that somehow they had met before he left England, as she showed me a letter from him which read
Sunday October 5th
All well had lunch here today. Wonderful time. Love Ron"

The card was of the Umfalanga Rocks Hotel outside Durban where I was to stay often in the 1960/70's. It had been posted on 10 October 1941.

The following article had appeared in the local press in Kettering
"Reported missing in the Middle East is Staff Captain R.V.Bellamy R.A.S.C. of Larch Road, Kettering. Captain Bellamy who also served in France before going to the Middle East was in the R.A.S.C. during the last war and early took up his commission again when this war broke out. As a commercial traveller he was well known over a wide area.
A son, Lionel, on finishing his college career at the end of last year, volunteered for and has joined the Royal Tank Corps."

In March we were informed that he a was a Prisoner of War. On 17 April 1942, Vatican Radio reported that he was in Camp 35 in Italy and broadcast the following message:
"No news yet. Very anxious. Don't worry. I am fit and well. much love to all. Ron."

This message was sent to Auntie Edna. Meanwhile my mother, Auntie Edna and many others were writing to him and sending him Red Cross parcels. I wrote to him as well but it was not easy living in a barrack block as I was. I was lucky with my weekend leave passes, which I always spent in London with my mother and grandmother. They were both very proud of me and I often brought soldier friends up to stay, who were made most welcome. Working at Smithfield, although she did not get extra rations of meat, my mother often brought home liver or kidneys, great delicacies in wartime, and much appreciated by us all! The raids were sporadic and not too bad at this time as Hitler was very pre-occupied with the war in Russia.

I passed out of my initial training in the summer and was promoted, becoming a Provisional Unpaid Lance-Corporal. The promotion was valuable because it entitled me to take a week's leave. I was granted a railway warrant to Kettering and then stayed at Havencourt. I then visited all my relations, the school, feeling frightfully important in my uniform. I returned to camp via London. I passed my Board for a commission and Sandhurst followed. I had more freedom there, so I spent evenings in London as well, when money permitted. We were paid 2 shillings a day at that time which didn't go far, but I still had 10 shillings per week allowance which was an amazing help.

On 15 March 1942 I passed out at Sandhurst and was gazetted as a Cornet in the 8th Kings Royal Irish Hussars. My mother was invited to the Passing Out Parade. She arrived in a stunning hat and dress which defied the economies and drabness of the war. Despite the cold March day, her ever present illness (she was injecting herself four hourly at this time), and her worry that her only child was now likely to join in the fighting, she brought joy to the event. After the Parade we all celebrated with tea and cakes in the Old Building. During this party, Captain Ward, my Troop Officer, came over and asked me if that pretty woman really was my mother! I felt very proud of her.

During that first leave, I spent time in London and then returned to Kettering. Whilst there, I caught the bus out to Woodford to surprise the Charltons, especially I hoped, Franny. I was in my service dress, brilliant polished buttons, glossy Sam Browne belt and my green and gold side hat, I felt quite something. As I walked up the drive Eleanor greeted me and said that her mother was at home but everyone else was away. That was rather a disappointment, but I was received with great affection and congratulated on my commission. After tea I led the subject round to Franny and was told that she was now at a Catering College. I asked where, but somehow the answer was never forthcoming and when I left I was no wiser. I did eventually discover from Yvonne that it was in Leicester but not the actual address. I was unhappy at the time but the message was fairly clear; I was upset but I was very occupied and did not pursue it further.

I spent the next few months helping to train other regiments to compete with the intricacies of tanks and armoured cars. They were converting a number of Infantry Regiments into Reconnaisance Regiments. Not an unqualified success! I had no further leave until June when I went down to Kettering unannounced, on a long weekend pass. It was a hot day, I walked up from the station and decided to enter by the back door at Kenilworth. I noticed that the sitting room doors were open, glanced along the passage and was astonished to see my father sitting on the sofa. He had been at Kenilworth for a couple of days to recover from the journey back to England and was as pleased to see me as I was him. During the next two days I learnt all about his imprisonment, his unexpected release and the joy of spending a few weeks in Cairo getting over the trauma. I thought that he was very well and we spent our time together, talking, walking and visiting local friends. He was feted everywhere he went. He had not yet told my mother and said that he would do so when he had totally recovered. She had sent him many letters and he spoke kindly of her.

A photograph of him appeared in the local press later with the caption "*Kettering Officer chats with "Posthumous" V.C.*", plus photograph and the following:-

"*Captain R.V.Bellamy, brother of Mr Leslie Bellamy and of Mrs B.G.Shrive, of Tennyson Road, Kettering, who was taken prisoner in the Middle East seen chatting with Major Le Patourel V.C. in Cairo shortly after their repatriation from Italy. Taken prisoner last January, Captain Bellamy had been in hospital for some time. He was aide-de-camp to Viscount Bennet when Canada's ex-Premier visited Kettering to receive the "Evening Telegraph" Spitfire campaign cheques.*
Major de Patourel, who comes from Guernsey, was awarded the V.C."posthumously". He was later found to be a prisoner of war."

My father and I spent the last evening of my leave with Uncle Bernard down at the Royal Hotel and then I went back to Kenilworth with them, so it was quite late when I left there. I walked down the London road to return to Havencourt, all was in pitch darkness, as of course there were no street lamps and few cars about. I was just passing the Langleys house, when I heard a woman screaming. I ran quickly down the London Road towards the noise and as I reached Pipers Hill Way, then only a cinder track, I heard the doors and windows of the two end houses on each side of it shutting. "*You're on your own*" I thought "*Nobody wants to know*". I could hear a struggle going on in the middle of the dirt road, I rushed over and found that it was a woman screaming at the top of her voice, with a large man lying on top of her. I was nonplussed to start with and I remember tapping him on the shoulder and shouting that he should stop. He

151

then looked up at me. He was a black man with a moustache wearing American Air Force uniform and looked very vicious. I grabbed his shoulder and tried to heave him off her. He twisted sideways and he started to get to his feet. It was then, that I realised how big he was and at the same time I saw the glint of a knife in his right hand. I stepped back and kicked him in the face with all the force that I could muster. He staggered to his feet and fell back against the wooden fencing by the side of the track. The girl, sobbing, was scrambling to her feet and so I just grabbed her and supporting her, I ran across the road towards the house opposite as fast as I could. They had heard the row and opened their door as we tumbled inside and they locked it again. It was the Pearson family, I knew their two daughters who were at school with cousin Mary and they rang for the police.

I discovered that the woman, the wife of a serviceman, had been at a pub in the town and as she passed the top of St Mary's Road, had realised that a man was following her. She thought that she had outpaced him, but suddenly as she entered Pipers Hill Road, he had grabbed her from behind, and pulled her down onto the ground. She was in a complete state of shock and wouldn't let go of my hand. Apparently he had threatened her with the knife, then he used it to try to cut her underclothes away. She refused to go home and wouldn't release my hand, so eventually, accompanied by the police, I took her to Havencourt. Auntie Peggy refused to allow her to sleep in one of her beds, *("You never know where she's been!")* so she lay on the small sofa in the sitting room whilst I sat by her in an armchair and held her hand all night. She just shook and shook with shock and fear. I took her home in the morning and left her with her neighbours, as I had to return to my unit that evening.

I heard later that they apprehended the man on our description, as he was the only black man in the Grafton Underwood American Airforce Base with a moustache and broken front teeth. He was sent back to the U.S.A., dishonourably dismissed the service and sentenced to hard labour. I probably saved his life! I was notified by the Commanding Officer of the 9th Battalion the Manchester Regiment with whom I was then billeted that a Commendation and a letter of thanks had been received from both the Police and from the U.S.A.F. but I never saw either, nor were they placed with my records. My posting came through within a couple of days and I was ordered to join the 8th Hussars in Benghazi.

I was granted a five days embarcation leave. It was in early September 1943 and I decided to go back to my school to say goodbye, then Kettering and finish up in London. I was due to meet my draft at St Pancras on 12 September. I had a warm welcome at the school, supper with Yvonne, compline at 8 pm as always, then I was invited out for a quick drink at Wakerley with my section of the Home Guard. I was never very good at holding my drink and apparently they virtually carried me back to school, where Fr Henry and Yvonne undressed me and put me to bed! I felt very ashamed in the morning but nobody seemed to be very upset.

My father was staying with Auntie Edna whilst I went to Havencourt as usual. He was touring the country at this time giving pep talks to factories. Not a task that he relished much. Repatriated prisoners of war had to be employed in non-combatant jobs as part of the terms of their release, luckily the Red Cross were after him to help with their fund raising and he soon went to join them at Winchfield. We spent an evening at the Royal in the snug which was Uncle Bernard's special place. It was great fun and all his friends were all very complimentary and kind to me. Some of them were not a little jealous of the 8th Hussar green and gold side hat which was a smash hit in Kettering and definitely turned a few heads. Many people thought that I was Polish!

My father had invited me to spend the last two days in London with him and we stayed at a small hotel near to Kensington station. Together, we visited my mother and I told her that I was off to the Middle East. We stayed for lunch I remember. After lunch, I looked out into the hall and saw her with her arms round my father's neck obviously hopeful that all would be well from now on. She looked very small, appealing and vulnerable and I was very moved by the gesture. My father wasn't brusque with her but equally he wasn't forthcoming and I felt desperately sad for her and disappointed too. My father had arranged for a farewell celebration that night, so to avoid complications, we had agreed that we should say that this was my last days leave and that I was departing on the train that afternoon. I felt an absolute swine when I carried this through. My mother was very upset to see me off to the war, and, clearly, she was disillusioned to find that my father still wanted the separation; it was an emotional situation in any one's book. On the other hand, I was torn with dual loyalties, and felt acutely ashamed because I knew that we were going to the theatre that night, and that I had another days leave ahead of me. I have never forgiven myself for this and retribution followed very swiftly.

We returned to our hotel and then he took me to meet Joanna. It was obvious that he was totally at home in her flat, which was close to Kensington station. She had another friend from the W.A.A.F, staying there for the night and the four of us had dinner together and then went off to the Theatre to see "The Little Dog Laughed". In the foyer I bumped into one of my Torquay

Prudential girls, Diana, who lived in Turnham Green and knew my mother. We exchanged courtesies and shortly afterwards, she saw my mother out shopping and said how happy I had looked. I think that this finally destroyed any faith or hope that she had in reconciliation with my father as well as giving her doubts about me. It was fortunate that on my return from the Middle East I was able to spend time with her in London and restore her faith in me a little.

I came back from the Middle East with a severe case of jaundice after having contracted dysentry. It was clear that I was not really suited to the tropics! I found myself in Broadgreen Hospital, Liverpool for Christmas which was a bit too far for anybody from my family to visit me. They were marvellous to us in the hospital and dozens of kind people gave up their time to make us enjoy it as best as we could. Carols, small gifts, visits by Friends of the hospital and then of course, the genuine care and affection given to us all by the devoted and much bombed staff. I was released on a month's convalescent leave on 14 January 1944. I was dreadfully bored and I wrote several poems, none very good but they reflected my mood:-

Time - like a dream rising out of the mist of ages, growing
Through eternity from a seed in the mind of God, formless
vaste, immeasureable, yet slow and tedious to those who live
beneath it's spell --- Away! Let us float in creamy space, apart
From temperate evils -- cast off this binding and sink
timeless into an everlasting present.

I arrived back in London on Friday evening, tired, not very well and clearly, very moody. What a mixture. My mother and grandmother were marvellous and I had a wonderful reception, all was at ease as far as my mother was concerned, clearly, she had come to terms both with my father's attitude and my deceit. She was only too delighted to see me home from a 'Theatre of War'. I spent a very happy two days with them and then, giving up my leave, I went back to rejoin the Regiment at West Tofts in Norfolk. I have never been any good at idleness and I think that I really needed a challenge to get me back on my feet. I certainly found that I was very occupied when I returned to soldiering. I did not see my father at that time, as he was travelling still, but I arranged to go to stay with him at Winchfield Lodge, the Red Cross Centre from which he was working, if I got any leave again.

Between January and May 1944, when we were finally bottled up prior to the invasion, I spent several happy weekends with both of my parents but separately. I was now established in the Regiment, very junior of course, but some of the adolescent silliness had gone and I was better company than before. I was also financially independent, my allowance stopped when I was commissioned, and I paid my corner. My mother loved my visits, we didn't do anything very exciting but we were together and we both found great happpiness in that. Sometimes we went to the "Kew" Theatre, we always had a drink in the "Goldhawk" on Sunday mornings, and all the time we talked. In the evenings we took to going next door to visit the del Renzios where we gossiped or drew. They were a fascinating couple, as despite the war, their lives revolved around stage scenery, backcloths, especially opera and the like, which was a total change from the Blitz, Shortages, Second Front and Blackout! They taught us to play the old ink blob game. You put an ink blot on a sheet of cartridge paper, then fold and press it. On opening the paper up, the ink makes a pattern which suggests something to you and you then draw and paint what it represents. We spent hours doing this and it was great fun. I found one of my mother's doodles, framed, down in the air raid shelter when we closed up Fairfax Road in 1954. My son, Giles, now has it.

I talked deeply with my mother about my future, about my religion and especially about family and marriage. I was disillusioned with marriage and it certainly didn't rank high in my list of priorities. She however felt that a good marriage was the most wonderful thing. She had not enjoyed it herself but it certainly didn't give her a jaundiced view of it as a desirable state. She hoped that I would marry one day, when I was older, and I think that she saw herself as a grandmother. Perhaps, to some extent, this was her motivating force. In April, during my last short leave, she showed me the grandfather clock and several pieces of furniture purchased by her or given to her by her father which she had put on one side for me as a start of my "bottom drawer". I felt very moved and loved her for her thoughtfulness. That was the last time that I was to see my mother.

The two days spent with my father were equally quiet, as the house, Winchfield Lodge, was right out in the country and we spent our evenings there. We talked a great deal about the past and what the future would hold for me. I had no question in my mind. I knew that I wanted to serve with the 8th Hussars until I retired. I wanted to be granted a Regular Commission and my ambition was to command the Regiment, after that I hadn't really thought. I think this pleased my father very much as he too loved the army. I was with him for a couple of days and then returned to Bognor.He told me that he was considering a move abroad when all this had finished as *"there was nothing to hold him in England if I was in the Army."*

After that leave I can't say that I gave my parents a great deal of thought as the excitement of the pending invasion took over as the focus of our lives.

Bill Serving in Middle East 1943

24C Troop Sandhurst 1943

Ronald Bellamy and his German Air Force prisoners!

CHAPTER 10
The End of a Generation

The invasion and the subsequent battles are described in some detail in my book "Troop Leader". In Chapter Nine of that book, I recorded the news of the death of my mother who was killed by a V2 on 6 March 1945, the very day after I had been decorated by Field-Marshal Montgomery in Eindhoven. I had just returned to the Regiment at Grevenbicht in Holland and in the book I wrote as follows:-

"During the afternoon of 7 March, I was changing my clothes in my billet in a small Dutch house, when Bob Ames walked in looking very grim. I made some facetious remark and then I saw that he was holding out a signal for me to read. I imagined that it was my posting but before I read it he said very gently "Sit down and listen to me" and then "Your mother was killed in London yesterday in a bombing raid".
I suppose looking back on it I was very strung up at the time and Tony, the Padre and the Doctor were probably right in their diagnosis (They felt that I was becoming "Bomb happy".) However on receiving this news, I was totally overwhelmed with grief and with the feeling of desolation that accompanied it. Perhaps I had never valued my mother as much as I did at that moment when I realised that I would never see her again. All my shortcomings in my attitude to her and my relationship with her poured into my mind; I was consumed with misery and with my feelings of guilt."

I was given every assistance to return home and arrived at 45, Fairfax Road to find that her funeral had just finished and everyone had gathered there for tea. My father was staying with Granny and I did the same. They told me that she had been killed by a V2 rocket, which fell directly on her offices near Smithfield Market. I believe that about 160 people died in the blast. She had been dead when they had pulled her out of the rubble. Her rings and any jewellery that she was wearing had been stolen. I was consumed with hate for a short time for the Germans who had caused her death and the thief who robbed dead bodies. She was buried in the Fulham Road Cemetery alongside her father, but I gather that some years later all memorial stones were moved to the side and the area has now become a children's playground. The obituary in the local London paper read as follows and was a fine brief statement of my mother's great qualities:-

"The death by enemy action of Olive Helen Louise Bellamy on March 6th last is mourned by a large circle of friends. Born at Askew Road where her father, the late Frederick A Gale, was in business as a tobacconist, she spent the most of her life in the Borough loved by all who knew her. A personality so vivid and endearing with such a talent for friendship is rare indeed and

her passing is a real loss to those who knew her. She was buried at Hammersmith Old Cemetry in the family grave. Wreaths included".

Later, amongst my grandmother's papers I found this couplet which she had written:-
"Somewhere within my quiet and lonely heart
Somewhere surrounded by my love,
She lives – and smiles with me again"

I was ill when I arrived home and rapidly getting worse. My father suggested that I went to the M.O. at Winchfield. Somehow I couldn't bear to be with them all and I said that I would go down to Bognor and stay with my girlfriend, Audrey, as there was a big Military Hospital in nearby Chichester.

I realise now how low I was and how much the loss of my mother affected me. I was put into hospital, became engaged to Audrey, spent two days with my father and Audrey up at Winchfield and then discharged myself from hospital and went back to rejoin the Regiment. It was not a time to make major decisions. I was strung up with emotion, the effects of the fighting and the general tension of everything. In becoming engaged, I acted entirely on the spur of the moment, and behaved grossly unfairly to Audrey, causing her much unhappiness. We broke off our engagement within twelve months.

The Regiment, having crossed the Rhine, were now involved in the battle for Hamburg. This ended in March when we entered that city and then carried on up into Schleswig-Holstein. The European war ended at the beginning of May and we were then moved to Berlin, which in itself was an extraordinary experience, before returning to the more mundane tasks in our role as part of the Army of Occupation. We were stationed at Lingen/ Ems on the Dutch border. To my undisguised delight, my commission into the Regular Army came through in 1946, and I saw an exciting career ahead of me.

Early that year my father went out to Haifa in Palestine to run the Officers Club there. He thoroughly enjoyed the work and, whilst there, fell in love with a very attractive young Syrian woman. He wrote to me later in the year with a photograph of her and asking what I would feel about him remarrying. I replied that I had no objection to him remarrying but that he should seek somebody more of his own age. I don't think it was a well couched reply as he didn't respond but re-surfaced in six months time as the Supplies Officer for the Kuwaiti Oil Company, a job that he held until the middle of 1947. He returned to England and married Irene Mitchell in September 1947, at the Registry Office in Dorking. I was unable to attend the wedding but sent roses which were displayed at the wedding breakfast.

I believe that at the age of 50, my father was finding it difficult to settle down to work again. He had fought through two wars, his health was moderate and he believed that with his savings and Irene's income, they would be able to live quietly and in reasonable comfort. They set up house in Dorking and when Irene's mother, Mrs Mitchell, died in 1949, my father sold the Dorking house and bought Little Corner, Riverside, Shaldon near Teignmouth. Unfortunately Mrs Mitchell's income derived from investments in the Argentine, and the Peron Regime and consequent falling values, caused her income to fall dramatically. She continued to live in great style but used up much of the capital so, as her will provided for an equal division of assets between three daughters, little enough remained. My father and Irene were soon living in fairly reduced circumstances. Having spent all of his capital on buying the house, to his chagrin, he became dependent on Irene for every penny. I was unaware of this at the time.

During the four years from 1945 to 1950, I returned to England very rarely, as I was spending most of my leaves with the de Smet family in Belgium.It was true to say that I did not get on well with Irene who I found to be both possessive of my father, and very proper. We tried one holiday together, going to the South of Ireland, but that ended in disaster and was never repeated. Irene's "old maid" behaviour brought out the worst in me. I was young and fairly uninhibited, my life was mainly spent in a male society and I shared a robust sense of humour with my father. Irene was jealous of my father's obvious affection for me and had no sense of humour at all. Not a good mixture!

This time, after four days of real effort to make it all work and really genuinely trying to be sensitive to her concerns, my father and I broke out. He was toying with the idea of finding a house in Ireland, as living was so much cheaper there. We were staying in Killarney at the time so this gave us the opportunity of setting up a meeting with an estate agent there. Irene declined to come, although warmly invited. That memorable morning we rolled up at his office in the back of a shop at about 10 o'clock. *"Would you be wanting a jar"* he said affably as we walked in. *"Yes, indeed"* replied my father and that was it! I can't remember talking much about houses, although it is true to say that they did visit one in Tralee later in the week. We were very relaxed, discussed wide issues, laughed a lot and drank alternate rounds at a bewildering pace. The drinks were all fetched from the shop next door by his secretary, who seemed to be quite at home with this method of trading. At about 1.15 pm the door was thrown open and in marched a furious Irene, her face making thunder clouds look like blue sky! She ordered my father out and as we all staggered to our feet, so our new friend offered her a jar as well! This really put the lid on it and we spent the rest of the day ostracised in silent detention, both with bad heads. During the night, I thought it best if I left them to it so next morning I departed on my own, in cowardly fashion, leaving my father to face the music and hid in the hills of Kerry where I fished.

I was lucky to find a room in a small hotel in Glencar with the most hospitable Daly family. I shared the fishing with a West Cork Circuit Judge, Judge O'Brien, and was ghillied by a retired Irish cavalry sergeant. We all had a famous time on the salmon, white trout and the brownies. We fished night and day, mainly fly, but some spinning and plenty of the "white maggot". There were rivers, streams and small lakes, so we enjoyed plenty of variety. There were many stories to tell of this idyllic week, from encounters with phantom fish on Lake Acoos assisted by my very inebriated cavalry friend, to a serious introduction to the consumption of "Poteen", or walking miles across the Macgillicuddy Reeks to serve mass in an isolated hamlet and so-on, but my favourite story related to the penultimate morning of my holiday. *"We must fish for the last time together tomorrow"* said my friend the Judge. *"I am not due in Court in Killarney until 11.am ,"* Next morning, we were on the river by 8 o'clock and to my joy, I had landed an 8lb salmon by 8.30 a.m. Judge O'Brien had no luck until his last cast (knowing him, probably the twentieth last cast!) when "Bang" and he was into a good fish. At the time he was fishing "The Joinings", a point where the river divided round an island. He was standing on the right bank and despite all his efforts, his fish ran like a demon straight up the left hand stream, eventually snagging the line in some tree roots there. There was no bridge for a mile or so and no boat, so, urged on by his Honour, I offed with my clothes, waded across the river in the freezing water, found the snagged line, chased the fish downstream to a more civilised area and then, still naked, netted it. Quite a party! It weighed over 10lbs, was the best fish of the week and was clean run and silver. After I had dressed, in elated mood, together, we walked back to Glencar, which was about one and a half miles, both very ready for our breakfast. By this time it was well past 10 o'clock, so Judge O'Brien asked if I would ring the Clerk to the Court on his behalf, explaining that the Judge's car was playing up and rearrange for Court to open at 2.15pm. When I telephoned, the Clerk replied *" Sure, Sir, I'll do that with pleasure, but tell me Sir, was it a big one?"!*

In 1946, after a series of Squadron and Regimental tasks at Lingen, I had been selected to join the Staff of 7th Armoured Brigade as a Staff-Captain. Initially, Brigade H.Q. was billetted in Wahrendorf near Bielefeld and then, for the last two and a half years, at Bad Lippespringe near Paderborn. I remained with them in various roles with both "A" Branch and "Q" Branch, until the end of 1949, when I returned to the 8th Hussars in Leicester.

Life for me in Germany was wonderful. I had two horses for £2 and 10 shillings per month each. I was Secretary first of all to the 8th Hussar Beagle Pack, then later to the Warman Hunt with whom I enjoyed two days of fox hunting per week. I had access to superb wild fowling up on the North coast of Germany, Langeland and the surrounding islands. In addition, there were flocks of geese and duck on the Ems at Lingen. We enjoyed good pheasant, hare and woodcock shooting with occasional organised sorties into the forests with German game keepers shooting driven boar and deer. In addition to all this, latterly, we had the river Lippe flowing through the Headquarters compound and enjoyed excellent trout fishing on a three to four mile stretch of good water.

I had a wide coterie of excellent friends, served under and enjoyed the friendship of two remarkable Brigadiers, Perry Harding of the Skins and "Fairy" Foot of the Royal Tanks and, all in all, lived the life of Reilly for nearly four years. My mentor during much of this time was Colonel Peter Gregson, R.H.A., who coached me in all these sporting skills and with his wife, Oriel, taught me much of how to handle the social side of life in the Regular Army. As with so many people in my life, I owe them both a great debt of gratitude.

I rose daily at about 5.30 am and rode for an hour and a half. I worked very hard at my job, but managed to fit in all the "extra-mural" activities and went to bed when the party was over. Female company did not play a very large part in our lives, although I was rarely without a girl friend to take to the many parties which seemed to be going on all the time. We thought nothing of driving fifty miles or more for a cocktail party! I was Brigade Mess Secretary for two years and acquired a great reputation for running imaginative parties. As an illustration of party life, when I left Brigade H.Q after nearly four years, I was the longest serving officer in it and my farewell party included a guest list of nearly 200 people. The party started at 7pm on Friday, finishing early on the following Sunday morning. Incidentally my old Brigadier, Perry Harding, came back for it, especially to be with us, and he was still operational at 7.30 on the Saturday morning! The mess was decorated to represent a French town and the food was served off imitation market stalls with all the civilian mess staff dressed as peasants in costume. My faithful G.C.L.O. (German Civil Labour Organisation) did all of this, to my design, in their spare time and at little cost. They were not only wonderful scroungers but imaginative and innovative. I built a Catholic Chapel for instance. It needed stained glass windows and they made excellent stained glass by using colours mixed with vaseline!. They were mainly in my area of command for several years. I was always addressed as "Herr Rittmeister", a signal honour for a very moderate horseman!

The other part of this enchanted life was spent during weekend or long leaves, with the family de Smet either in Ghent or in their country house near Lathem St Martin. In "Troop Leader" I tell of how Madame DeSmet came and took me out of hospital in January 1945 and how close we became. A year after my mother had died she "adopted" me and from then on I called her Mammy. Her three children became as brothers and sister to me and an ever closer friendship, which began in 1945, exists with their descendents to this day. They are a wealthy family, very loving and very generous. I had my own room in both houses and life was composed of tennis, swimming, riding, marvellous soirées and house parties at the weekends. When her second son, Yvan, died of cancer in the 1950's, immediately, Mammy said that I had been sent by God as his replacement and she treated me as if I truly was. Happily, the affection and relationship between the two families has continued into the next generation. I was devastated by Mammy's death and retain the very fondest of memories of her and her husband.

In December 1949 I handed over to my successor at Brigade H.Q. and returned to England for Christmas. My posting back to the Regiment was operational from mid-January when I was to take up the appointment as Second in Command of A Squadron and then that of Adjutant. In January I was to return to Germany for two weeks to complete some handover details. I decided to leave my kit with the Regiment at Leicester, contact my father and ask him if I could spend Christmas with them. With Irene's approval, he agreed and we spent a week together, firstly at Shaldon and then, for the three days of Christmas, with his sister in laws, Jessie Thoms, and Kitty Mitchell, at Cadgewith in Cornwall. They were very nice to me but I found them to be very staid old maids and it was difficult, after my more extrovert life, to really enjoy their company.

I was preparing to leave after New Year but on New Years Eve, which was to be spent at home in Shaldon, a young officer, Chris Coldrey, who had recently joined the Regiment, rang up and invited me to go to a dance at the Imperial Hotel in Torquay. He would provide a partner for me, and we would all meet there. I did all I could to wriggle out of it but eventually agreed to go.

I arrived and was introduced to my partner for the evening, a very agreeable girl but not particularily exciting. As we went over to our table, Chris' young brother

Bill appeared with a chestnut haired girl beside him. I took one look, thought that she was beautiful and without even speaking to her, fell in love with her. It was the complete *"coup de foudre"!* I was quite astonished by the intensity of my feeling, made no pretence about dancing with my partner but moved in and took her away from Bill. She told me that she was Ann Burbury, the eldest daughter of Chris' father's partner, a Doctor, and lived in Teignmouth. We danced together throughout the whole evening. I immediately changed my plans and stayed in Shaldon until she had to return to London, where she worked as a radiographer at the London Hospital. I then returned to London in the train with her and from then onwards, we spent all our free time together.

During March 1950 I organised the move of the Regiment from Leicester to Tidworth. Ann and I became engaged on 30 April 1950. Shortly after this we were put on standby for the war in Korea and I began the long and arduous process of mobilising the Regiment for war. Mobilising a Regiment in peacetime is desperately hard work and I rarely left the Orderly Room before 3 o'clock in the morning. At one point the total intake of reservists gave us a strength of over 1200 men, and, for instance, amongst these there were many compassionate cases requiring individual careful investigation with a view to their possible release from service. New officers were coming in from the reserve as well as from other Cavalry or Tank Regiments and all the time new equipment, training programmes, revised structural organisation and volumes of instructions or demands from Brigade, Division and the War Office. The organisation was going well however and, despite all the uncertainties, Ann and I decided that we would get married before I left for Korea. Then one night I collapsed in the Orderly Room and was rushed into hospital. After a series of tests, it was discovered that I had a fifth severe bout of jaundice which, because of my medical history, was life-threatening. I was boarded and down graded to Home Service only.

I don't think that in my whole life I have ever been so devastated by any event as much as by this one. My beloved Regiment where I was now well re-established, the mobilisation procedures which I was master minding, the prospect of fighting again in the company of such people and then suddenly "Home Service only" - there was no way out. I was sent away on two months sick leave at the end of which, I was to be reboarded. There was even a possibility that I would be discharged. I was in despair and I don't know what I would have done if Ann hadn't been there both to help me through the aftermath of my illness and to restore my shattered morale. I have never really recovered from or forgotten this incident which greatly affected the rest of my life. Incidentally, the doctors sent for Ann and told her that if I had one more attack then I was likely to die! Not a good start to a long marriage.

Ann and I were married on 14 September in the Church of Our Lady and St Patrick, Teignmouth. We honeymooned, intensely happily, but in somewhat straightened circumstances, in Devon and Cornwall. In October I was re-boarded and graded as L.E. which meant that I could serve in temperate climates. I immediately applied to rejoin the Regiment, but Korea was not considered as temperate so I was then posted to the Northamptonshire Yeomanry as Adjutant, joining them on 1 November 1950. We found a very nice small quarter at 7, Manfield Way off the Kettering Road in Northampton and settled down to married life. The pay of a Captain at that time was not generous and I kept scrupulous accounts to help us to cope. I still have the original account books from 1950-1957, and see that my Army pay for December 1950 was £35 and six pence, for the following January - £41 and three shillings and February - £38. Despite the frugality we managed and had a wonderful time. I worked very hard to help to make the Yeomanry into the best Territorial Regiment in the country. They were all very keen and I think that the general consensus over the next four years confirms that we suceeded in our aim.

On 6 June 1951, our first child, Simon Jonathan, was born, this somewhat unexpectedly! We were a bit naive about pregnancies and on, what proved to be, the hottest day of a very hot summer and late in her eighth month, I took Ann for a drive to Gloucester in our old Lanchester. It was a fine car but bounced up and down over any small bump and the roads were not as smooth as they are today. Next morning, Ann was sweeping the stairs with a brush and pan doubled up with a "tummy-ache"! By chance, our Doctor, Jimmy Myles, a wonderful old friend who had been out in the Desert with my father, arrived for coffee. He was horrified, rushed her into the Nursing Home and Simon arrived quite soon afterwards.

Life was hectic in the Yeomanry. Basically, I was responsible for everything that happened. I attended training evenings three times each week for instance, these took place in Northampton, Kettering, Towcester and Brackley. We held Annual camps in Pembroke, Salisbury Plain and West Tofts, Norfolk which needed a lot of organising. National Service was in full swing and there was a constant flow of new recruits. There were various messes to run, pay to be sorted out, G1098 stores to control, tanks and a variety of arms to maintain, plus a host of peripheral matters to deal with. I enjoyed it all and made many life time friends during these years. The Regiment peaked at a strength of 950 all ranks, with a permanent staff of three civilians and around fifteen soldiers to help to run it. Early in 1952 we were honoured to provide a small contingent to attend the burial of King George the VIth.

Our second child, Timothy James, was born on 27 July 1952 and our house was becoming too small, so we moved to a very nice quarter, Southolm, in the adjacent village of Long Buckby. We engaged an "au pair" to help Ann and entertained a great deal. There was a large garden for the children to play in and I kept a fruitful vegetable garden and poultry. We sold the surplus to add to our income.

I spent weeks during the weekends of May 1953 training a body of officers and men for the Coronation of Queen Elizabeth. I marched them endlessly around the lanes with drawn swords, causing much interest and mirth. Coronation day itself, was a dramatic day for both Ann and I. We went up to London to stay for the night before the Parade with my grandmother. I was appointed to be on duty at the Admiralty Arch and Ann had a seat there. We arrived in London in the early evening only to find that I had left my blues trousers in Northampton! We telephoned the Tisdalls who were at Staff College in Camberley and I drove down there in our very rickety old car, borrowed St Clair Tisdall's blues trousers, and arrived back in London in time to have a few hours sleep before going on parade at 5.30 am. We took the Tube to St James and as we debouched onto the platform, I was pressed back against the train by the crowd. The Tube doors then closed whilst my sword was still in them. I had visions of being dragged down into the tunnel, but luckily it pulled out although my scabbard was badly dented! It was lucky that it came out at all! On arrival at the Stand, Ann in her beautiful and expensive green grosgrain coat was sitting next to an equally elegant lady who promptly tipped the contents of her coffee flask over both of them! Despite that they enjoyed an excellent view of it all.

The other major Regimental event of 1953 took place on 3 October when we held a parade at Althorp during which the Duke of Gloucester presented the Regiment with its new Guidon. It was a splendid sunny, autumn day. We had 250 Officers and Men on parade with the band of the Life Guards to help us. I was responsible for the whole parade including the drill, administration and catering whilst Lord Jack Spencer and I prepared the background layout of the scene together.

The whole parade was excellent, there were no hitches, and all who took part, treasured the memory of a very special day. The Duke was most fulsome in his praise and I was invited by Lord Jack Spencer to sign the Althorp

"Distinguished visitors' book", and did so immediately after the Duke. It began a good friendship with Lord Jack which lasted until his death in 1971.

On 11 October 1953, Ann produced another baby boy, Andrew Nicholas who was actually born at home. My parents-in-law were not very pleased at the speed at which our family was growing! Ann and I both wanted a large family so despite the murmurings were not deterred. Later that year we organised a Yeomanry Ball at Althorp which we greatly enjoyed. By this time I was working in preparation for my Staff College Entrance Examinations which were due to be taken in 1954. Successs was vital for my future career and I worked as hard as the time and other commitments permitted.

In 1954 I went out to Germany as an umpire on various exercises, as well as running the Regiment and working at night studying. Shortly after taking the exam, our Colonel, Sir John Baldwin, invited me to accompany him on an official visit to the 8th Hussars. I was to act as a supernumerary A.D.C. to Prince Phillip for the day. He was to inspect the Regiment and then on to the Cameron Highlanders. We flew out in a Dove of the Queen's Flight and spent a wonderful three days with the Regiment, renewing old friendships and talking about the future. Prince Phillip was very pre-occupied, rather abrupt and clearly running on a tight schedule. However just as he was about to take off in his plane on his way to Austria, where he was to stay with his cousins, the door of the plane opened and a cardboard box was handed out to me. *"Take care of this"* I was told *"deliver it to Buck House."* The box had the words "Molyneux" printed on it so I imagined that it contained a present for the Queen, as Prince Phillip had just been to Paris.

I then flew back with Sir John and with the Comptroller of the Household, General "Boy" Browning, who had commanded the British forces at Arnhem. The plane was flying at a very bumpy 3000 feet and I began to feel terribly queasy. This was noticed by Sir John, who immediately instructed the pilot to take the plane up to 6000 feet where it would be much calmer. As we started to go higher, so the box which I was guarding carefully on my knees fell to the floor and burst open. I hardly dared to look, but when I did I discovered that it contained Prince Phillip's Cameron kilt and not a romantic present for Her Majesty! We flew on and as we reached the Arnhem area, General Browning asked if we would like to view the landing sites and have the basis of the battle explained to us from the air. We eagerly agreed and it was a most interesting experience.

On 14 June the Staff College results were published and I found that I had passed comfortably. We were both elated. I received a telegram from the Regiment which read -"*Congratulations on passing Staff College examination. Colonel and all Officers*". Staff College was a key to advancement and I felt that now our joint future was assured. During the next months between Annual Camp and the various activities which occupied me, we made our plans for the move. I received warning of my posting to "C" Division at Minley and we were allocated a quarter in Farnham, which pleased us, as it was near to Burnham Beeches where Ann had lived at the beginning of the war.

Then came the bombshell. In October, I was medical boarded again as a matter of routine and, to my horror, graded as L.E. but in a category which virtually ensured home service only. This meant that as I could never serve abroad, my future army career would be extremely restricted. I appealed to H.Q. 44 Division, and General Herbert intervened personally, giving me a glowing reference. This, although I was unaware of it at the time, caused some offence at my A.G.Branch and they immediately arranged for another Medical Board. This took place on 2 November and confirmed the findings of the first Board; in fact rather underlined them sending me home to "*Await War Office Instructions*". I then drove up to Stanmore to see the Officer in charge of my Branch, A.G.17. I didn't find him helpful but, instead of doing the sensible thing, saying nothing and getting in touch with the Commanding Officer of the 8th Hussars, I said words to the effect that "*if that was the best they could do, then I would rather leave the army.*" My "retirement" papers came through immediately, dated 5 November 1954, "*to retire with gratuity (£1,300) on 31 December 1954*". I had grossly mishandled it, overestimated my importance to the army and learned a very hard lesson. Perhaps I finished up with a little more humility!

My replacement, Dick Randall, an admirable choice by the Regiment, was then nominated to commence on 1 January 1955. I was out of a job, with a wife, three children, £1,300 in the Bank, an invalid pension of £56.00 p.a. and nowhere to live. I was astonished and delighted to find that I was offered a number of jobs by local firms. I was totally ignorant of commercial matters but evidentally they felt that I would learn quickly. In the event I accepted the position as trainee Company Secretary with Phipps and Son Ltd. They were a small privately owned shoe components supplier in Guildhall Road, Northampton. The prospects looked interesting because the then Company Secretary was due to retire in several years time. Also, one of the Directors who was about to be appointed, was my close friend in the Yeomanry, Tom Boardman, later Lord Boardman, but at that time, an up and coming commercial solicitor in Northampton.

Granny Gale then asked whether she could sell up in London and come to Northampton and live with us. She said that she wished to retire as she was then 75 years old. She also said that she would *"like to come up to die, dear,"* but evidently she didn't anticipate a long life ahead. Granny loved our family and felt that she could thus assist us in furnishing our first house. Ann and I were very happy at the idea which was certainly immensely helpful. Neither of the parents felt able to help us financially. In fact at this time my father and Irene had sold "Little Corner" and moved to "Yew Tree House" near Yeovil in which they had set up a small tea room. It was just beginning to show a modest profit and thus was helping them with their income problems.

Our immediate need was to find a house which we could afford. A town house, 21 Park Avenue North, was available, and appealed to us because it was within walking distance of my new offices, near to a good school and opposite the Catholic Church, the only problem was the price which was £1,200. The bankers to my new company were Lloyds and at that time they had a most exceptional manager, who was to become my mentor in banking matters. I went to see him and although I had not yet started work he advanced the funds necessary to buy the house and we moved there at the beginning of December. Granny joined us and we celebrated our first Christmas together there.

I started at Phipps on 3 January 1955. It was all very strange; I was treated with considerable suspicion and had a difficult first year. I was soon aware that although commercial life was different to that of the army my training as a Staff Officer made me more articulate, better able to express myself and more analytical than any of my colleagues. I had the additional advantage of fluent French and reasonable German. I wrote a long letter to my father, thanking him for the sacrifices that he had made to ensure that I was well educated and thus capable of taking on such a task. Very soon I was to thank God that I had done this and not put it off until later. I found life in the Secretary's Office absolute hell as she took every opportunity of "putting me down" and belittling my knowledge. However despite the strain of the petty persecution, the whispering and the bickering, and greatly comforted by Ann, I decided to stick it out.

During the summer my father asked whether the two older children, Simon and James, could come down to Yeovil and stay with them. We were delighted and they collected them from Long Buckby whilst later we drove down and picked them up. Their house was very nice, a stone cottage with a pretty garden. In it, they had laid out their silver and porcelain in the tea room and furnished it with dark antique tables and chairs. Irene was using her hand embroidered cloths and the whole thing was in good taste and very attractive. Irene was a good cook and all the scones and cakes were made by her, whilst my father used his considerable charm to bring in regular custom. It was a team effort and by the looks of it had the makings of success. My father said that it was becoming the place to go. I had a long talk to him and found him to be happier than he had been for some time. He was suffering from a bad stomach but felt that this was as much from the strain of moving and starting a new lifestyle as from anything organic. He looked well.

On November the 4th I attended a Regimental Dinner at the Cavalry Club, where I was still a member. Prince Philip was present. During the dinner I received a telephone call to say that Ann had gone into the Nursing Home. I was talking to Prince Philip at the time, it was a rule that we were not able to leave until he had left and it was still quite early in the evening... *"You'd better go home early"* he said *"and if it's a boy don't call it Philip."* Peter Giles, was born on the morning of 5 November 1955. We couldn't believe that we would have had a fourth son although of course my grandparents had had four boys and a girl in that order. Ann coped magnificently with our large family, she received some help from Granny and at that time we always had an au pair which made a considerable difference. The first au pair who we welcomed into that house, was our much loved Fini Coumou who came over from Holland, and who, with her husband Jan, is still visiting us now in 2009.

Christmas 1955 was held under somewhat straightened financial circumstances and we hadn't enough money to buy a turkey. However, to our great delight we won second prize in the Phipps Christmas Raffle! It was a large cockerel and Ann spun it out to last us throughout Christmas. Frankly it didn't seem to matter and we all enjoyed a wonderful time.

We were very surprised and saddened to hear on 29 December that Auntie Peggy had died in Kettering. Uncle Leslie and she had been very good to me when I was a child, they were frequent visitors to our house and her death was the first of the other "elders" in my life. She was cremated at the Kettering crematorium and I found it to be rather a soul-less service for such a nice person. Uncle Leslie sold "Havencourt" and in November 1956 married Pat Robinson, a widow. Initially, they lived in the Market Square in Higham Ferrers before moving to Brigstock, not far from where his grandparents had lived in the 1800's.

I returned to work in the New Year and on 31 January, a Thursday, my father telephoned, whilst I was in my office, to say that they had asked him to go to

Kings College Hospital in London for an operation. Apparently they suspected that he was suffering from stomach ulcers and although it wasn't considered to be very serious, he felt that I should know. I felt very concerned, and telephoned my father in law, a fine doctor, whose opinions on such matters I greatly respected. As a result I decided that I must go to the hospital.

Next morning having been given the day off so that I could visit him, I arrived at Kings at about 3 p.m. and met up with Irene. Daddy was still in the operating theatre, so we sat and waited in the ante-room. At about 6pm. he was returned to the ward and we were allowed to see him. Initially, he seemed fairly lucid and looked remarkably well, considering that he had just endured an operation. I then realised that he must be heavily sedated, as he thought that I was his brother, Uncle Leslie, and he was equally confused about Irene. Sister then came in and asked if I would go down to the theatre where the surgeon would like a word. I was shown into a side room where I found the surgeon standing still wearing an operating gown. He said *"I am sorry that I could not see you before, but I have only just finished today's list. I won't beat about the bush, I'm afraid that your father has no chance of survival. He has extensive cancer which has spread throughout his stomach and other organs. His case was totally inoperable and I just sewed him back up again. I cannot understand how he has lived with so little discomfort for the past twelve months. Although that is little comfort to you, at least he has been spared suffering. I deeply regret that I have to tell you this and that I could do nothing to save him."* I was totally taken aback, thanked him and made my tearful way back to collect Irene. She was absolutely devastated and I had a job to convince her that it was true. We were then told that we could stay the night in the ante-room, so we sat there in armchairs and tried to comfort each other. He died, delirious and without us present at 6.30 a.m. I had seen a lot of violent deaths but my father's was the first that I had experienced as the result of illness and I felt wretched because it seemed so unjust at his age, he was only fifty-eight years old. It added to my growing realisation that you don't know how big a part people play in your life and how much you will miss them until they have gone. In the case of my father, with whom both in childhood and adolescence, I had so much shared experience I felt totally bereft. His funeral, at Irene's insistence, was in South London Crematorium and his ashes were scattered on Plot J 52 in the Garden of Remembrance there, near to the hospital. I find it quite impersonal as I lack both a stone and a defined grave site, and, as is now the case with my mother, whose graveyard has been turned into a playground, there is nowhere I can go to mourn. It is a sad lesson to me.

In the autumn of 1956 matters were at a low ebb between the Company Secretary and I. She had no time for me and wanted me to be removed. It was decided that I should go up to London for three months to train at an affiliated company, a Confirming House, where I would be assesssed by their Chief Executive, Peter Bayliss, whose judgement was well respected by her. At the end of the three months, he asked me to remain with him and offered me the post of Assistant Managing Director. I refused it but on my return it caused a further storm.

On 6 February 1957, our daughter, Sarah Gale, was born. There were scenes of triumph at the Barratt Maternity Home that night!

February was always a difficult month at work as the year end accounts were in course of preparation and in 1957, for the second year running, the company was in loss. I had the temerity to cast doubts on the current costing system and to attribute the losses to that. The Company Secretary was incensed, as it was a system designed by her, which I hadn't realised when I made the remark. The upshot of it was, that somewhat ill advisedly, she went to the Chairman and said that she would resign if I continued to be employed by the Company. The Chairman accepted her resignation on the spot and I took over as Company Secretary on 14 April 1957.

My first action on being appointed was to take the door closing device off the office door to indicate that all was open from now on. There had been a "secretarial clique" which had always appalled me and I was determined to eradicate it. I am glad to say that my rather direct method was a total success. My salary was increased a little on my appointment as Secretary which certainly eased the domestic stricture a little and, as we had never felt really happy living in the town, Ann and I began looking for a house with a suitably large garden for our children in the country.

For some months we had no luck, then one night in September, as we returned from dinner with a young surveyor Philip Blacklee and his wife, Sylvia, the phone rang. It was nearly one o'clock in the morning, it was Philip. *"I forgot to tell you just now"* he said *"but there is an old stone house out at Great Brington, Folly House, it is in bad condition and I don't recommend it, but it might be worth looking at. It has not yet been advertised for sale."* The madness of youth! We dressed again immediately, told Granny that she was back on duty as our baby sitter and drove straight out to Great Brington arriving there at about 1.30 am. We sat in our car at the top of the Whilton Road and just gazed down at this beautiful stone house which, at the time, was brightly lit by a wonderful full moon. We had no hesitation about it, rang the owners next morning, Saturday, had a tour of the house, fell totally

171

in love with it, despite all the horrors of damp and poor condition, and offered them £3,250 on the spot. This was not accepted.

Nevertheless I knew somehow that we had to have it, so, on the following day, as we came out of mass, seeing Pat Phelan, our Estate Agent, I said that we were putting our house in Park Avenue North on the market. *"No hope of a quick sale"* he replied *"Town houses there aren't moving well at present."* I must confess that I returned home somewhat depressed. Half and hour later, the telephone rang, it was Pat, *" I am with Eric, the head brewer from Phipps Brewery, in The Cock Hotel"* he said *"He has a bad back, wants to give up his present house which has a large garden, and especially wants a house in Park Avenue North. Is this the power of prayer or what have you trodden in! Can we come round?"* They came, he liked the house, brought his wife back for tea and bought it subject to them moving in on 1 November. It was then the middle of September 1957.

Two weeks passed with no progress being made on the purchase of Folly House, the Arnolds or their solicitor prevaricating at every point. I went to see Tom Boardman, explained the problem and he offered me a house in Thornby as a fall back. He then picked up the phone, rang the owners solicitors and told them that if our final offer of £3,300 was not accepted by four o'clock that afternoon, then it would be withdrawn. I passed a very uncomfortable hour and a half, then the phone rang *"We accept"* said the solicitor. I was elated, grateful and very relieved. Ann and I started work on the interior of the house during October and actually moved in on 1 November meeting our deadline.

Our lives then really blossomed. We were the proud owners of a lovely but very dilapitated new house. There was much to be done in every way but we were extremely happy with our young family whether we were working on the house or tryng to sort out the garden. People were very kind to us in the village and we felt really welcome. The children were soon at home, walking daily to Little Brington to the excellent school and all looking fit and well. Surprisingly Granny Gale had settled in the country and was busy sewing covers and curtains. The house was a hive of activity and this was reflected in the quality of my office work which went from strength to strength. I installed a new costing system immediately and in 1958 the financial results of Phipps had risen from a loss of £16,000 to profits of £156,000. This of course enhanced my status in the company and in 1959 I took over the role of Assistant Managing Director with Tom Phipps. Tom Boardman and I had already started on a planned expansion programme at home and abroad. From 1960 onwards, this took us round the world setting up subsidiaries and eventually led to us floating the company in 1964.

As the children grew older, so their schooling pattern changed from the village school to Spratton Preparatory School. Simon, the eldest, was accepted for Westminster Cathedral Choir School and departed for London and subsequently went to Blackfriar's School, Laxton (my old school). In the 1960's James went first to Llanarth Preparatory School near Abergavenny, then also to Blackfriars School. Andrew and Giles went to Llanarth Preparatory School. Simon and James, followed by Andrew and Giles, then completed schooling at Belmont Abbey, Hereford. All of them in turn distinguished themselves by becoming Head Boy. Meanwhile Sarah went to Farnborough Hill, a convent where my old friends the Charlton girls had been educated. She was not really cut out for boarding school and in retrospect we should have tried another route. However like all things you make your judgements at the time and only see what you should have done after the event!

At home, Folly House began to benefit from a wide range of improvements and in 1971 we were able to demolish the semi ruined out-buildings and erect the new, four car garage and garden sheds in Duston stone. My company, in 1969, merged with Chamberlains in order to rationalise the footwear supply industry. It was a good merger but the two philosophies in respect of employee values and treatment were very different. I operated best in independence and ran my companies as if they were a regiment, on a personal and caring basis. I was not essentially a "bottom line" manager although Phipps profits had shown constant growth. In the end I became Chairman and Managing Director of all the non-footwear activities in Chamberlain Phipps and was a main Board member, I did my best to influence the personnel policies in the other Divisions. I had some success but at great personal cost. I was very happy to retire in 1983.

My remaining Bellamy relations were ageing, and in April 1971, Uncle Bernard died as the result of a car crash in which he was the innocent party. It was a sad loss and his funeral in the Church of St Peter and Paul in Kettering showed what an immensely popular man he had been. The church was full and the service was vibrant and somehow very satisfying. He was followed by Uncle Leslie who died in 1976 his widow Pat staying on in the house in Brigstock.

Just after the war, Auntie Edna and Uncle Bernard had moved into a large house, number 3, Queensberry Road, Kettering. At this time, she was still very fit but after his death, age and the isolation began to tell on her and eventually she had, for her own protection, to be placed in an old people's home. Her household possessions were divided up, and to my surprise and delight, I found that she had left instructions that I should share the contents with her children.

It was she who, as her two surviving brothers divested themselves of their parents' assets such as pictures or china, purchased and housed them. She wanted to ensure that their direct descendants benefited equally. It was a wonderful gesture and I appreciated it greatly, as I believe so strongly in tradition and in the passing on of inherited family objects. She died in the home in Welton in March 1980 and was buried near her beloved parents in Kettering Cemetery. The funeral service was held in the Toller Congregational Chapel, where my grandparents and direct ancestors had played such a major role. It was well attended and to me very nostalgic.

Granny Gale lived on in Folly House until 1976. She was dearly loved by the whole family and continued to play a big part in all of our lives. She had always enjoyed parties and even when still in her nineties, rarely left before the last guest. She suffered a lot from rheumatism and the general debility which comes with age but remained uncomplaining. Eventually in 1976, Ann, who had been a wonderful support to her for twenty years, found that for medical reasons, she needed professional nursing. Granny opted to move to Nazareth House in Northampton and was very happy there for the remaining months. We visited her on most days but as Giles was then working from home, she saw a lot more of him than of the other children. A few days after her 97th birthday in 1976, she told me that she had decided not to take her pills that night. Apparently the sister had tried gently to persuade her to do so but she was determined, so sister did not push the matter. Granny then asked that Giles should visit her which he did. Sister, sensing that this forecast the end, arranged for two of the older sisters, her friends, to come and have a cup of chocolate with her at nine o'clock. *"Oh how lovely, we are having a party"* said Granny! They telephoned us at 2.00 a.m. to say that she had died in her sleep.

She died as she had lived, a gentle, kind hearted peacemaker, whose life was devoted to the service of others. A woman of strong principle, she chided me on her death bed for not having suggested that she should have become a Catholic. I always felt that her goodness was such that any change would have been almost an insult. I experienced the peace of death in her passing and lost the fear and apprehension which the brutality of my mother's death and the suddenness of my father's had engendered. This was her last and perhaps her most precious gift to her grandson. Her service, Catholic, was held in the chapel at Nazareth House and she is buried in the graveyard at Great Brington. Her inscription reads "beloved of five generations" and that tells it all.

So, the generation which had endured and survived two world wars and seen so much radical change taking place in the world, passed away. They left many precious memories and undoubtedly their influence is still felt in our lives today. We, the next generation, also live in a life of radical change, both moral and temporal. We should take heart from the way in which our predecessors faced their difficulties and should endeavour to leave, as they did, examples, which in their different ways, have a message of hope for those who follow. As I said in the introduction to this book, quoting the words of St Teresa's "Patient endurance attaineth to all things". Faith, Hope and Charity are always there, but only we, the present generations, can actually ensure that they are put into practice.

Family Tree - Bellamy Family (19th & 20th Centuries)

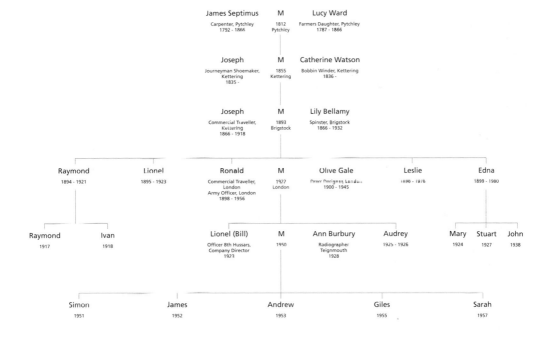

Ann and Bill engagement – April 1950

Ann and Bill's Children Folly House 1959

Ann and Bill's Children Folly House Garden 1965

Feb: the 19 1696 (140)

In the name of god Amen I William Belamy
now being taken ~~and~~ weakly ill but very
sensible and of perfect memory blessed be
god for it I doe here comit my soul into the
hands of god through the Lord Jesus Christ
and my Body after death to be buryed according to the Christchen Buriall and my
Lands and goods to be disposed of as followeth
I doe Appoynt Aline Belamy my wife and William
Belamy my son my soul Executors of this
my Last Will I giue unto my son Samuel
the sum of fiu (5) score pounds with an Abroginon
I giue to my son John A hundred pounds: to be
paid in this years time I giue unto my son
James A hundred pounds: to be paid in two
years time: I giue unto my son Thomas the
the sum of fiu pounds: I giue to my son Samuel
the soureth horse: I giue unto William King my
grandchild fiu pounds to put him to prentise
I giue unto Anne Chandler and Elisabeth her daughter
and Will: Chandler her son three shillings I giue
unto Elisabeth Chanon my daughter Ann Elisabeth
her daughter and Peter her son three shillings
I giue unto Margery Palmer my daughter
and John King her son two shillings I giue
unto Sarah Belamy my daughter one shilling
and this my Last will to be performed by them
how I haue Aboue menshioned my Executors
the day and year aboue Witten in witnes
hear unto I haue sett my hand and seale
Sealed and delivered
in the presents of
The ~~Chandler~~   william Belamy
William Leigh
Jane Rennington

Probatum est for W Flambton
his ~~or~~ to nominat Executor
administ Bonis Coram   Sam: Saunders Surrog:

March 21 170[?]

A Inventory taken of the goods and chattels
of William Bellamy [...] at his death is as
followeth ————

Two [...] beddinges ———— 00 — 13 — 00
one Wooll bed ———— 00 — 02 — 00
[...] blankets ———— 00 — 06 — 06
two Botters ———— 00 — 07 — 06
three Tables ———— 00 — 05 — 00
five Stooles ———— 00 — 05 — 00
Tenn Chaires ———— 00 — 04 — 00
Two Coffers ———— 00 — 03 — 00
one pot [...] ———— 00 — 08 — 00
[...] dishes ———— 00 — [...] — 00
one [...] ———— 01 — 05 — 00
other [...] ———— 00 — 06 — 06
one pillow two Blankets ———— 00 — 09 — 00
one [...] hangings ———— 00 — 04 — 00
one chest of drawers ———— [...] — 03 — 00
Two chests ———— 00 — [...] — 00
five Sheets ———— 01 — [...] — 00
the [...] ———— 01 — [...] — 00
two Barrells small Barrells ———— 00 — 02 — 06
the Linnen ———— 01 — 00 — 00
[...] and apparell ———— 02 — 00 — 00
                        [...] — 17 — 00

This Taken by us [...]
the Day [...]
Above written ———

John Miller
William Leigh [...]

Translation of Inventory of William Bellamy 1704/5

March 21 1704/5

The Inventory taken of the goods and chattels of William Bellamy Senior at his death is as followeth

	£	s	d
Two Bedstedes and Certinrods	00	13	00
One Wooll bed	00	02	00
Three blankets	00	07	06
Two Bolsters	00	06	00
Three Tabulls	00	07	06
Five Stooles	00	05	00
Tenn Chares	00	05	00
Two Cettells	00	04	00
One pote and scelit	00	03	00
Six plates fore deshes	00	08	00
One poset pote	00	01	00
One fether Bed	01	05	00
One pillow two blankets	00	06	06
One Coverled and Certings	00	09	00
One Chest of drawerers	00	07	00
Two Chestes	00	03	00
Five Sheep	01	00	00
The fierwood	01	00	00
Two Barells small Barells	00	02	06
The Linen	01	00	00
Pors and Aparell	02	00	00
	£	s	d
The sum is	10	04	06

This taken by us and aprased
The day And year
Above Wretten
John Miller
William Leigh Senior

viz: A true and perfect Inventory of all
the Goods and Creditt Chattel and Whattots of
William Billamy of Kingstock in the County
of Northampton Lately Deceased

	£	s	d
Purse and Apparell - - - - - - - - - - -	10	00	00
The furniture of the parlor - - - - - -	04	00	00
The pewter and other things in ye pantree - -	02	15	00
The Clock and tables in ye Hall - - - - -	01	13	00
The Copper and Brass and Irons in ye Kitchin	08	15	00
The tubs and vessills in ye Cellars - - - -	01	15	00
Some pease one Bed in ye Kitchen Chamber - -	04	00	00
The Garrett two Beds & some other things - -	02	05	00
The Chamber over ye parlor 1 Bed & a Glass - -	08	00	00
The Chamber over ye Hall a paire of Draws 1 Bed	02	15	00
The Chamber over ye Bread house one Bed & Chest	05	00	00
Cow Plate - - - - - - - - - - -	13	00	00
The Linnen - - - - - - - - - -	08	00	00
The metorialls in ye Bake house - - - -	01	15	00
The Wood in ye yard - - - - -	04	00	00
The Wheat and pease - - - - -	08	08	00
The horses - - - - - - -	12	05	00
Two Hoggs - - - - - -	01	12	00
Two Leathers and a fann - - - -	01	00	00
Cow ye Beast and Hay and things - -	31	10	00
Ow ynterest money and Debtt - - - -	00	00	00

Apprized by us whose - - £ 415   Totall: 157 : 10 : 00

Robert Hester }
Tho: Rowlatt }   Elizabetha Billamy vidua
Guilielmi Billamy Jurata fuit
martij 1710 Cord me Higood Surrogate

Translation of Inventory of William Bellamy 1719/20

Viz: A true and perfet Inventory of all the Goods and Credits Chattel and Chattells of William Bellamy of Bridgstock in the County of Northampton Lately Deceased.

	£	s	d
Purse and Apparell	10	00	00
The furniture of the parlor	04	00	00
The pewter and other things in the pantree	02	15	00
The Clock and tables in the Hall	01	13	00
The Copper and Brass and irons in the kitchen	03	05	10
The tubs and vessells in the Cellars	01	15	00
Some pease one Bed in the Kitchen Chamber	04	00	00
The Garrots two Beds and some other things	02	05	00
The Chamber over the parlor 1 Bed and a glass	08	00	00
The Chamber over the Hall a pair of draws 1 bed	02	15	00
The Chamber over the Bread house One bed and Chears	05	00	00
For plate	13	00	00
The Linnen	08	00	00
The meterialls in the Bake house	01	15	00
The Wood in the yard	04	00	00
The Wheat and pease	08	08	00
The horses	12	05	00
Two Hoggs	01	12	00
Two Leathers and a fann	01	00	00
For the Beast and Hay and Sheep	31	10	00
For interest money and debts	30	00	00
Total	157	10	00

Apprized by us March the 3rd 1719
Robert Foster
Thomas Rowlatt

Elizabeth Bellamy widow and administratix Of the above-named William Bellamy was sworn on the ninth day of March 1719 before me
H Goode, surrogate

CHILDREN'S FREE BREAKFASTS

At the Mission Hall, Tanner's Lane, Winter 1887-8.

FINANCIAL STATEMENT.

RECEIPTS

	£	s.	d.
By Subscriptions	40	2	10

EXPENDITURE.

	£	s.	d.
Bread Buns ...	23	8	2
Extra ditto ...	0	8	0
Milk ...	2	9	0
Cocoa and Sugar ...	6	19	2
Printing Tickets ...	0	7	0
Financial Statements ...	0	5	0
Weekly and General Cleaning ...	1	8	6
Mugs ...	1	6	3
Extra provisions ...	0	2	0
Utensils ...	0	6	0
Use of Hall and Gas ...	0	10	0
Hire of Copper ...	0	3	6
Balance in Treasurer's hands ...	2	0	0
	£40	2	10

Audited and found correct,

THOMAS WIDDOWSON.

O. ROBINSON, Treasurer.
JOSEPH BELLAMY, Jun., Hon. Secretary.

TOTAL BREAKFASTS GIVEN, 5761.

[Kettering.

APPENDIX D
Myasthenia Gravis

These notes do not pretend to give a scientific background to the disease but reflect the situation as I understood it affected my mother.

Myasthenia gravis is a form of paralysis which causes tasks such as eating, speaking, use of limbs, even turning over in bed, for instance, increasingly difficult. It attacks unexpectedly so that one day all is well and then for no apparent reason a particular function does not work. The effects can be dramatic and I can recall my mother just collapsing when out walking. When my parents were first married, it was relatively speaking an unknown disease on which no basic studies had been made. It was defined under the general term "nervous complaint" and as such attracted the stigma attributed to it by the Bellamy family. They considered all nervous complaints were controllable given sufficient "backbone". This contributed to the isolation of Uncle Lionel, who as a result of the war, was a bundle of nerves and eventually resorted to alcohol for his solace. He and my mother had much in common, suffered together and had a deep understanding of their mutual difficulties. I think that her fondness and sympathy for him caused her to promise to name me after him should I turn out to be a boy.

I do not know what operations were carried out on my mother but she was certainly aware that to have children would be dangerous for her. This was shown by the problems which she experienced at my birth and then again at the birth of Audrey in 1925. I believe that, amongst other things, she had a hysterectomy but have no documentary proof. She was operated on in London on the 20th of May 1925, prior to Audrey's birth. (Chapter 3, page 46, contains her letter to her parents).   Her daily treatment, as I understand it, consisted of injections and I know that later in the Thirties she was injecting herself every four hours with a variety of drugs including Ephedrine and Belladonna but eventually Prostmin.

As medical knowledge progressed so it was discovered that the cause of myasthenia gravis lay in the failure to transmit certain chemicals to the nerve endings. The chemical transmitter concerned was identified as ascetylcholine and, until the late 1930's no drug had been found which helped the situation very much. Then in about 1935 there was a breakthrough with the discovery that Neostigmine had dramatic effects in some cases. I have a report in front of me concerning a 28 year old woman in 1935 who had tried everything gold, thyroid extract, ephedrine and etc with no avail and then in February 1935 was given Neostigmine. *"Then came the day I shall always remember. I was lying on the sofa after tea and my fiancée came in late, saying that he had yet another possible remedy. I submitted to the injection with complete indifference and within a few minutes began to feel very strange .... It was wonderful and we danced twice around the room. It was my first experience of Neostigmine and we have never since been separated".* Note that this was written in the 1970's.

I do not know whether this drug was used by my mother but to the end of her life she still suffered in varying degrees and always carried a syringe and emergency instructions with her.

During much of the time she attended the private clinic of Dr Laurent at the Hammersmith Hospital. He became a friend and was in constant touch with her on medical matters. She co-operated with him as a case study for his students and took part in a number of drug trials. I have a number of his letters to her, written in the 1942/3 period when he had been evacuated to the Park Prewitt Hospital in Basingstoke. This was the time when they discovered that the removal of the thymus gland was giving hope for myasthenia sufferers. It was a tricky operation and in the U.K. was being carried out at the Hospital for Nervous Diseases in Bloomsbury. The first operation being completed in 1941 and by 1942 a further 19, all successful as to survival. My mother was told about these and evidently contacted Dr Laurent, as on the 15th of Januarry 1942 he wrote :-

"Dear Mrs Bellamy, I was so glad to hear from you and to know that you are keeping fit. Your account of the meeting with Dr Rodriguez (the Doctor at Bloomsbury) is very interesting. I think that I can answer all the questions that his statements must have raised in your mind.

1. The gland that he referred to is the thymus gland. This is enlarged in about 40 out of every 100 cases of myasthenia. This cannot be the cause of the disease since 60 out of every 100 cases have no sign of trouble with that gland. Removal of the gland involves a very severe operation and no improvement can be guaranteed. The gland can also be destroyed by X-Ray treatment, but no improvement followed this treatment in five cases of mine where this was done.

2. The question of eating salads, fruit and vitamin C arose in this way. Many years ago a patient attending Dr Symond's at Guys Hospital, suddenly took a liking for lemons and took the juice of six every day. His myasthenia gradually got better and the improvement was written up in a medical journal and put down to Vitamin C in the lemons.Unfortunately this patient's myasthenia has since returned and even twelve lemons a day have failed to improve him this time. I have tried lemons, vitamin C and fresh fruit in many cases without the slightest result.

3. Many doctors at various times have had the idea that the suprarenal glands might be at fault. In 1929 I was in Paris and had many talks with French specialists who were using suprarenal extracts with apparent good results in a few cases. I brought back the extract with me but could not get any improvement in my cases.

So you see I don't sound too optimistic, but nevertheless I should like you to attend Dr Rodriguez and have any treatment he suggests, except an operation.

Before you try this treatment I have got something new I would like you to try. It is a substance called guanidine which is taken by mouth. Some cases do very well on it. If you let me know whether you get Prostigmin from Dr Elliott at the hospital or from your doctor, I will write and tell whoever is attending you how to get the stuff and how much to give you.

You can take the Prostigmin at the same time and might find that injections last much longer. Write soon Yours sincerely.   L.E.Laurent."

The next letter I have is dated 11th of April 1943 in which he asks her to write up a detailed history of her illness as he was writing a Medical Paper on myasthenia. He then outlines his requirements in this respect and ends with a P.S. *"Do you take ephedrine or potassium as well?* (as Prostignum) The next letter thanks her for her" *very full and clear letter"* and then goes on - *"I did not realise that you had myasthenia before you had your babies. Pregnancy often has a definite effect on myasthenia in one way or another. Could you tell me how it has effected you in each case? .... also if you got better or worse in the few weeks after delivery. Any detail of how long each labour lasted and whether anaesthetics or forceps were used would be a help."* He then asks again if she is taking potassium or ephedrine. I know that when I was born I was very late, nearly ten months my mother said, and I was definitely a forceps baby as I still have the mark under my left eye.

On the 2nd of July 1943 he wrote again and refers to the fact that Dr Westropp has told him that she has not been *"too well"* and he asked to see her at the King Edward Hospital in Ealing. She was to say that she *"was a private patient or a friend so as to spare her the interview with the Almoner"*. He went on to say that if she couldn't manage it then he would visit her at home. I have no further correspondence. Granny Gale said that he was in constant touch with her from that point on and that she was his "prize patient" because she had survived for so long with the disease. Clearly myasthenia gravis was a difficult disease to endure and she suffered a great deal, continuously and with little support from her husband and his family. That this was through ignorance is without question, but it does give added reason to her flight to London where she had the loving and consistent support of her mother as well as a more sophisticated medical back-up.

Her mother wrote to Dr Laurent with the news of her death and received the following reply:-

"We were all deeply shocked to hear of Mrs Bellamy's death, we were so fond of her, I myself feel it as a personal loss. It is some comfort that she was saved any suffering. She always bore her own ill health so courageously. Thank you for writing to me and I have forwarded your letter to Dr Laurent".

Troop Leader

A Tank Commander's Story

Commissioned out of Sandhurst in 1943, nineteen-year-old Bill Bellamy joined the 8th King's Royal Irish Hussars. Following the Normandy landings in June 1944, he was involved in the great tank battles around the town of Caen, the battle of Mont Pincon and then the Allied breakout into Belgium. There followed the advance into Holland and onwards to the River Maas. In October 1944, during this phase of the fighting, he was awarded an immediate Military Cross for bravery during the battle to secure the Dutch village of Doornhoek. In the spring of 1945, the 8th Hussars thrust into Germany and on towards Hamburg, eventually winding up at the very heart of Hitler's Reich, Berlin.

Bill kept diaries and notes of his experiences, and shortly after the war he used them to write up a series of articles recounting his part as a junior officer in the hard-fought battles to free Europe from the Nazis. Bill's narrative is fresh and open, and his descriptions of battle are vivid. He saw many of his contemporaries killed in action, and this life-altering experience clearly informs his narrative. His accounts of tank fighting in the leafy Normandy bocage at the height of the summer, or in the iron-hard fields of Holland in winter, are graphic and compelling.

This unique personal account of a British tank commander in the battles for Normandy and the Low Countries is illustrated with archive and personal photographs, some never previously published.

Sutton Publishing
www.suttonpublishing.co.uk
ISBN 0-7509-3979-6